CLASSICAL TURKISH COOKING

TRADITIONAL TURKISH FOOD FOR THE AMERICAN KITCHEN

AYLA ALGAR

HarperCollins*Publishers*

FIRST EDITION

Designed by Helene Berinsky

LIBRARY OF CONGRESS CATALOG CARD NUMBER 91-55096

ISBN 0-06-016317-8

91 92 93 94 95 AC/RRD 10 9 8 7 6 5 4 3 2 1

To Hamid and my sons, Dennis, James, Larry, and Selim

CONTENTS

✳✳✳✳✳✳✳✳✳✳✳✳✳✳✳✳✳✳✳✳✳✳✳✳✳✳✳✳✳✳✳✳✳✳✳

ACKNOWLEDGMENTS

My gratitude goes first to the hard-working women of my
country who devote themselves utterly to their families,
keeping homes where the sweet smell of cooking provides constant
reassurance and a source of strength. It is in this spirit that I think
affectionately of my grandmother, mother, and aunts, whose cooking has nourished me, body and soul, and left me with many precious memories.

I am forever grateful to my husband for all his varied help,
without which this book could never have been written.

Among the scholars who have written on Turkish and Middle
Eastern food and food history, I feel particularly indebted to Alan
Davidson, perhaps the first Westerner to take a serious interest in
Turkish cuisine; Charles Perry, whose diligent researches have clar-
ified many an obscure point of etymology and food history; and the
Kuts, Günay and Turgut, scholars of literary history who have not
disdained the study of Ottoman culinary texts.

I express my heartfelt gratitude to Gülsen Kahraman of the
Turkish Ministry of Culture and Tourism who kindly provided much
needed help in gaining access to restaurants and bakeries. My appreciation goes also to Kamil Toygar of the same ministry for his
generous assistance in finding books relating to food history.

I carry a particularly heavy debt of gratitude to the staff of
numerous restaurants and bakeries in Turkey. Special thanks go to
owner Nurettin Doğanbey, pastry chef Abdullah Akkuş, and baklava
chef Abdulbaki Yazgalı of Konyalı Restaurant; Beyti Güler of the
Beyti Restaurant; Hristo Çobanoğlu and chef Ismail Demir of Pandeli
Restaurant; the director and kitchen staff of Kalyon Hotel; chef Süleyman Özgen of the Divan Oteli; Abdurrahman Seçer and all the

bakers at the simit bakery in Tahtakale—all in Istanbul—and the bakers at the Doğu bakery in Ankara, especially Ömer Aslan and Hacı Çoban.

I thank my young friend Hatice Aynur of the University of the Bosphorus for promptly obtaining for me the urgently needed photocopy of the nineteenth-century classic cookbook of Mehmet Kamil.

Thanks, too, and fond good wishes to my dear friends, Mine Mengi, Türkan Ersin, and Gülumay Özbay, for all their help and suggestions.

I am indebted to my agent, Susan Lescher, for her generous encouragement and her faith in this book. Heartfelt thanks to Susan Friedland, senior editor at HarperCollins, for her patient, diligent, and persistent work on the book. Finally, I am very grateful to my friend Florence Myer for typing an immaculate manuscript, in conformity with her usual high standards.

PREFACE

L ike all major culinary traditions, that of Turkey is marked simultaneously by unity and diversity. The unity derives ultimately from the traditions of the Ottoman palace, which, filtering down to the population at large in modified form, became the foundation for a common national cuisine. This classic cuisine has always been cultivated in its fullest form in Istanbul, and from there conveyed to the provinces through family ties or other linkages with that great metropolis.

The assimilation of the food of Istanbul by the provinces has, however, been subject to significant regional variations. Local tastes as well as availability of ingredients have often dictated the use of certain foods in preference to others. Thus the meat dolmas of Gaziantep in southeastern Turkey tend to be spicier than elsewhere because of their heavier use of cumin, peppers, and garlic, while the yogurt soups of eastern Anatolia substitute sweet basil for mint and wheat for rice. In the Aegean area there is a tendency to cook everything in olive oil—even *baklava*, in violation of the national consensus that it should be cooked in butter. Furthermore, the popularity of certain dishes is uneven throughout the country. Olive oil dishes, for example, are rare in central and eastern Anatolia, areas with a strong preference for meat dishes, and are cooked mostly by those with an Istanbul background. In addition to these regional variations on Istanbul cuisine, fully distinct regional traditions of great richness and antiquity also exist. Collectively, these might be designated as Anatolian cuisine, for they owe nothing to the cuisine of Istanbul, although they are to be found side by side with it. Anatolian cuisine deserves separate and detailed treatment; we will concentrate in this book on the cuisine shared by the whole country, offering only a few glimpses of regional specialties.

My richest source of recipes and food lore has been my family in Turkey; many of the dishes included here evoke strong personal memories. Since for professional reasons my father traveled widely across Turkey, I had the good fortune to stay in various parts of Anatolia and learn something of their distinctive culinary traditions. This exposed me to a variety of tastes and helped me to appreciate the relationship between the classic cuisine and its regional variants. In more recent years I have benefited from the expertise of numerous chefs and bakers kind enough to take me into their kitchens.

Through extensive reading and research I have also studied all the available Turkish cookbooks, including those published in the nineteenth century in the Ottoman script, as well as a wide range of sources—lexicons, poetry, historical texts, memoirs, books by European travelers—that serve to illuminate the historical and cultural background of Turkish food.

CLASSICAL TURKISH COOKING

INTRODUCTION

Turkish History in the Mirror of Food

One should not pass over these things, simply saying they are food. They are in reality a complete civilization.
—Abdülhak Şinasi, *Çamlıcadaki Eniştemiz* (1944)

The task of the culinary historian is in many ways akin to that of the archeologist. Both must work with fragmentary materials, scrutinizing them for indications of origin in place and time, and correlating their sometimes scanty evidence with linguistic, literary, and historical data. But just as the skillful archeologist conjures up a lost civilization from what appears to the layman as unpromising scraps of evidence, the historian is able to turn the commonplace subject of food into a mirror that reflects the history and culture of a nation with remarkably little distortion. The ingredients, dishes, and cooking techniques of a cuisine, together with the names used to designate them, all offer abundant clues to the historical growth of a nation, its religious loyalties and cultural affinities, its changing economic fortunes, and the general interplay of change and continuity within its life. As Margaret Visser has recently written, echoing Byron, "Much depends on dinner."*

The archeological concept of strata may also be applied to certain major cuisines that can be seen to have traversed fairly distinct stages of evolution, successively superimposed on each other as the edifice of taste and consumption gradually attains definitive form. Thus in Turkish cuisine one can discern Far Eastern, Central Asian, Iranian, Anatolian, and Mediterranean layers, each of them mirror-

* *See her book of the same title* (New York, 1986).

ing one stage in the long and complex history of migration that has enabled the Turks both to exert and to receive influence all across Eurasia.

TURKISH ORIGINS IN CENTRAL ASIA

The comparison with archeology is particularly apt for the earliest period of Turkish history, one characterized by nomadic wanderings in the marches of China. We can only surmise what the primitive diet of these Turks may have been. However, from the earliest important Turkish literary monuments, inscriptions from the eighth century found in Northern Mongolia, we know that deer and hare were consumed, and that dead rulers were bidden farewell with massive funerary feasts.* Venison disappeared from the Turkish menu quite swiftly, once animal herding replaced hunting as the mainstay of the alimentary economy. The fact that the consumption of hare is now regarded in Turkey with quasireligious abhorrence, despite the absence of a prohibition in Islam, may point to the gradual emergence of a taboo in pre-Islamic times.

The earliest settled Turkish culture of note was that of the Uyghurs, who established their kingdom in the mid-eighth century in what is now known as Xingjiang. The Uyghurs were under the strong cultural influence of China, and it is most likely during the period of their flourishing that *mantı* entered the diet of the Turks. A kind of dumpling still eaten with enthusiasm by virtually all the Turkish peoples, this dish derives its name from the Chinese.† It should not be thought, however, that culinary influences flowed in only one direction. The delight taken in stuffing not only pasta but also intestines and vegetables is so widespread and constant a feature of Turkish cuisine that it is difficult to regard it as a mere borrowing. The presence of stuffed dishes in the cuisine of Northern China may

* Wilhelm Radloff, *Die alttürkischen Inschriften der Mongolei* (St. Petersburg, 1895).
† Gerhard Doerfer, *Die mongolischen und türkischen Elemente im Neupersischen* (Wiesbaden, 1965), Vol. 4, pt. 1, 23.

well be a symptom of Turkish influence, although it is possible that the transmission took place in the era of Mongol dominion, some six centuries later.* In any event, the Uyghurs proclaimed their gastronomic independence from the Chinese in at least one significant way: they ate on low tables, a custom still encountered in the villages of Anatolia.†

❀ EARLY CONTACT WITH ISLAM

The emergence of the Turks as a principal factor in world history is linked indissolubly to their conversion to Islam, a process as much political and civilizational as religious in its consequences. Although some Turkish peoples have remained the neighbors of the Chinese down to the present, the conversion of almost all of them to Islam irrevocably detached them from the cultural sphere of East Asia and oriented them westward to the classical world of Islam.

The first important literary monument of the Muslim Turks is a remarkable Turkish-Arabic dictionary, the *Diwan Lughat al-Turk,* composed in the late eleventh century by Mahmud al-Kashghari.‡ Replete with precious information on the material culture of the Turks, this dictionary demonstrates among other things the ancient lineage of much of present-day Turkish cuisine. Mahmud al-Kashghari lists terms relating to the preparation of bread and other dough products: varieties of bread such as *yufka, ak ekmek, kara ekmek* and *kevşek;* implements such as the *oklava* (rolling pin); and methods of cooking such as the use of the *tandır* (clay oven), and the *sac* (griddle), as well as burying the dough in warm ashes (*gömmeç*). We also learn from this source that a fondness for milk products such as yogurt, *ayran* (yogurt drink), and various types of cheese—something definitely alien to the culinary traditions of China—was already well established among the Turks. Yogurt and its by-products were to become one of the principal contributions of the

* See Françoise Sabban, "Court Cuisine in Fourteenth-Century Imperial China: Some Culinary Aspects of Hu Sihui's *Yinshan Zhengyao,*" *Food and Foodways* 1 (1986): 161–96.
† Annemarie von Gabain, *Das Leben im uigurischen Konigreich* (Wiesbaden, 1973), 91, 94.
‡ A full and critical edition of this work is now available in three volumes, with English translation, prepared by Robert Dankoff and titled *Compendium of the Turkic Dialects* (Cambridge, Mass., 1984). The ancient forms of the words quoted here differ from their modern counterparts. The food-related material of this work has been correlated with other evidence by Bahaeddin Ögel in *Türk Kültür Tarihine Giriş,* Vol. 4 (Ankara, 1985).

Turks to the culinary resources of Europe as well as the Islamic Middle East. Although yogurt is recorded to have existed in the ancient Near East, it was the Turks who gave great impetus to its consumption, and the name by which they designated it has entered all the major languages of Europe. Finally, we find in this important dictionary charming stories about the origins of certain foods, such as *tutmaç* and *börek,* which may indeed be apocryphal but testify to the ancient origin of these dishes and the prestige they enjoyed (see pages 174–75, 185).

As the Turks moved westward through Central Asia toward the Islamic Middle East, they came into contact with the highly evolved and sophisticated urban culture of the Iranians. This was to leave an indelible Iranian imprint on the language and literature of the Turks, as well as on many other aspects of their cultural life. But despite their far-reaching subordination to Iranian models, the Turks maintained their autonomy in culinary matters. This was particularly remarkable given the high prestige of Iranian cuisine in the early Islamic world. Many of the words found in the most ancient Arabic cookbooks are Persian, and the Caliphs of Baghdad always prided themselves on the consumption of elaborate Iranian dishes.* The Turks, too, were not immune to the attractions of Iranian cuisine. They came to appreciate, for example, stews in which fruits and meats were combined, and a few dishes answering this description are to be found even in Ottoman cookbooks of the nineteenth century and still survive to some degree in Anatolia (see pages 93, 100). Vegetable stews, known as *yakhni,* were also absorbed from the Iranians into Turkish cuisine.

In addition, the word *kebab* is of Persian origin, which suggests that the Turks learned something about grilling meats from the Iranians. However, Mahmud al-Kashghari informs us that the Turks were already acquainted with the art of cooking meat on skewers, and it stands to reason that the nomadic Turks should have practiced this convenient and easy method of cooking even before making the acquaintance of the Iranians. So although the Iranians supplied the generic name for kebab dishes, there is no reason to attribute to them all the various kinds of kebab. Certainly the

* See Maxim Rodinson, "Recherches sur les documents arabes relatifs à la cuisine," *Revue des Etudes Islamiques* (1949), and Peter Heine, *Kulinarische Studien: Untersuchungen zur Kochkunst im arabisch-islamischen Mittelalter* (Wiesbaden, 1988).

present-day cuisine of Turkey offers far more types of kebab than its Iranian counterpart.

Similar remarks apply to *pilav* (pilaf). The word itself is the Turkicized version of the Persian *pulau,* and rice was cultivated in Iran, as well as elsewhere in the Middle East, long before the arrival there of the Turks, to whom it was originally unknown in Central Asia. But in early Iranian and Iranian-influenced Arab cuisine, rice was chiefly used in desserts and as a starch accompaniment to fish.* The emergence of pilaf dishes, in all their rich variety, seems to have accompanied the rise to prominence of the Turkish element in the Islamic world. One indication of this—relatively late—is that virtually all the rice dishes listed by the seventeenth-century Iranian philosopher Molla Sadra bear Turkish names.†

Apart from all this, it is known that a number of purely Turkish dishes found great favor in the Persian-speaking world, even being celebrated in verse. Thus *tutmaç,* a kind of thick soup made with noodles and lentils, was praised by a thirteenth-century poet as "the caliph of the world of appetite"; he claimed that "all the way from the limits of Iraq to Khurasan, you can find no one who will deny its deliciousness."‡ The Turkish dish known as *buğra* (which may or may not have been the ancestor of present-day *börek*) was also known and appreciated; there is evidence suggesting it may even have been a delicacy unrivaled by any other dish until the rise of pilaf.§ More generally, the prevalence of dishes relying on flour, dough, and noodles, and others involving intestines and tripe, may fairly be traced to Turkish influence, given the names used to designate them even in Persian. ‖

In sum, the confluence of Iranian and Turkish elements led gradually, both in the westerly regions of Central Asia and in Iran itself, to the emergence of a composite cuisine in which Turkish elements came to predominate by the fifteenth century at the latest. This was the cuisine that the Moghuls transplanted to India, where

* See Marius Canard, "Le riz dans le proche orient aux premiers siècles de l'Islam," *Arabica* 6 (1959): 113–31.
† Quoted in Z. Sabitian, *Asnad va Namaha-yi Tarikhi-yi Daura-yi Safaviya* (Tehran, 1964), 371.
‡ Quoted in Zabihullah Safa, *Tarikh-i Adabiyat-dar Iran* (Tehran, 1961), Vol. 2, 852–56.
§ See the poem described by Ayla Algar in "Bushaq of Shiraz: Poet, Parasite, and Gastronome," *Petits Propos Culinaires* 31 (March 1989): 10.
‖ See the glossary to Abdulghani Mirzoev, *Abu Ishaq va Fa'aliyat-i Adabi-yi U* (Dushanbe, 1971).

it was further enriched and refined through the incorporation of distinctively Indian elements.

✸ ARRIVAL OF THE TURKS IN ANATOLIA

At about the same time that Mahmud al-Kashghari was compiling his dictionary in the distant confines of Eastern Central Asia, one branch of the Turkish peoples was beginning to settle in Anatolia. This was the start of a process that led to the Islamization and Turkicization of most of Anatolia and the triumphant installation of the Ottoman Turks in Istanbul, at the junction of Europe and Asia, where for centuries they determined the destinies of the Balkans, the Arab world, and much of the Mediterranean basin. The Ottoman centuries were to mark the apogee of Turkish history; under the auspices of the Ottoman dynasty there came into being a great imperial culture, which had, of course, its culinary dimension.

The chief predecessors of the Ottomans in the Turkicization of Anatolia were the Seljuqs, a branch of the great dynasty that had once ruled much of the eastern Islamic world. Their seat of rule was the city of Konya, a brilliant center of culture that attracted scholars, poets, and mystics from various regions of the Islamic world. The cuisine was correspondingly lavish and cosmopolitan. At a banquet given by Sultan 'Ala al-Din Kayqubad in 1237 a variety of kebabs were served, including duck and chicken broiled on spits, together with pepper-seasoned pilaf, a variety of vegetable dishes, stewed and fried, and the saffron-flavored rice pudding known as *zerde*.*

It is not, however, so much in the official chronicles of the court that culinary information on the Seljuq period is to be sought as in the works of the great mystic and poet Mevlana Jalal al-Din Rumi. This may come as a surprise to those who associate Sufism—Islamic mysticism—with world-abnegating asceticism, or who take as a literal truth stories of saints who survived on a chick-pea a day. As we shall see, the kitchen played an important role in the life of the Turkish Sufi hospice. At least in the case of Rumi, this positive interest in food should be taken not so much as a sign of sensuous indulgence as of a worldview that regarded all phenomena, from the lowliest to the highest, as integral parts of a universe replete with

* See M. Zeki Oral, "Selçuk Devri Yemekleri ve Ekmekleri: i," *Türk Etnografya Dergisi* 1, no. 2 (1956): 73.

spiritual and symbolic meaning. In any event, thanks to Rumi, we know that a whole variety of vegetables, pulses, nuts, fruits, breads, buns, pastries, sweets, milk products, and pickles were available in Seljuq Anatolia.* Sultan Veled, Rumi's eldest son, inherited from his father, it appears, some of his interest in food. One of his poems has as its opening line *qarnum açdur, qarnum açdur, qarnum aç* ("I am hungry, I am hungry, I am hungry!"), although the next line immediately makes clear that it is the "food of paradise" (*uçmaq aşı*) for which he hungers.†

The evidence before us is incomplete, but it seems that the transition from the inherited cuisine of Central Asia to the richer, more varied and elegant cuisine that was fully elaborated by the Ottomans had already begun in Seljuq times. For in Anatolia, the Turks gained access to many new types of food: fruits, vegetables, and herbs generally unavailable in Central Asia, olive oil in abundance, and seafood. The dishes concocted using these were combined with established fare of Central Asian origin—breads, dough products, kebabs, and so on—to produce a cuisine unrivaled for its profusion of taste and variety of ingredients.

The arrival of the Turks in Anatolia in Seljuq times made them close and intimate neighbors of the Greeks, themselves heirs to culinary traditions of great antiquity, although these had no doubt declined with the general weakening of Byzantine institutions. It has been suggested that during the formative period of Turkish culture in Anatolia substantial borrowings from the Greeks took place in various areas of material culture, including cuisine, and Greek loanwords referring to the making of bread have been cited as evidence.‡ However, hardly any of the words in question ever attained broad currency and, as we have seen, the essential methods for the baking of bread, together with a purely Turkish vocabulary to describe them, had been recorded by Mahmud al-Kashghari in eleventh-century Central Asia. The baking of round loaves of bread, as distinct from the flat bread of Central Asia, was on the other hand a tribute to Greek influence.

The case of baklava presents a special problem. There is no

* For a full analysis of food in the writings of Rumi, see Annemarie Schimmel, *The Triumphal Sun: A Study of the Works of Jalaladdin Rumi* (London and The Hague, 1978), 138–48.
† Sultan Veled, *Divan-i Turki,* ed. Veled Çelebi (Istanbul, 1922), 12.
‡ Speros Vryonis, *The Decline of Mediaeval Hellenism in Asia Minor* (Berkeley and Los Angeles, 1971), 482–83.

evidence that it existed among the Byzantine Greeks, even under a different name, and the word *baklava* is not Greek.* Equally we cannot with any confidence assign it a Turkish origin. The word occurs in sixteenth-century Turkish texts in the archaic form *baqlagu,* but this cannot be connected with any primordial Turkish root. The fact that the word occurs only in the Turkish of Anatolia, among all the Turkish languages, is suspicious and points to the possibility of a foreign origin.†

The only clear etymological evidence for a Greek influence on the evolution of Turkish cuisine in the Seljuq and early Ottoman periods (eleventh to fourteenth centuries) is furnished by the numerous loanwords of Greek provenance that designate fish and seafood in Turkish.

We suggest, therefore, that the additions and refinements that took place in Turkish cuisine after the arrival of the Turks in Anatolia and, more particularly, after the establishment of the Ottoman Empire was due less to the absorption of foreign influences than to the availability of a profusion of new ingredients and, still more, to the massive impetus given by the emergence of an imperial culture under the aegis of the Ottomans. It was the prestige of this culture and of the capital city that was its chief embodiment, Istanbul, that caused Turkish cuisine to be admired and imitated throughout the Balkans and the Near East, thus giving rise to the culinary similarities still observable today.

❋ ISTANBUL, IMPERIAL CAPITAL OF THE OTTOMANS

The splendor of Istanbul, although much tarnished by the passage of time, still impresses the foreign visitor who has the good fortune to glimpse the silhouette of the city as he approaches it by sea. In earlier centuries, the prospect induced positive rapture in many a traveler. A sixteenth-century ambassador, Busbecq, remarked of Istanbul: "Nature seems to have created this place as the capital of the world . . . I cannot imagine a better place to build a city."‡ At the turn of the nineteenth century another visitor, Ed-

---

* Charles Perry, "Baklava Not Proven Greek," *Petits Propos Culinaires* 27 (October 1987): 47–48.
† Communication from Dr. Talat Tekin, Professor of Turkology at Hacettepe University, Ankara.
‡ Ogier Ghislain de Busbecq, *Vier Briefe aus der Türkei* (Erlangen, 1926), 33.

mondo de Amicis, waxed still more lyrical. After describing with enthusiasm and sensitivity the composition of Istanbul's magnificent panorama, he proclaimed: "To deny this is the most beautiful sight on earth would be churlish indeed, as ungrateful toward God as it would be unjust to His creation; and it is certain that anything more beautiful would surpass mankind's powers of enjoyment."*

For the Turks, as for many neighboring peoples in the Near East and the Mediterranean, the enjoyment of food has always gone together with other forms of esthetic pleasure, especially that afforded by impressive and harmonious landscapes, whether urban or rustic. But the significance of Istanbul for Turkish cuisine has been infinitely more than that of a backdrop against which to enjoy the pleasures of the table. As the capital of the vast Ottoman Empire, an entrepot where all the varied produce of its lands was available, from Wallachia in the north to Yemen in the south, not to mention delicacies brought from Western Europe and spices from the Orient, Istanbul came to resemble a vast food market; the variety and profusion of foodstuffs found in the city mirrored the variety of tongues, races, and religions that were held together by Ottoman rule. As still another European admirer of Istanbul, Joseph Pitton de Tournefort, explained, "It seems that the Dardanelles and the Bosphorus exist expressly for the purpose of conveying to Istanbul treasures from all parts of the world."†

❉ FOOD IN THE OTTOMAN PALACE

The foremost beneficiaries of all this abundance were the Ottoman sultans themselves. The importance they assigned to culinary matters was apparent in the time of Sultan Mehmed Fatih in the fifteenth century. When some twenty years after his conquest of Istanbul in 1453 he began the construction of the celebrated Topkapi Palace, a huge kitchen surmounted by four domes came to form a principal part of the structure. About one century later, the Ottoman Empire reached its zenith of splendor and power in the reign of Sultan Süleyman the Magnificent. The organization of the court became more elaborate and the people dwelling in the palace

* Edmondo de Amicis, *Constantinople* (Philadelphia, 1896), Vol. 1, 31.
† Quoted on the cover of *Istanbul,* an anthology of extracts from European writers, ed. Esther Gallwitz (Frankfurt, 1981).

more numerous, which necessitated the construction of additional kitchen space, this time a building with six domes. This building was known as the Helvahane, "the House of Helva," but jams, sherbets, and herbal remedies were prepared there, in addition to numerous varieties of helva, or halvah. The final stage in the expansion of the royal kitchens came during the reign of Sultan Selim II when a portion of the palace was destroyed by fire and advantage was taken of the rebuilding operations to add ten further sections to the kitchens.*

The staff employed in the kitchens underwent similar inflation with the passage of time. At the end of the sixteenth century, no more than two hundred servants were employed in the preparation of food, but only fifty years later the kitchen staff had swollen to 1,370, all of them housed within the palace grounds.† In keeping with the genius for administrative hierarchy that pervaded Ottoman state and society, this horde of food craftsmen was organized into a pyramid headed by the *matbah emini,* the trustee or supervisor of the royal kitchens. He was responsible for supervising the whole operation, from the purchase of foodstuffs to the serving of the finished product. His principal aides were the *matbah kahyası,* who watched over expenditures and the food entering and leaving the kitchen, and the *kilercibaşı,* whose job it was to ensure that the vast pantries of the palace were properly stocked at all times.‡

Particularly remarkable about the palace kitchens was their high degree of specialization. The preparation of soups, kebabs, pilafs, vegetable dishes, fish, breads, pastries, candy and helva, syrup and jam, drinks such as *hoşaf,* sherbet, and *boza,* each represented a separate skill to be learned as an apprentice and refined in a lifetime of labor.§ So high was the degree of specialization that by the mideighteenth century each of six varieties of helva was assigned to a separate master chef, with a hundred apprentices working under him. ‖ From the meticulous records that were kept on all aspects of life in the palace, it appears that certain regions of the country began to specialize in producing masters of different aspects of the culinary

* Gülcan Kongaz, "Topkapı Sarayı Mutfakları," *Tarih ve Toplum* 15 (March 1985), 22–24.
† İsmail Hakkı Uzunçarşılı, *Osmanlı Devletinin Saray Teşkilatı* (Ankara, 1945), 380, 382.
‡ Ibid., 379, and H. A. R. Gibb and Harold Bowen, *Islamic Society and the West* (London, 1950), Vol. I, part 1, 357–58.
§ Emin Cenkman, *Osmanlı Sarayı ve Kıyafetleri* (Istanbul, 1948), 145–55.
‖ Uzunçarşılı, *Saray Teşkilatı,* 460.

art; thus kebab specialists tended to be recruited from Bolu, in central Anatolia, and pilaf experts from Istanbul itself.* This indicates how the culinary standards set at the court and the eating habits of the country at large came to influence each other.

There are also records on the amount of money spent for the upkeep of the royal kitchens. In addition, many foodstuffs were simply gathered and sent from the provinces in obedience to an imperial decree. Statistics for the annual meat supply of the palace in 1723 list 30,000 head of beef, 60,000 of mutton, 20,000 of veal, 10,000 of kid, 200,000 fowl, 100,000 pigeons, and 3,000 turkeys. We also have a list from 1661 that includes 36,000 bushels of rice, 3,000 pounds of noodles, 500,000 bushels of chick-peas, 6,000 loaves of sugar, and 12,000 pounds of salt.†

It is tempting to see these gargantuan amounts of food prepared and consumed in the Topkapi Palace as nothing more than the opulence and self-indulgence of a powerful sovereign and his court. But it should be remembered that the number of persons fed each day in the palace might be as high as 10,000 and that in addition food might be sent outside its walls to certain select recipients as a sign of royal favor.

The culinary arrangements of the palace had in fact an important aspect of ritual and protocol, designed to emphasize the unique power and status of the sultan. Before the conquest of Istanbul endowed the Ottomans with all the trappings of imperial might, the sultans used to eat relatively simply, often in the company of men of religion and ministers of state. But in the fifteenth century Sultan Mehmed Fatih declared, with austere imperial arrogance, "It is not my practice to have anyone eat in the company of my noble person, unless it be one of my family."‡ When vassal rulers were invited to dine in the presence of the sultan, they were seated at a lower level although in the same room. This insistence of the sultan on eating alone—a signal exception to the sociability generally associated in Turkey with dining—was a measure of the lofty heights to which the Ottoman rulers had ascended, of the distance they had traversed, in the words of a German historian, "from the tent of the shepherd to the Sublime Porte."

* Kongaz, "Topkapı Sarayı Mutfakları," 24.
† Barnette Miller, *Beyond the Sublime Porte: The Grand Seraglio of Stambul* (New Haven, 1931), 192–94.
‡ Ali Seydi Bey, *Teşrifat ve Teşkilatımız* (Istanbul, n.d.), 92.

✸ FOOD AND OTTOMAN INSTITUTIONS

Food played an important role in two other institutions, each of which—in its own way—contributed to the formation and preservation of Ottoman state and society; the corps of Janissaries, for many centuries the military elite of the empire, and the *tarikats,* the Sufi brotherhoods.

The commander of each of the three divisions of the Janissaries was known as the *çorbacı* (soupman) and other ranks were designed as *aşçıbaşı* (chief cook), *karakullukçu* (scullion), *çörekçi* (baker of round loaves of bread), and *gözlemeci* (pancake maker). In their application to the Janissaries, these terms came to lose all connection with the actual preparation of food, although they must originally have borne their literal meaning. However, the symbolic focus of each Janissary division remained at all times its *kazgan,* the huge cauldron in which pilaf was cooked; whenever the Janissaries decided to revolt—which happened with increasing frequency—they would overturn their *kazgans.** Conversely, the ties of obedience that in normal times linked the Janissaries to the sultan were reflected in the trays of baklava they collected from the palace every year on the fifteenth day of Ramadan.†

Although it originated in the Seljuq period, under the auspices of Rumi and his descendants, the Mevlevi *tarikat* may be regarded as the most quintessentially Ottoman of all the Sufi brotherhoods. The kitchen held an important place in the communal life of the Mevlevis, serving as a place of training and initiation. The purpose was not only utilitarian but also symbolic; the process of cooking was held to be analogous to the maturing of man's soul, in accordance with the well-known statement of Rumi, "I was raw, then I was cooked, then I burned." (This of course should not be taken to imply that Mevlevis liked their food burned!) A complex hierarchy of kitchen-related ranks existed among the Mevlevis, and the running of each of their hospices was supervised by a triumvirate consisting of the *kazancı dede* (cauldron elder), the *aşçı dede* (chief cook), and the *bulaşıkçı dede* (elder in charge of dishwashing).‡

Similar remarks apply to the Bektashis, a brotherhood that arose

---

* Gibb and Bowen, *Islamic Society,* 319–21.
† Reşad Ekrem Koçu, *Topkapu Sarayı* (Istanbul, n.d.), 52.
‡ See Hamit Zübeyr, "Mevlevilikte Mutfak Terbiyesi," *Türk Yurdu,* Vol. 5, no. 28 (March 1927), 280–86.

at roughly the same time and in the same milieu as the Mevlevis.*
Other *tarikat*s did not place the same emphasis on the ritual dimensions of food preparation, but most maintained in their hospices soup kitchens for feeding the poor and the wayfarer.

✸ FOOD MARKETS AND THE FOOD OF THE STREET

The palace enjoyed, no doubt, an exceptional degree of culinary riches, but what we know of the food markets of Istanbul, which in normal times were abundantly stocked with a wide variety of items, points to a high level of gastronomy among the general population. The preparation and sale of food in the markets were in the hands of specialized guilds, which served both as professional associations and as mechanisms for pricing and quality control.† In keeping with the Islamic belief that all the principal trades of man are sacred in origin, each of the different guilds stood under the patronage of a prophet or a companion of the Prophet Muhammad. Thus the patron of the cheesemakers was the Prophet Abraham, to whom was credited the invention of cheese. Evliya Çelebi, the celebrated seventeenth-century traveler, provides us with a detailed and vivid account of the food-related guilds of Istanbul. These included bakers and butchers, cheesemakers and yogurt merchants, pastry chefs and pickle makers, and fishmongers and sausage merchants. Together with the other guilds, they participated in the spectacular parades that formed such an impressive feature of Istanbul life; mounted on floats drawn by oxen, they displayed their skills to the public and distributed free samples of their wares.‡

Certain markets, above all the Egyptian Spice Bazaar, still functioning and described in detail below, had a central function in provisioning the whole city. At the same time, many districts of the city were famous for one or more particular commodity, so that the truly discriminating shopper had to tour much of the city to find all his needs: Çukurçeşme was celebrated for its pickles, Eyüb for its

* See Ayla Algar, "Bektaşilik'te Yemeğin Yeri," *İkinci Milletlerarası Yemek Kongresi Tebliğleri* (Konya, 1989), 20–24, and "Food in the Life of the Tekke," in *The Dervish Lodge in Ottoman Turkey,* ed. R. Lifchez (Berkeley and Los Angeles, in press).
† Concerning the regulation of the food markets, see Roger Mantran, *Istanbul dans la deuxième moitié du xviième siècle* (Paris, 1962), 331–35.
‡ Evliya Çelebi, *Seyahatname,* ed. Zuhuri Danışman (Istanbul, 1969), Vol. 2, 231–58. The gastronomical data supplied by Evliya Çelebi have been attractively summarized by Alexander Pallis in his *In the Days of the Janissaries* (London, 1951), 216–24.

clotted cream, Kanlıca for its yogurt, Karaköy for its *poğaça* (enriched flaky rolls), and so on.* Many of these associations still hold true, and it would be entirely possible to organize an eating tour of Istanbul for those robust of stomach and leg.

Yet another diffuse presence of food in Istanbul came from the ubiquitous street vendors who sold the most diverse foods to the accompaniment of distinctive cries. Much reduced in number, these vendors are still to be encountered, particularly in places like Karaköy that are the hubs of urban transport where people wait patiently for their buses or ferries.

❀ TRADITIONAL EATING ARRANGEMENTS

At the height of their opulence and sophistication, the Ottomans had elaborate ways of serving food. They carefully arranged precious artifacts both indigenous and imported on richly embroidered cloths. Purely for the sake of nostalgia, let us cite a vivid passage from the memoirs of Leyla Saz, once a tutor to the Ottoman royal family:

> Dinner was set on the floor on one side of the room. First a heavy round gold-embroidered cloth was spread out, and a six-legged silver stand was placed on top of it and covered with a cloth identical to the first. On top of this second cloth was put a round silver tray, adorned with salads, caviar, fish roe, olives and cheeses. In the middle of the tray would be placed a silver trivet, and around it were arranged jewel-encrusted salt, pepper, and cinnamon shakers, and a crystal jug filled with lemonade. Around the edges of the tray were placed sets of three napkins, made of delicate cloth with embroidered fringes, and on top of each set of napkins went a gold soup and pilav spoon and mother-of-pearl dessert spoons with stems made of coral and encrusted with small jewels. . . .
>
> Food would be taken from dishes of silver or Saxon china, using only the tips of three fingers with such delicacy and care that they would barely be soiled by the grease. Afterwards a servant standing ready with a silver jug and bowl would slowly pour water over our hands, and we would dry them on towels embroidered with gold thread.†

* For more complete lists of the wares of different localities in Istanbul, see Emir Mustafa, *Ramazanname*, ed. Amil Çelebioğlu (Istanbul, n.d.), passim, and Abdülhakk Şinasi Hisar, *Çamlıcadaki Eniştemiz* (Istanbul, 1978), 87.
† *Haremin İçyüzü* (Istanbul, 1974), 206, 213.

The use of the knife and fork is a fairly modern development in Turkey, but the spoon is fully traditional. Turks always use spoons for soups, pilafs, *hoşaf*s, or compotes (page 250–52), and desserts such as milk puddings, *aşure* (page 230), and *zerde* (page 226); a different kind of spoon would be used for each. While the spoons of the common people were generally made of wood, those of the rich were fashioned from costly and exotic materials:

> The most striking implements used at dinner were, without doubt, the spoons. The spoons of different size and designs that were used for soup, pilav, desserts and *hoşaf*s, were all masterpieces, made out of such varied materials as gold, silver, mother-of-pearl, ivory, coral, ebony, rhinoceros horn, walnut, tortoise shell, jade, amber, and often encrusted with rubies, emeralds and other jewels. Then there were napkins, soaped and sprinkled with rose-water, lying in small bowls and dishes.[*]

Virtually nothing remains of all this splendor, and there is little distinctive about the way today's Turks eat their meals. A few traces of tradition persist in rural areas where the time-honored low table is still brought out at mealtimes and in the absence of running water a pitcher and bowl are passed around for people to wash their hands. In general, however, the eating arrangements of modern Turkey are identical with those of the West.

❀ MODERN DEVELOPMENTS

When in 1888 the railroad between Istanbul and Vienna was completed, a European resident of the Ottoman capital interpreted the event as marking "the conquest of the city by foreign thought and enterprise" and its "annexation to the Western world."[†] His estimate was perhaps exaggerated, but there is no denying that the Westernization of Turkish culture and society, powerfully accelerated by the collapse of the Ottoman Empire in World War I and its replacement by the Turkish Republic, was already underway in the late nineteenth century. One symptom of this was the decline of the traditional neighborhoods of Istanbul and the corresponding rise to prominence of Pera (now known as Beyoğlu). Formerly the preserve

[*] Samiha Ayverdi, *İbrahim Efendi Konağı* (Istanbul, 1982), 19.
[†] A. van Millingen, *Constantinople* (London, 1906), 205.

of the Christian minorities and the European diplomatic community, Pera, with its prosperity and amenities, began to attract not only foreign travelers but also members of the Ottoman elite who came to patronize its European-style cafés and restaurants. The emergence of the Turkish restaurant must, in fact, be dated to this period. In traditional Turkish society, the idea of eating a complete meal outside the home as a matter of pure recreation, unconnected with the exigencies of travel or the exchange of hospitality, was unknown. The café, as we point out elsewhere in this book, originated as a Turkish institution, but it is significant that the earliest Turkish word for a restaurant, *lokanta,* is taken from the Italian *locanda,* meaning an inn. (The word *lokanta* now has an old-fashioned ring to it, and it has been largely replaced by the international term *restoran*).

The genesis of the restaurant can be taken as an indication of new patterns of consumption and taste; not merely the context in which food was consumed but also to some degree the range and type of the cuisine became modified. Thus we find in menus from the turn of the century French dishes such as asparagus with *sauce hollandaise* intermingled with Turkish classics like *börek* and pilaf. But this, like many other aspects of Westernization, especially in its earliest phases, affected principally the lives of the affluent elite.

Now matters are changing, and it is increasingly common in urban areas for families to eat in restaurants. Not coincidentally, the food provided by the restaurants is also changing. Very few now cook good traditional Turkish food, most offering instead a mixture of Turkish and Western dishes. A still more disturbing development is the proliferation of fast-food places that offer pizza and hamburgers, a sure sign that Turkey is entering the orbit of the multinational corporations.

In their own homes, however, Turks continue to be steadfastly conservative in their culinary habits. Chronic economic difficulties have combined with the pace of modern life to reduce the gastronomic possibilities available to most families. Nevertheless, food continues to be one of the principal axes on which social and family life turns, and the preferred dishes, for both everyday meals and special occasions, are with few exceptions traditional.

The cohesiveness of the family is still regularly expressed at the dinner table. It is unthinkable that as a matter of course teenage children should eat at a separate time of their own choosing, and equally unlikely that a mother should make her often tiring work outside the home a reason for failing to prepare a meal. (It should be noted, however, that grocery shopping is often a male duty, in accordance with tradition.) Furthermore, it is not a disaster, to be masked with uneasy pleasantries, if an unexpected guest chances by at dinnertime. Room is made at the table, and the opportunity to feed a guest is indeed greeted as a chance to earn merit. It may even be claimed that the social role of food has been reinforced in modern times. Faced with the dual pressures of economic hardship and the stress induced by life in congested cities that defy all attempts to regulate their growth, Turks find solace and strength in the ties of family and friendship that are both expressed and reinforced through the simple act of eating together. Seen in this light, the preparation, offering, and consumption of food reveal themselves to be among the principal mainstays of a profound social solidarity.

Discussing the drastic changes that have affected Turkish life in the twentieth century, the writer Ahmet Hamdi Tanpınar astutely observed: "Side by side with those many things which are lost when one passes from one civilization to another, there are others which themselves ruling over time are the true and lasting monarchies of this world."* It is not an exaggeration to regard the rich traditions of Turkish cuisine, with their profound historical and cultural roots, as one of those precious and imperishable monarchies.

* Quoted by Gürol Sözen in *Bin Çeşit İstanbul ve Boğaziçi Yalıları* (Istanbul, 1989), 93.

Turkish Food in the Cycle of Time

Upon reflection, the calendar turns out to be far more than a mathematical means of marking the passage of time. With its festivals and special occasions, it is, on the contrary, a way of planting islands of meaning in the inexorable flow of days and months, times that are to be both remembered and anticipated in their punctual and welcome recurrence. On such occasions, the link between food and sociability, always strong in Turkish culture, comes fully to the fore as special dishes and foods are prepared for both family and friends.

It is only an apparent paradox that Ramadan, the month of dawn-to-dusk fasting obligatory for all Muslims, should also be a month of extraordinary culinary activity. It is not only that the appetite and the sense of taste are sharpened by the experience of fasting; Ramadan is also a month of hospitality and charity, in which the obligation to feed the hungry is taken more seriously than usual. It should also be noted that fasting is experienced not as a deprivation but as a gift, a source of abundance; the whole month, not merely the festival itself that marks its end, is joyous, and the sense of renewal that comes to those who observe it finds a natural expression in the meals taken together at the end of each day.

Each day's fast is also preceded by a meal known as *sahur,* taken before the dawn prayer, intended to fortify one against the rigors of the fast (which might last as long as fifteen hours, if Ramadan falls in the summer). Traditionally, pilaf dishes, *börek,* and poached meat served cold and sliced (*söğüş*) would be favored for *sahur,* but now people generally content themselves with leftovers from the previous day's dinner, or the regular fare eaten for breakfast.

Even the traditional *sahur* was a frugal affair compared with the quantity and variety of foods prepared in Ottoman times for breaking the fast (*iftar*) as soon as the sun had set beneath the horizon. The treasures that had been accumulated in the pantry in the weeks leading up to Ramadan would be brought forth in rich and hierarchic splendor to delight the palate of the faster. Samiha Ayverdi, the well-known contemporary writer, recalls how during her childhood in an aristocratic family foods would be gathered in advance of Ramadan from all the corners of the Ottoman realm—still a vast area, despite the progressive amputation of its outlying territories:

dates from Baghdad, rice from Egypt, clarified butter from Aleppo and Trabzon, baklava from Gaziantep, dried apricots from Malatya, kasseri cheese from the Balkans, honey from Ankara, caviar from the Black Sea, figs from Izmir, cheese aged in skins from eastern Anatolia.

The time for breaking the fast was traditionally announced by the firing of a cannon in big cities or the beating of a drum in smaller localities. This was the signal to bring out an array of small dishes containing a variety of cheeses, pickles and jams, dates, and slices of sausage (*sucuk*) and dried pressed meat (*pastırma*), accompanied by sesame rings (*simit*), and a special type of *pide* baked for the season. After this prelude to the day's feast, the sunset prayer would be offered, before proceeding to the next stage of the evening meal, consisting of either rice or vermicelli soup and eggs cooked with onion or *pastırma,* a dish which for all its simplicity had originated in the kitchens of the palace. Even this did not mark the end of the proceedings, for then came a variety of meat and vegetable dishes, *börek,* and desserts. The most favored dessert during Ramadan was *güllaç,* a creamy and delicate concoction flavored with rose water, that set off to perfection the heavy meal just completed. Then pipes and coffee were prepared, serving to dissipate postprandial languor.

Outside the home, eating places would remain open throughout the night, and the special prayers performed during Ramadan, known as *teravih,* would often be followed by an outing to a locality of Istanbul renowned for a certain kind of food.

Constraints of time and finance have combined to reduce the lavishness with which *iftar* is prepared, but the three-tiered arrangements—an array of small dishes followed first by soup and then by a dinner with several dishes—is still preserved, as are, of more importance, the festive and communal aspects of the meal.

Ramadan is brought to an end with a festival known popularly as Şeker Bayramı, the Festival of Things Sweet. On that day candy and confectionery as well as traditional desserts such as *kadayıf* and baklava are offered to guests and relatives who come to pay their compliments. A special meal may also be cooked for the occasion, consisting of heavy foods not customarily eaten, such as stuffed chicken or turkey and a dish of meat and wheat known as *keşkek.*

The other chief festival of the Islamic calendar is known as Kurban Bayramı, the Festival of Sacrifice. On this day Muslims everywhere—especially those performing the *hajj,* or pilgrimage to Mecca—slaughter an animal both in commemoration of the readiness of Abraham to sacrifice his son Ishmael and as an act of charity. The meat of the animal slaughtered is to be distributed, in fixed proportions, to relatives, neighbors, and the poor. In Turkey it is almost always a sheep that is sacrificed, and the approach of the festival is marked by the appearance of sheep in the most unlikely metropolitan settings, tied to a tree and awaiting their fate. The meat is roasted in a dish known as *kavurma.* Dolmas, *börek,* and various desserts—baklava and *kadayif* in particular—are also eaten on this occasion. It is customary in addition to prepare helva using the fat of the slaughtered animal.

Şeker Bayramı and Kurban Bayramı belong to the official calendar of Muslims all over the world. Distinctively Turkish, by contrast, is the celebration of six nights distributed through the calendar known as Kandil Geceleri (Lamp Nights). Each of these nights is of religious significance for all Muslims, but only in Turkey (and in some countries once ruled by the Ottomans) are they given this collective designation, which refers to the illumination of the mosques and the stringing of rows of lights between their minarets. These nights are marked gastronomically by the preparation of various special desserts, primarily *lokma* but sometimes helva, and distinctive *çöreks* adorned with sesame seeds.

The tenth day of Muharram, the first month in the Islamic lunar calendar, has also held an important place in the popular religion of the Turks. It has given rise to a sweet soup, known like the day itself as *aşure.* (See page 230 for a detailed discussion.)

Since the Islamic calendar is lunar, it regresses ten days in each year in respect to the solar calendar, and the religious festivals that are set in accordance with it move gradually from one season to another. Other festive occasions, and their gastronomic accompaniments, are fully seasonal in nature: the cherry harvest, the weaning of lambs, the beginning of the ramming season. Not surprisingly, these festivals are confined almost exclusively to the countryside, and even there they are gradually dying out. Still celebrated is the Festival of Hıdırellez, a celebration of the arrival of spring held on May 5 and 6. The name of this festival comes from a compounding of Hıdır and Ilyas, two figures that symbolize fertility and immortality in popular Islamic tradition. People go picnicking on foods as varied as hard-boiled eggs, grape-leaf dolmas, lettuce salads, and different kinds of *börek* and *çörek*. Sometimes a lamb may be slaughtered, and its meat roasted and eaten with bulgur pilaf.

A seasonal celebration of a quite different type, one that I remember from my own childhood, belonged to an urban milieu. During the forty coldest days of winter (reckoned to begin on December 22 and end on January 30), friends would invite each other to their homes to while away the long winter evenings eating helva—hence the name of the occasion, *helva sohbetleri* "helva conversations"—and listening to poetry. Other substantial foods would also be prepared for the occasion, such as stuffed turkey and *börek*. At the end of the winter, all those who had survived the cold season without falling sick would sacrifice an animal and organize additional "helva conversations"—an excuse for more eating and conviviality!

Both these categories of festival, the religious and the seasonal, serve to fix the pattern of social and communal life. A third set of occasions serve as landmarks in the life of the individual and the family; their particular quality, too, is marked by appropriate gifts of food and drink.

This pertains particularly to marriage and all the carefully calibrated stages that have traditionally led up to it. In the past, when verbal agreement was made between the families of bride and groom, sherbet was served, followed by sweet coffee, *lokum,* and candy, the hope being that all this sweetness would somehow be reflected in the marriage-to-be. The formal announcement of engagement was similarly accompanied by much sweetness! On the night that the bride was taken to the bathhouse and the following night when she was adorned with henna, a substantial meal was served, consisting of pilaf and meat dishes, rich desserts, fruits, and roasted nuts. A similar ample repast would be prepared on the day of the wedding itself; essential elements of this feast were a meat pilaf, a warm vegetable dish, and *tepsi böreği*. If all went well on the wedding night, the family of the bridegroom would send a tray of desserts to the family of the bride the next day.

The procedures leading up to marriage in modern Turkey have been telescoped into a few simple stages, and not many people can afford the money and time required to provide such repeated hospitality on so lavish a scale. Nonetheless, the wedding and its preliminaries are still the occasion for much cooking, eating, and drinking.

A birth is, of course, a festive occasion, but it is not celebrated with the same ceremony as the circumcision of a male child, which traditionally takes place when the boy is at least four or five years old. Then he is dressed in a white suit and crown of velvet and gold thread, to help him forget his discomfort, and the guests are served a meal that should traditionally contain a meat pilaf, helva, and a saffron-flavored rice dessert (*zerde*) that is now almost entirely forgotten in Turkey.

Even death, the somber counterpart of the processes of generation and birth, has its culinary consequences. As the Turkish writer Nezihe Araz puts it with characteristic grace, human beings have never been able to accustom themselves to death, despite the grim regularity of its occurrence, and "those who seek to modify the nature of death by means of various ceremonies, to soften its impact, naturally have recourse to food in their efforts." Even now, it is customary in Turkey for neighbors and friends to send food to a bereaved household for three days after the occurrence of death. The trays they send will always include warm soups, but never the sweets and desserts associated with joyous occasions. However, on the evening after the funeral, helva is prepared by female friends and relatives of the family, to the accompaniment of prayers, and it is then distributed in the neighborhood, with the request that everyone pray for the departed in whose name it has been prepared. Seven days after the funeral, *lokma* is made and similarly eaten in memory of the departed.

Many of the rich traditions described here have diminished or been forgotten in recent times. Changes in material culture, in living arrangements, and in the overall atmosphere of society have combined to make impossible the retention of the former leisurely way of life with its ornate and sumptuous celebration of special occasions. But it may be thought that the essential has been preserved: the celebration of continuity in patterns of religious devotion, in the cycle of the seasons, and in the life and death of the individual, by means of food that nurtures the heart and the spirit even more than the body.

Markets Magnificent and Modest

My way led me first through the spice bazaar, where all the scents of Arabia came streaming towards me. Even the entry to this bazaar was mystical, and the light effects had a picturesque effect. There was light only immediately beneath the roof, and it was cool, despite the great heat outside. . . .*

Thus opens the description of Istanbul's Mısır Çarsısı, the Egyptian Spice Bazaar, as it appeared to a German traveler in the late nineteenth century. Plainly little had changed since its inception in the mid-seventeenth century by Turhan Sultan, the Russian wife of Sultan Ibrahim and mother of Sultan Mehmed IV. Turhan Sultan was also responsible for the building of the nearby Yeni Cami (known also, in her memory, as Valide Sultan Camii, the Mosque of the Queen Mother). The great fires that frequently ravaged Ottoman Istanbul did not spare the interior of the Spice Bazaar, but the shops were always rebuilt, and the lofty shell of the bazaar, surmounted with domes, has survived down to the present. There are two explanations for the name of the market: either that spices and other goods imported from Egypt were sold there (Egypt serving then as a great entrepot for the spice trade) or that the tax revenues of Cairo were used for its upkeep. Remarkably, a spice market stood on almost exactly the same site in Byzantine times, so that the present-day market is in fact the descendant of a tradition going back to the pre-Ottoman period.

Entering the Spice Bazaar today is still a dramatic experience. With little transition from the street to the entrance, which is festooned with the gaudy displays of the newspaper and magazine sellers, one leaves behind the bustle and the often inclement weather of the outside world—heat and dust in the summer, rain and mud in the winter—to be enveloped immediately in a vast, dimly lit realm redolent with hundreds of scents. Apart from the often dazzling electric lights that highlight the displays in each shop, light is provided only by glass-covered apertures high in the vaulted ceiling that arches over the market. On each side of a walkway broad enough to take two lanes of traffic stand hundreds of shops offering the most varied kinds of foodstuffs. The Spice Bazaar is in fact like a perma-

* Anna Grosser-Rilke, *Nieverwehte Klänge* (Leipzig and Berlin, 1937).

nent exhibition of Turkish foodstuffs. Here you will find not only every type of spice both familiar and unfamiliar but also dried roots and barks used for medicinal purposes; a great variety of cheeses; *sucuk* and *pastırma;* honey, in both jars and honeycomb; black and green olives; almonds, walnuts, hazelnuts and pistachios; dried fruit and herbs; rice and other grains; clarified butter; rose water and bergamot oil; and a host of other items the precise nature and use of which are a mystery to the uninitiated. Use is made of every available inch: items are piled high on marble-topped counters, hung from the ceiling by string, threaten to disgorge from open-mouthed sacks, and swim on the surface of barrels.

The Spice Bazaar is, in a way, an outpost of Anatolia situated in the heart of Istanbul. Most of the wares sold there originate in Anatolia, and the dominant atmosphere is the same one of business-like sobriety that prevails in so many small Anatolian towns. Many of the shopkeepers are themselves from Anatolia, as their accents and somewhat darker complexions reveal, and although the younger members of the family take quickly to the modernity of the Istanbul milieu, the patriarch sitting impassively by the cash register obviously remains true to his origins.

If you walk straight through the Spice Bazaar you will come to Mahmudpaşa, a complex of steep streets selling all kinds of clothing that in turn merges with the environs of the great Covered Market (a place of great interest, but largely irrelevant to the gastronome). If, on the other hand, you retrace your steps toward the main entrance you may notice a staircase leading up to Pandeli's, the celebrated restaurant situated immediately over the entrance. Now operated by Hristo, son of the founder and a trained obstetrician before he took up his present profession, Pandeli's is open for lunch. It affords a splendid view over the busy confluence of the Golden Horn and the Sea of Marmara and is decorated with exquisite tiles.

A quite different ambiance from that of the Spice Bazaar prevails in the Cicek Pasajı (the Flower Passage), which is situated in Beyoğlu on the other side of Istanbul. Less a traditional Turkish market than an arcade of European design, the Flower Passage reflects the spirit of old Pera, with its cosmopolitan mix of nationalities and love of entertainment.

This arcade, first built in 1876, was put to various uses until it acquired its present designation in the aftermath of World War I.

Then White Russian refugee girls, selling flowers in the streets of Istanbul to eke out a living, would run down this passageway to escape the importunate advances of the British and French troops then occupying Istanbul—or so it is said! The Flower Passage came fully into its own as a center of eating, drinking, and merriment in the 1940s, when a cluster of taverns and beer shops sprang up along it. These attracted not only the literary intelligentsia and the occasional visiting celebrity (such as Maria Callas), but also a host of people who would both entertain and prey on the revelers: violin and accordion players, young gypsy girls dancing on the tables, matrons measuring the blood pressure of elderly reprobates to warn them against too much excitement, fortune-tellers, cardsharps, lottery ticket sellers, all kinds of mountebanks. Men would come to drink and discuss with equal passion the great (or seemingly great) political questions of the day and the merits of their favorite soccer teams.

The novelist Haldun Taner engagingly described the therapeutic effects of a visit to the Flower Passage in its heyday in the 1940s:

> On a careladen day, you might plunge into this passage from the Fish Market and advance slowly through the sea of people, pushing and shoving your way and often exchanging greetings with those against whom you were pushing and shoving, irrespective of whether you knew them or not, bumping into the stumbling drunkards that crossed your path, and pouring out your troubles to the hawkers who pestered you. You would then realise with astonishment that you had shed the anxieties that were contorting you a short while ago, the daily problems and accumulations of resentments, and that you could not even remember why you had been tormenting yourself.*

In May 1978, not long after a report of the Istanbul municipality proclaimed the passage structurally sound, much of it came tumbling down in the middle of the night, as if not only the passage of years but an excess of merrymaking had undermined it. Almost exactly ten years later, the process of restoration was completed but, as might have been predicted, much of the old atmosphere was lost forever. Gone, for example, was the jumble of nondescript chairs

* Quoted by Gürol Sözen in *Bin Çeşit İstanbul ve Boğaziçi Yalıları* (Istanbul, 1989), 74.

and tables strewn carelessly along and across the passage, replaced by uniform benches and tables screwed to the ground and arranged with mathematical precision.

Something, however, survives. The Flower Passage, even in its sanitized form, is still a place to go for distraction from one's cares, as I discovered when staying in a nearby hotel. Entering the passage, one is greeted with a pungent odor compounded of draught beer and mussels being fried in great vats of sizzling oil. Mussels are indeed the chief accompaniment to beer in the Flower Passage. The taverns and drinking places—now fashionably renamed "restaurants"—are interspersed with flower shops and greengrocers' stalls, where a profusion of fruits and vegetables spill out onto areas of the sidewalk not yet claimed by the screwed-down tables and benches. Walking through this profusion of color and smell, and assailed on every side by a cacophony of shopkeepers praising their wares, loud conversation at the tables, and the crying of children briefly separated from their mothers, one finds it hard indeed to remain deep in one's own thoughts.

❋　❋　❋

Burhaniye would not rank high on a list of tourist priorities in Turkey. But this little Aegean town—not quite as sleepy as it used to be a few years ago—has a special place in my personal image of Turkey, for my father maintains a summer residence at a nearby seaside settlement and I visit it almost annually.

There is not much that is remarkable about Burhaniye. Grouped along a single main thoroughfare are all the standard amenities of the Anatolian town—a bus station; a mosque with adjacent teahouse; a variety of kebab shops, pastry shops, and pharmacies; a square with a taxi stand. For most of the week, it is pretty somnolent, but on Mondays it comes to life for a day with the weekly open market held in a big walled enclosure not far from the mosque. It is this market in fact that constitutes virtually the sole reason for an outsider to venture into Burhaniye. A few sun-bleached and bewildered-looking German and Scandinavian tourists mingle with self-assured and businesslike crowds of shoppers from the resort settlements nearby, prosperous folk who spend most of the year in Ankara or Istanbul and are decked out now in their fashionable summer finery. Both groups of outsiders seem almost equally alien from the townsfolk.

From early morning the market is filled with all the produce of the region, one of the most fertile in Anatolia. Particularly impressive is the great quantity and variety of olives, heaped up glistening hillocks according to their size, shape, and color, which may be green, pink, brown, or black. (These varying colors are determined by factors such as the degree of ripeness when the olives were picked and in what kind of brine they were treated.) There is also an abundance of freshly pressed olive oil—again in many different colors—available either *en gros* in great barrels or bottled. So ubiquitous is the olive in this part of Turkey that many households have their own olive oil press, and people would be at a loss to understand the meaning of "virgin olive oil," this being the only variety with which they are acquainted.

Figs are, of course, another specialty of the region, which includes Izmir (or Smyrna, as it is still archaically known in conjunction with figs). These are sold for the most part by village women who have come to town for the day, squatting on the ground at the edge of the market with their wares displayed in baskets lined with grape leaves. The dry form in which Smyrna figs reach the West is a far cry from the luxuriant sweetness of these delicious golden, green, or rich purple fruits, which are a pleasure to the eye and the touch as well as the palate.

Overwhelmingly vivid taste characterizes virtually everything to be found in the market: the Morello cherries that make their appearance in the late spring; the strawberries that follow soon after; apricots and peaches that it is impossible to bite into, however delicately, without being drenched in juice; melons and watermelons lying on the ground in great heaps, with samples cut open to reveal their hidden treasure of fragrance and color.

Particularly noteworthy among the vegetables are the eggplants with their shiny, dark purple exteriors; they are similar in shape to the Italian eggplant, but somewhat longer and thicker, being about 1½ to 2 inches in diameter. The eggplants commonly available in the West are but a pale and distant echo of these masterpieces fed by the rich soil and sun of the Aegean.

Peppers, too, are numerous: both the long, thin, and very tender green peppers that can be snapped apart as easily as a pea pod and, sweet or hot, find a place in almost every summer meal; and green, red, or yellow bell peppers used for dolmas that can suffuse a whole neighborhood with their redolence when cooking.

Everything else the cook may need is also conveniently gathered together in the market: fresh herbs; fresh hazelnuts; fresh butter and cheeses, sometimes mixed with herbs; different varieties of rice, beans, and grains; and cookware that ranges from the most traditional to plastic.

Once the cook's purchases in the market are done, a visit to the butcher or the fishmonger completes the day's business. What remains is the fairly easy task of converting the generous and precious offerings of nature into a satisfying meal.

The Daily Eating Pattern

Turks take three meals a day. Breakfast is simple but fortifying. It consists of soft-boiled eggs, several varieties of cheese and olives, and jam and butter, all enjoyed with bread freshly baked that morning and copious quantities of tea. In winter the breakfast menu may be supplemented with *sucuk* (spicy sausage) and *pastırma* (cured beef flavored with garlic and spices).

Lunch is traditionally a hot meal, which used to be taken at home by the whole family. Nowadays, however, in urban areas both husband and wife are at work and children take their lunch at school. Dinner, therefore, is the main meal of the day.

A typical family dinner often begins with soup, especially in winter. A hot dish almost always follows, usually made with meat but sometimes with poultry or fish and perhaps including vegetables or legumes. If this dish includes starchy vegetables such as potatoes or is made with a rice filling (as with meat dolmas), it is served simply with bread; otherwise it may be accompanied by pilaf. Some dishes such as grilled meats and fried *köfte* may be accompanied by fried potatoes. In summer a garden salad will also be served, replaced by pickles in the winter.

After the hot dish, the much-loved olive oil dishes make their appearance, served either cold or at room temperature. Regarded as side dishes and not essential components of the menu, they keep well for many days and do not need reheating. It is common therefore to make two or three dishes of this type at the same time in large quantities for serving several days in succession. *Meze* also may be served as side dishes, as may *börek,* although some types of *börek* such as *Talaş Böreği* (page 212) may take the place of a hot meat dish. *Börek* are also taken as snacks at any time as well as being favored for breakfast. Side dishes are always presented in separate serving dishes and are never mixed together on the plate, either with each other or with the hot dish. The taste of each side dish deserves to be enjoyed individually. In many households it is even customary to change the plates after the hot dish has been eaten.

Some extremely substantial dishes such as *mantı* are satisfying enough to form complete meals in themselves and are therefore not followed by side dishes.

The most common desserts are seasonal fruits, light milk puddings, or fruit compotes. Syrupy, pastry-type desserts such as baklava are not part of a typical meal. They are enjoyed separately, as occasional treats taken with coffee or tea.

When designing your menu, be sure not to include dishes containing the same or similar ingredients; for example, it would be unwise to serve both a rice-filled meat dolma and a pilaf. Remember also to serve bread with all Turkish dishes except *mantı* and *börek*.

SOUPS

✤✤✤

Turks love soups, and so integral are they to their cuisine that it is difficult to conceive of *çorba,* the Turkish word for soup, as a borrowing. But respectable lexicographical authorities compel us to admit that it is derived from the Persian word *shurba,* composed of *shur,* meaning "salty, brackish," and *-ba,* a suffix indicating a food. The word *shurba* has long since disappeared from Persian usage, and the few soups found in Persian cuisine are nowadays designated as *sup,* an obvious borrowing from French. By contrast, *çorba* has not only maintained itself in Turkish but passed from it into the Balkan languages and into Arabic (giving rise to a false etymology based on the Arabic verb *shariba,* "to drink").

The countless varieties of soup found in Turkish cuisine offer a constant and loyal companionship that is particularly welcome and comforting on a cold winter's day or during times of sickness when the stomach refuses all else. Soup caresses the empty stomach at the end of each day's fast during Ramadan, and it also forms the vanguard of the banquets served on festive occasions. Above all, soup is an economical source of nourishment; even if nothing else can be found in the house, the ingredients to make some kind of soup will usually be available even in the humblest of homes.

Eastern Anatolian Yogurt Soup

4 TO 6 SERVINGS   [YOĞURT ÇORBASI]

Many of my most vivid childhood memories touch somehow on food. I remember, for instance, a snowbound village high in the mountains of Eastern Anatolia where I once visited a simple peasant house, accompanied by my father. We arrived in the village at dusk. The cattle were being driven back to the village, their lightly tinkling bells suggesting the movement of their hulks through the darkness, and the accumulated smoke from dozens of wood fires mixed acridly with the cold night air. But inside the house of our hosts—as, no doubt, elsewhere in the village—a warmth prevailed that owed less to the fire raging in the hearth than to the simple and robust hospitality of the villagers. The floor was of beaten earth, covered with *kilims* of lively color and design, and the walls were similarly stark, the monotony of the whitewash broken only by brightly burnished copper pots and utensils. Stacked in a corner were quilts that would soon be unfolded to guard us against the night chill. But first it was time for the evening meal, the yogurt soup that stood ready in a steaming cauldron next to the hearth. A low wooden table was placed in the center of the room, and we all ate generous portions of soup with those quintessentially Turkish wooden spoons. Accompanied by ovals of freshly baked flat bread, this soup formed an unforgettable meal, warming in senses both literal and figurative. Even now whenever I prepare yogurt soup in my California kitchen, the image of that charmed winter evening hovers through my mind.

There are many versions of this much-loved soup, which is made frequently in almost every home in the country. In eastern Turkey, particularly in the city of Erzurum and its environs, it is especially popular; the grain used in it there is hulled wheat. In other regions it is usually made with rice. Although it is flavored in most places with dried mint, cilantro is preferred in Erzurum.

6 cups good chicken or
    meat stock
⅔ cup hulled wheat
    (barley also works
    very well)
3½ cups plain yogurt
3 tablespoons flour
2 egg yolks
2 cups cold water
Salt
2 or 3 tablespoons
    unsalted butter
¼ cup dried mint leaves

Bring the stock to a boil in a large heavy pan, stir in the grain, cover, and simmer over medium heat for about 40 minutes, until the wheat is tender.

In a large bowl, with a wooden spoon, mix the yogurt with the flour and egg yolks until smooth. Gradually mix in the cold water. Stir this into the soup through a sieve. Season with salt. Cover and simmer the soup gently for 10 minutes.

Heat the butter in a small saucepan until frothy. Sprinkle in the mint leaves, crushing with your fingertips as you add them. Stir and let the mixture sizzle a second or two; pour this into the soup. Serve hot.

Sometimes instead of adding the mint to the butter I add it directly to the soup and omit the butter and it is still good. This soup keeps very well and can be reheated for subsequent servings. It thickens as it stands; thin with water.

Variation: Use ½ cup coarsely chopped fresh cilantro instead of mint, adding it directly to the soup just before removing it from the heat. It gives the soup an entirely different flavor.

Chick-pea–Red Pepper–Celery Root Soup with Cilantro

* *

4 SERVINGS

[NOHUT ÇORBASI]

2 tablespoons unsalted
    butter
1½ cups chopped onions
½ cup chopped carrots
½ cup diced celery root
1 large sweet red pepper,
    coarsely chopped
5 sprigs flat-leaf parsley
3 sprigs cilantro
1 cup chick-peas, soaked
    in water overnight
1 cup chicken or meat
    stock
Salt
1 cup half-and-half or
    milk
3 tablespoons chopped
    flat-leaf parsley
3 tablespoons chopped
    cilantro

This particularly delicious soup is a beautiful gold color with specks of red and green.

❋   ❋   ❋

Put the butter, onions, carrots, celery root, red pepper, and herb sprigs in a heavy pan, cover, and let the vegetables sweat over low heat until they are limp, about 10 minutes. If the mixture looks too dry, splash in some water to keep it from burning. Drain the chick-peas and stir them into the vegetables. Add enough water to cover, cover the pan, and simmer until the chick-peas are very tender. Remove from heat and put the soup through a sieve. Return to the pan and stir in 1 cup chicken or meat stock, season with salt, and 1 cup half-and-half or milk. Add the chopped parsley and cilantro, bring to a boil, and serve.

Creamy Red Lentil Soup

❋❋

4 SERVINGS

[KIRMIZI MERCİMEK ÇORBASI]

1 cup red lentils
1½ cups chopped onions
4 tablespoons unsalted
    butter
6½ cups good chicken or
    meat stock
2 tablespoons flour
1 or 2 egg yolks
1 cup milk
Salt
Croutons (recipe follows)

Red lentils, not used very often in the West, have an earthy, satisfying flavor; they do not require soaking and they cook fast. This soup has a lovely yellow color and velvety texture.

❋   ❋   ❋

Pick over the lentils, wash, drain, and reserve.

Sauté the onions in 2 tablespoons of the butter until golden. Add the stock and bring to a boil. Stir in the lentils, cover, and simmer gently for 25 or 30 minutes, until they are very soft. Pass the lentils through a sieve, pressing against them, and reserve, discarding the residue.

Melt the remaining butter in a heavy pan, add the flour and cook, stirring, for 2 minutes or so, until the flour turns deep golden. Stirring continuously with one hand, pour in the lentil liquid. Simmer the soup, stirring frequently, over low heat for 3 minutes. In a small bowl, whisk the egg yolk with the milk. Season with salt. Whisk some hot soup into the egg mixture and then pour it all back into the soup while stirring. Bring it to just under boiling and serve. The soup thickens as it stands and can be thinned with water or stock.

Croutons

❋❋❋❋❋❋❋❋❋❋❋❋❋

¾ cup small bread cubes
Butter

Fry the bread cubes in hot butter until golden and crispy.

Chicken Soup with Vermicelli

6 SERVINGS

[TAVUK SUYUYLA ŞEHRİYE ÇORBASI]

CHICKEN STOCK

One 4-pound chicken, cut into 8 or 10 pieces, including the feet (all fat removed), or 4 pounds chicken parts, such as backs, wings, and necks (all fat removed)
1½ cups coarsely chopped onions
1 cup chopped carrots
10 sprigs flat-leaf parsley
1 bay leaf
½ teaspoon peppercorns
1 teaspoon salt

SOUP

1½ to 2 ounces vermicelli
4 egg yolks
¼ cup lemon juice (or to taste)
Chopped flat-leaf parsley

This is the Turkish version of the chicken soup that many people instinctively feel to be curative. Like many other Turkish soups, it is finished with egg yolk and lemon juice binding.

Put all ingredients for the stock in a pot, cover with about 4 quarts cold water, and bring to a simmer. Periodically skim off the scum that rises to the surface. Let simmer for at least 3 hours. Strain and reserve the stock; if you have more than about 2 quarts, simmer to reduce.

Bring the stock to a gentle boil, taste for salt, and add the vermicelli. Cook until the pasta is tender. In a bowl, whisk the egg yolks with the lemon juice. Stir in some hot soup, whisking continuously, and pour it all into the soup while stirring. Adjust to taste with lemon juice, bring to just under boiling, and serve immediately, sprinkled with parsley.

Fresh Fava Bean Soup with Yogurt-Dill Cream

✳✳✳

4 SERVINGS

[TAZE BAKLA ÇORBASI]

3½ pounds fresh fava
   beans
1½ cups chopped onions
3 to 4 tablespoons olive
   oil
About 7½ cups water
Salt
3 tablespoons chopped
   fresh dill
Lemon juice
Yogurt-Dill Cream
   (recipe follows)
Lemon wedges

Shell fava beans and set aside.

Sauté the onions in the oil until limp. Add beans and turn them in the oil a minute or so. Add 6 cups of water and a little salt, cover, and simmer about 30 minutes, or until beans are very tender.

Stir in dill and simmer 1 or 2 additional minutes. Remove from heat and cool slightly. If beans get too dry as they cook, add a little water; almost all the water will be absorbed at the end of the cooking.

Put beans through a sieve, return puree to pan, and stir in enough water (about 1½ cups) to get a cream soup consistency. Simmer about 5 minutes. Correct seasoning with salt and a little lemon juice to taste. Serve hot with yogurt-dill cream. Pass some lemon wedges with the soup.

Yogurt-Dill Cream

✳✳✳✳✳✳✳✳✳✳✳✳

¾ cup Mellow Yogurt
   Cream (page 276), or
   crème fraîche
1 to 2 teaspoons chopped
   fresh dill

With a wooden spoon, mix yogurt cream or crème fraîche with dill until smooth.

Saffron-Perfumed Mussel Soup

✻✻✻

[MİDYE ÇORBASI]

⅓ cup chopped onion
⅓ cup chopped celery
⅓ cup chopped carrot
2 sprigs flat-leaf parsley
1 bay leaf
½ teaspoon black
   peppercorns
5 cups water
1 quart mussels
1 teaspoon saffron
   threads
2 tablespoons butter
1½ tablespoons flour
Salt
3 egg yolks
2 tablespoons lemon juice
Chopped chervil

This soup is inspired by a fish soup recorded in an anonymous eighteenth-century treatise on cookery. It was infused with saffron and finished with the familiar egg yolk and lemon juice binding.

✻ ✻ ✻

Put the vegetables with the parsley, bay leaf, and peppercorns in a pot, add water and simmer for 20 minutes.

Meanwhile, scrub the mussels and set aside. Soak the saffron in 3 tablespoons hot water and set aside. Bring the vegetable broth to a boil, stir in the mussels, and wait just until the mussels open. Remove them and strain the stock through a cheesecloth-lined sieve. Return the stock to the pan. Remove the mussels from the shells, reserve them, and discard the shells.

Heat the butter, then add the flour and cook, stirring, for about 2 minutes. Stir in the reserved stock and saffron water, season with salt, and simmer 7 or 8 minutes. In a bowl beat the egg yolks and lemon juice with a fork. Return the mussels to the simmering stock. Stir some of the hot stock into the egg and lemon mixture and pour it all into the soup. Bring to just below boiling and serve hot, sprinkled with chervil.

Bulgur and Lentil Soup with Red Peppers and Mint

4 TO 6 SERVINGS

[NANELİ KIRMIZI MERCİMEK VE BULGUR ÇORBASI]

¾ cup chopped onions
4 tablespoons unsalted butter
1 tablespoon tomato puree
7 cups chicken or meat stock
½ cup bulgur
½ cup red lentils
2 tablespoons flour
Salt
¼ cup dried mint, crushed
1 teaspoon dried thyme leaves
¼ teaspoon crushed red pepper flakes

Sauté onions in 2 tablespoons butter until limp. Stir in tomato puree until it blends with the onions. Add the stock, bulgur, and lentils, cover, and simmer until bulgur and lentils are thoroughly cooked. Remove from heat, cool slightly, put through a sieve, and set aside.

Melt 2 tablespoons butter in a pan, stir in the flour, and cook, stirring, about 2 minutes, until flour turns golden. Gradually whisk in the soup. Keep at a gentle simmer, and salt to taste. Stir in the mint, thyme, and pepper flakes; continue simmering for 1 or 2 minutes; serve hot.

MEZE

❋❋❋❋❋❋❋❋❋❋❋❋❋❋❋❋❋❋❋❋❋❋❋❋❋❋❋❋❋❋❋❋❋❋❋

The dawn is here; arise, my lovely one!
Pour slowly the wine and touch the lute.
For those who still are here will not stay long
While those departed never will return.

❋❋❋

Thus runs one of the poignant quatrains of Omar Khayyam, almost as well known in Turkey as in his native Iran. It reflects beautifully an attitude toward life shared by many peoples of the Balkans, Turkey, and the Middle East. Part of their shared culture and outlook on life is a determination to appreciate the varied pleasures of human existence. They have a keen appreciation of the transitory nature of life, of the fragile nature of the existence on which Westerners habitually lavish such proud and obsessive concern. This perception often induces a dignified melancholy that has a thousand cultural expressions and enhanced ability to enjoy a few simple pleasures, at the head of which stand eating and drinking in a leisurely manner and congenial company. From this has arisen the tradition of certain types of food known as *meze*, eaten leisurely to the accompaniment of drinking. This is a tradition at least as rich as *tapas* of Spain or the still largely unknown *zakuski* of Russia.

I have traced the possible origin of *meze* to ancient Persia, where wine was the center of an emotional and esthetic experience that also included other forms of enjoyment, notably food and music. The original *meze* of Persia appear to have been tart fruits, such as pomegranates, quinces, and citrons, designed to alleviate the bitter taste left by unripe wine. Later nuts and small pieces of roasted meat were added to the spread of the wine drinker.

Despite the Islamic prohibition against wine, it continued to be drunk by nonconformists, and the ancient habit of eating while drinking also persisted to be passed on from Iran to Turkey. Not surprisingly, this form of food—known universally by the original word *meze* and its derivatives—expanded and diversified greatly after its arrival in Anatolia, an area rich in the bounty of nature. In fact, *meze* may well be the category of Turkish cuisine that best exemplifies its Mediterranean character.

The home, then as now, was often the locus for convivial gatherings involving eating and drinking, but sometimes a different locale, specific to the purpose, was preferred. The café was probably the simplest and most universal of such places; it should not be forgotten that the café originated in Turkey. There is also the drinking place, a marginal institution no doubt in Muslim countries (nonexistent in some), but nonetheless widespread throughout the area. In Turkish poetry as well as in its Persian sources of inspiration, the tavern with all its accoutrements was often praised, and so fixed a topos of poetry did it become that it finally acquired a symbolical and mystical meaning: the tavern stood for the Sufi hospice.

But even short of such rarefied interpretations, the tavern has not, on the whole, been a sinister place, dedicated to the sole purpose of quick and efficient intoxication. Food is consumed with wine, which is drunk gradually not by solitary drinkers but by men conversing on a variety of subjects. The tavern should not be idealized into a debating chamber for high philosophical discourse, but it functioned as a place where the inescapable burdens of worldly existence could be gently discarded for a few precious hours.

The setting of a tavern, café, or restaurant in which *meze* is consumed is important. It is often a place of natural beauty, with running water nearby to heighten the sense of tranquillity. The scenery combines with the pleasures of the palate to produce a complete hedonistic experience.

A noisy but picturesque setting for the consumption of *meze* is provided by the little fish restaurants nestling beneath the Galata Bridge in Istanbul, a pontoon bridge built in 1913 that somehow defies all prediction of imminent collapse. While the fish of your choice is being grilled in the kitchen, you watch the ceaseless traffic of steamers that connect the city with the islands in the Sea of Marmara and the resorts along the Bosphorus, and sharpen your appetite on an array of simple *meze* such as a slice of fragrant melon dripping with natural sugar, a slab of creamy white tangy cheese, a small bowl of glistening black olives from the Aegean, a quarter of a good baguette, and maybe some cranberry bean *plaki* simmered in olive oil, lemon juice, tomatoes, garlic cloves, and parsley. The liveliness of the scene itself sharpens your senses.

Were you to take one of those steamers that dock at the Galata Bridge, you could alight somewhere along the Bosphorus and visit a small café restaurant surrounded by chestnut and acacia trees and jutting out into the water. Nearby, you will see a narrow cobbled path leading down to the water's edge and little boys playing with stray cats, and notice an abandoned wooden boat tied to a tree stump, rocking endlessly back and forth in the water. The sparkle of the Bosphorus contrasts vividly with the air of gentle decay exuded by the old wooden houses (*yalıs*) standing on the shore—houses that once saw a life of elegant opulence that inspired European artists and writers such as Pierre Loti.

An array of little *meze* dishes is spread in front of you, containing mostly seafood. Typical is a mussel *plaki*—fleshy mussels stewed in their own juice and olive oil with tomatoes, celeriac, yellow potatoes, whole garlic cloves, and parsley and served with lemon juice at room temperature in their shiny black shells. Another favorite seafood *meze* is deep-fried golden squid rings or mussel brochettes, crispy and light, served with a pungent walnut-garlic-vinegar sauce called *tarator*. A good accompaniment would be a salad made with dried haricot beans, red onions, garnished with yellow and white slices of hard-boiled eggs, shiny black olives, and parsley, dressed in fruity olive oil and vinegar. Never lacking, here or elsewhere, are generous slices of fresh, crusty bread, the type that everyone in Turkey, rich or poor, takes for granted, but that has to be queued for here at a handful of special bakeries.

All this you can enjoy while breathing in the intoxicating sea air and watching the gulls circling in the hope of catching scraps discarded by fishermen from their bobbing boats, as the ships proceed up the Bosphorus against the background of the green hills of Asia.

In Izmir, a long street called Kordon Boyu runs along the shores of the Aegean. Lined with fashionable apartment houses and expensive restaurants, it is an ideal vantage point to watch the violent red sun of summer sink mercifully and dramatically beneath the horizon. After dark, you hear the soft murmur of laughter and conversation from the balconies of apartments overlooking the sea, together with the gentle clinking of silverware and bone china. The *meze* most likely to accompany the drinks of these well-heeled people is smoked sturgeon, juicy morsels of grilled shrimp brochettes, glistening blue-black mussels, tiny red glossy peppers, deep purple eggplants stuffed with rice, currants, toasted pine nuts, and fresh herbs, simmered in olive oil and served chilled and sharpened with lemon juice, and deep-fried paper-thin pastries with a variety of savory fillings.

At the restaurants and sidewalk cafés on the street below, closed now to all traffic but horse-drawn carriages, people also are enjoying their *meze* and drinks as gypsy street musicians pass by playing cheerful tunes. A matchless aroma arises from the juices of swordfish and lamb dripping onto the fire, the roasting eggplants, the piquant long green peppers, fresh cut cucumbers, melons, pounded garlic, chopped thyme, and the unmistakable fragrance of *rakı* (the Turkish equivalent of ouzo)—all intermingled with each other.

The *meze* I shall tell you how to prepare need not be consumed in any of the settings I have described. You can improvise your own setting: the essential is good company and the willingness to spend a few hours of leisurely eating and drinking with your guests.

Let me stress that *meze* do not form a fixed or closed category of food. *Meze* are in fact drawn from different categories of food, and the *meze* I describe here can also be served as side dishes. Conversely, some dishes that I have chosen to include in other sections of this book might also be used as *meze*. The word *meze* signifies an eclectic, flexible, and often personal choice of foods that are a suitable accompaniment to the consumption of *rakı* and other alcoholic drinks.

The *meze* most commonly favored are meatless vegetables made with olive oil and served cold or at room temperature. All meatless dolmas (pages 121–34) are good choices for *meze*, as are Small Eggplants Stuffed with Garlic Cloves, Tomatoes and Parsley, known in the West by its Turkish name, *İmam Bayıldı* (page 122), Artichoke Hearts Cooked with Dill (page 124), and Puree of Fava Beans with Olive Oil–Lemon-Dill Sauce (page 126). White Beans Stewed with Garlic Cloves and Olive Oil (page 128) is particularly favored. Various salads also make excellent *meze*. Examples are White Bean Salad (page 147), eggplant salads (pages 150 and 152), Beet Salad with Yogurt (page 150), Roasted Eggplant and Chili Salad (page 52), and Lentil and Bulgur Salad (page 153).

Grilled tidbits of meat such as grilled or fried *köfte* and fish or shellfish also make good *meze*, examples being Grilled Bulgur *Köfte* with Herbs and Chilies (page 115) and Fried Fresh Anchovies (page 80).

Fingertip *börek* are always found on *meze* tables, especially Filo Cheese Rolls (page 62), Circassian *Börek* (page 210), and Filo

Triangles with Spicy Filling of Meat and Pine Nuts (page 214).

Failing these, a bowl of freshly roasted salted nuts, a slab of white cheese or kasseri cheese, or a slice of melon can all serve as *meze*.

Here, for your inspiration, is an account of a *rakı* and *meze* evening in late Ottoman times:

The news that the kitchens dreaded was when my grandfather decided to invite his friends to a *rakı* evening. He had many friends and acquaintances who graced his table, but he had a very select small group with whom he drank. These would be exclusively men, and the table would be set up in the garden, which, being on the Asian side afforded a glorious view of Topkapi and the minarets of the mosques. Drinking in Ottoman times was taken seriously. It was a lengthy affair, there was nothing to hurry for, no last train or boat to catch, no telephone call from Suadiye or Singapore to interrupt one's thoughts or privacy. One drank with one's special friends, to hear them discourse, at times seriously, at other times flippantly.

Poetry was sure to be recited, and one was expected to answer one poem with another. The *rakı* evening started about an hour before sunset, to appreciate the sunset behind the outline of the city. The table was laid out with *rakı*, ice, and water, olives, dried fruit, and raisins being the only food. Next would come white cheese and melon, a delightful combination and then slowly, when all the guests had arrived, a succession of different cheeses, and salads, a dish or two at a time, just sufficient for the number of the guests to take a spoonful of each. Dishes would be left on the table, one ate and drank at one's own pace.

After the preliminary assortment of dried and prepared foods, came those on which the kitchen staff had been working all day. At first there were cold dishes, the dolmas, eggplant in various ways, liver Albanian style, cold vegetables in olive oil. To follow came the hot dishes, some grilled or fried fish, meat balls, *börek* with cheese or minced meat, and so it went on, for between four or five hours. To let the guests know the evening was coming to an end, a plate of fruit, all peeled and sliced, appeared, and the guests could linger over this as long as the convivial atmosphere lasted. Finally, coffee was served and the guests would leave, merry certainly, inebriated never, or they would never be asked to grace that table again.*

* F. M. Katırcıoğlu, "Ottoman Culinary Habits," *Birinci Milletlerarası Yemek Kongresi Tebliğleri* (Istanbul, 1986), 165.

Circassian Chicken in Paprika-Laced Walnut Sauce

✹✹

8 TO 10 SERVINGS   [ÇERKEZ TAVUĞU]

One of the centerpieces of classical Turkish cuisine, this dish conjures up by its very name images of Circassian beauties languidly reclining in the gilded captivity of the harem. Circassia, a region of the northern Caucasus still noted for the beauty of its womenfolk, for many generations supplied the palaces of uxorious potentates with the choicest of its daughters. It was not for culinary skills that Circassian women were so highly esteemed, and it is a mystery why the name of their homeland should be linked to this dish, unless it was felt to be as voluptuously appealing as they were.

In the old days, one had to grind the walnuts in a meat grinder and collect the red-tinted oil that dripped from the mouth of the grinder. This process was time consuming and tedious. Nowadays one can create this splendid dish in a minimal time by using a blender or food processor.

Before making this dish you must make sure to have sweet-tasting walnuts and good-quality paprika. Both of these ingredients can sometimes be old or of poor quality. Taste the walnuts to make sure they do not have a rancid, harsh aftertaste.

The chicken is cooked first in an aromatic liquid, in as short a time as possible and cooled in its own liquid; the longer it is cooked the more flavor it loses.

One 3-pound chicken, cut
  into serving pieces
½ cup chopped onion
½ cup coarsely chopped
  carrots
8 black peppercorns
Salt
2 bay leaves
6 sprigs parsley

PAPRIKA OIL

3 tablespoons walnut oil
2 teaspoons good paprika

WALNUT SAUCE

2 ounces French bread
  (2 or 3 slices), crusts
  removed
Milk
¾ pound walnuts (about
  3 cups)
1½ tablespoons crushed
  garlic (page 286)
¼ cup plus 2 tablespoons
  minced onion
1 tablespoon plus 2 tea-
  spoons good paprika
1 teaspoon cayenne
  pepper
Salt

Walnut halves for
  garnish

Rinse the chicken pieces and pat dry; reserve. Put 1½ quarts water into a pot with the onion, carrots, peppercorns, salt, bay leaves, and parsley and simmer gently for 20 minutes. Add chicken pieces and simmer in the broth gently for 20 minutes, just until done. Cool in the cooking liquid. Remove the pieces from the pot; skin and bone them. Discard the skin and bones; divide the meat into bite-sized pieces and reserve. Strain the chicken stock and reserve.

Meanwhile, infuse the walnut oil with paprika by heating the oil until warm and stirring in the paprika. Leave this mixture on a warm spot on the stove.

To make the walnut sauce, soak the bread in a little milk until soft. Then squeeze it dry and set aside.

Grind the walnuts in a food processor or blender until fine. Put them in a large bowl. Crumble in the bread. Stir in the garlic, onion, paprika, cayenne, salt, and 2 cups of the strained defatted chicken stock. Mix and process in batches to make a smooth sauce. Adjust taste with salt; add a little more chicken stock if necessary to make a thick pouring consistency.

Mix half of the sauce well with the chicken pieces. Arrange the mixture on a serving platter and pour the remaining walnut sauce over it. Decorate with the walnut halves and the paprika-infused oil. Serve cold or at room temperature. It will keep several days in the refrigerator.

Roasted Eggplant and Chili Salad

4 SERVINGS

[PATLICAN VE BIBER SALATASI]

1 pound Japanese
  eggplants, roasted and
  peeled (1¾ cups
  cooked and chopped;
  pages 279–80)
2 small poblano chilies,
  roasted, peeled, and
  seeded (page 281)
¾ cup chopped onions
¼ cup olive oil
1 tomato, peeled and
  chopped
1 tablespoon garlic puree
Pinch of sugar
Salt
Pinch of crushed red
  pepper flakes
½ cup chopped flat-leaf
  parsley
2 teaspoons red wine
  vinegar

Chop eggplant and poblanos finely and set aside.

Cook onions in oil until almost reddish brown. Add tomato, garlic, sugar, salt, and red pepper flakes; cook 2 to 3 minutes. Add eggplant and poblanos, and ¼ cup parsley; cover and simmer about 10 minutes, until eggplant is very tender. Stir in vinegar, taste, and adjust with salt and vinegar. Serve cold or at room temperature, sprinkled with remaining parsley.

Fried Eggplant with Fresh Tomato-Garlic Vinegar Sauce

[DOMATESLI PATLICAN TAVASI]

1½-pound eggplant
Salt
Olive oil
1½ pounds fresh ripe
    tomatoes, peeled and
    minced
1 tablespoon crushed
    garlic (page 286)
3 teaspoons vinegar

Peel eggplant lengthwise in a striped fashion and remove the stem. Quarter it lengthwise and cut into ¼-inch-thick slices. Sprinkle generously with salt and let stand at least 1 hour. (See pages 279–80).

Rinse eggplant in plenty of water, squeeze each slice dry, and fry in 1 cup hot olive oil until golden brown on both sides. Drain on paper towels.

To make the sauce, pour off any remaining oil from the frying pan and put in 1 tablespoon fresh olive oil. Add tomatoes and sprinkle with a little salt; simmer until tomatoes form a sauce, mashing them down with a fork. Stir in garlic and vinegar and remove from heat. Taste and adjust with salt and vinegar. Place the eggplant in a serving bowl and cover with the sauce. Serve cold or at room temperature with crusty bread.

Roasted Red Peppers with Garlic and Vinegar

6 SERVINGS

[SIRKELI SARMISAKLI BİBER IZGARA]

6 sweet red peppers
1 tablespoon minced
    garlic
¾ cup red wine vinegar
Salt to taste
Fresh thyme leaves

Roast the peppers directly over a gas flame or charcoal grill, turning frequently (see page 282 for different ways of roasting) until charred all over. Transfer to a plastic bag to steam for 5 or 10 minutes, scrape off the charred skin, removed the stem and seeds, and cut lengthwise into 4 or 5 pieces. Put the peppers and any juices in a bowl.

Combine the garlic, vinegar, and salt. Pour over the peppers and sprinkle the thyme leaves on top. Refrigerate several hours, arrange on a serving dish, and serve at room temperature.

Fresh Cranberry Beans Stewed in Olive Oil

❋❋❋

4 SERVINGS

[TAZE BARBUNA PİLAKİSİ]

2 pounds fresh cranberry
   beans in pods
1½ cups finely chopped
   onions
½ cup fine olive oil
1 large tomato, peeled
   and chopped
2 or 3 tender long green
   peppers, if available
   (see page 281), or 2
   small Anaheim chilies,
   seeded and cut into
   rings
Salt
1 tablespoon sugar
Chopped flat-leaf parsley
Lemon juice
Lemon wedges for
   garnish

Shell the beans and boil them in water to cover for only 5 minutes; drain.

Cook the onions in the oil until limp. Add the tomato and cook 5 minutes longer, until the tomato is soft. Stir in the beans, peppers, a little salt, sugar, and about 1½ cups water, enough to be almost at the same level as the beans. Cover and simmer for 1 hour, until the beans are very tender. As they cook, maintain water a little under the level of the beans. Stir in a handful of parsley, cook a few minutes longer, and remove from heat. Cool, and serve cold or at room temperature, sprinkled with parsley and lemon juice to taste, accompanied by lemon wedges and crusty bread.

Crispy-Fried Squid with Garlic-Vinegar Sauce

✻✻

4 SERVINGS

[KALAMAR TAVA]

2 pounds squid, cleaned
    and washed
Salt

BEER BATTER
½ cup cornstarch
½ cup flour
Salt and pepper
2 cups light beer
2 eggs, separated

Flour for dusting
Peanut oil for deep-frying
Garlic-Vinegar Sauce
    (recipe follows)

Drain the squid and cut into ¼-inch rings. Put in a bowl and sprinkle with salt.

To make the batter, sift the cornstarch and flour with salt and pepper. Mix in the beer and egg yolks and beat with a whisk until smooth. Beat the egg whites to soft peaks and fold into the batter.

In a large skillet or wok, heat oil to 350 degrees.

Put about 2 cups flour in a bowl. Toss a handful of squid rings with the flour, then shake in a sieve to remove excess. Drop the rings into the batter. Lift with cupped fingertips, letting excess batter fall back into the bowl. Fry in hot oil until dark golden brown. Don't crowd the pan. Drain on paper towels and serve immediately. Pass sauce separately.

Garlic-Vinegar Sauce

✻✻

MAKES 1½ CUPS

[SARMISAKLI SİRKELİ SALÇA]

5 ½-inch-thick slices
    French bread, crusts
    removed
1 small head of garlic
Salt
¾ cup good olive oil
¼ cup red wine vinegar

Soak bread in water to cover. Squeeze dry and set aside. Peel garlic cloves and pound them in a mortar with some salt until thoroughly pureed. Stir in the bread and blend with the garlic. Gradually stir in olive oil and then vinegar. Adjust salt and vinegar to taste. This sauce will keep in the refrigerator for several days. Thin with water to desired consistency.

Cabbage Dolmas Stuffed with Rice, Pine Nuts, Currants, and Herbs

✳✳✳

8 SERVINGS

[LAHANA DOLMASI ZEYTINYAĞLI]

Rice, Pine Nut, and
  Currant Filling (page
  130)
1 green cabbage
Salt
¼ cup fine olive oil
Lemon juice
Lemon wedges

Make the filling and set aside.

Penetrating to a depth of 1 inch, remove part of the cabbage core with a small knife. Bring a quart of salted water to a boil and cook cabbage for 4 minutes. Remove from the pan and refresh with cold water. Remove as many leaves as you can. Put the remaining cabbage back in the boiling water and cook about 10 minutes longer. Rinse with cold water and remove remaining leaves. Drain the leaves in a colander.

To stuff the leaves, place one on a dinner plate, core end facing you, and cut out a V-shaped piece to remove hard part of the center. Place some filling along the bottom edge of the leaf and shape into a ½- to 1-inch roll, depending on the size of the leaf. Turn the sides over the filling and roll the whole thing up, creating a cylinder. Stuff the leaves until all the filling is used. Place some unused whole leaves in the bottom of a heavy shallow pan and arrange the stuffed dolmas side by side in layers. Mix 1 cup water, a little salt, the olive oil, and 2 tablespoons lemon juice and pour over the dolmas. Place an inverted plate over them to keep them in place, simmer about 1 hour, or until the leaves are cooked, adding water in small quantities if necessary. Let cool.

Serve the dolmas cold or at room temperature, sprinkled with lemon juice. Decorate with lemon wedges.

Variation: Use grape leaves in place of cabbage leaves. When using grape leaves bought in jars, there is no need to precook them. Rinse them in cold water, drain, and stuff them following the directions for cabbage dolmas.

Mussel Brochettes with Walnut *Tarator*

✱✱

4 SERVINGS

[MİDYE TAVASI]

About 3 dozen large
  mussels, scrubbed and
  bearded
Bamboo sticks
2 large bottles (2 quarts)
  unflavored,
  unsweetened soda
Salt
Flour to coat the mussels
Peanut oil or other
  vegetable oil for deep-
  frying
Walnut Tarator (page
  58)

Steaming hot, golden nuggets of deep-fried sweet mussels on tiny wooden skewers are part of the lively street food scene of Istanbul. You find vendors frying them on portable braziers set on glass-enclosed carts. As you stand waiting for your order in the circle of eager customers surrounding the cart, the vendor prepares it with an air of self-assured calm and good-naturedness and asks whether you want your mussels in a piece of bread or not, and with or without *tarator*.

As I was testing the dish in my California kitchen, threading slippery mussels onto bamboo sticks and frying them in hot, bubbling, splattering oil, I thought of those vendors, preparing who knows how many sticks of mussels all day. I wondered whether they were really as calm as they appeared.

Once you shuck the mussels, the rest is very easy and the result delicious. However, I must warn you: there is a bit of cleaning up to do afterward!

✱   ✱   ✱

Open mussel shells (see directions on page 61) and remove flesh. Break the bamboo sticks to measure about 7½ inches; any longer and they won't fit into the wok or other frying utensil. Thread 3 or 4 large mussels on each stick. Put the soda in a large bowl, place the threaded sticks in it, and let them soak for 30 minutes.

Meanwhile, take enough flour to cover the bottom of a cookie sheet, to a depth of 1 inch, and mix with a little salt. Put a wok or other utensil suitable for deep-frying on the stove. Then set the bowl containing the mussels next to the cookie sheet with the flour. Heat the oil until it is hot enough for deep-frying (when a small cube of bread dropped into it turns golden in 30 seconds). Roll one stick of mussels in the flour, dip it briefly in the soda, and roll again lightly in flour. Shake off the excess flour and drop it gently into the hot oil. Fry about 3 or 4 sticks at a time; do not crowd the pan. Deep-fry the mussels until they turn golden brown on both sides. This will take only 1 to 1½ minutes. Drain on paper towels and serve immediately, plain or with Walnut *Tarator*.

Walnut *Tarator*

✺✺

[CEVİZLİ TARATOR]

1 cup walnuts
2 teaspoons minced
  garlic
1¾ cups fresh French
  bread crumbs (about
  3½ to 4 ounces)
About ¾ cup water
¼ cup fine olive oil
Salt
3 to 4 tablespoons
  balsamic and wine
  vinegar in equal
  proportions

*T*arator is the general designation for a variety of sauces made basically with nuts and flavored with garlic and lemon juice or vinegar. They are usually served with poached, grilled, or fried fish and shellfish, as well as with steamed or fried vegetables. *Tarator* is a lively sauce and on the whole an assertive one, its pungency regulated by the amount of garlic and lemon juice or vinegar used to complement the food on which it is served. It can even be quite delicate, as in the case of the almond sauce served on poached sea bass, grouper, or salmon (page 74). Sometimes a particularly pungent *tarator* can transform a bland-tasting fish or vegetable and at other times it adds another dimension to an already assertive flavor.

Usually walnut and hazelnut *tarator*s are made with vinegars and almond and pine nut *tarator*s with lemon juice. Although a *tarator* usually includes garlic in varying degrees, sometimes it does not.

Its texture also varies from slightly crunchy to creamy. If made with a mortar and pestle, the resulting sauce will have a granular texture, and if made in a blender or food processor it will be very smooth and creamy.

Finally, a few words on the use of vinegars in making *tarator*. Certain vinegars result in a strongly and unpleasantly acidic, almost metallic taste. In Turkey, vinegars are deliciously strong and sharp, with a slightly sweet undertone. In the following recipe, therefore, I suggest using a combination of balsamic and wine vinegar in equal proportions.

✺   ✺   ✺

Grind walnuts finely and pound in a mortar with garlic and bread crumbs, adding a little water to moisten. Finally, mix in the olive oil, season with salt and vinegar, and thin to a creamy consistency with the remaining water. Allow at least 2 hours for the flavors to blend and mature before serving. Taste just before serving and adjust with vinegar if necessary. The sauce thickens as it stands, and may be thinned with water.

Alternatively, process ground walnuts, garlic, bread crumbs, and water in a food processor. Mix in olive oil and season with salt and vinegar.

Gülümay's Walnut-Garlic Spread with Hot and Sweet Peppers and Pomegranate Syrup

❋❋❋

ABOUT 1 ¾ CUPS   [MUHAMMARA]

2 large sweet red peppers
   (12 oz.)
1 tablespoon water
⅔ cup walnuts
1 tablespoon crushed
   garlic
⅔ cup toasted sourdough
   bread crumbs
1 or 2 red jalapeños,
   seeded and minced
¼ cup fine olive oil
1½ teaspoons coarsely
   ground cumin seeds
¼ to ½ teaspoon crushed
   red pepper flakes
2 teaspoons pomegranate
   syrup (see Glossary)
2 tablespoons lemon juice

This is an utterly delicious spread with lively flavors. It comes from southeast Turkey, where red peppers and cumin seeds are used abundantly and pomegranate syrup is a staple ingredient used as a souring agent. Although there is no real substitute for the sweet and sour flavor of pomegranate syrup, lemon juice will be adequate.

❋   ❋   ❋

Roast peppers over a grill or gas flame, turning frequently until charred all over. Seal 10 minutes in a plastic bag, peel, seed, and chop (see page 282). In a food processor, mix chopped peppers with 1 tablespoon water. Process to a moist paste. Set aside.

Pound walnuts with garlic in a mortar. Stir in bread crumbs and jalapeños. Continue pounding until all ingredients are blended. Mix in the pureed peppers. Gradually mix in the olive oil and season with cumin, red pepper flakes, pomegranate syrup, and lemon juice (use additional lemon juice if pomegranate syrup is unavailable). Taste and adjust with salt and lemon juice. (Alternatively, you can make the whole dish in a food processor.) Let stand several hours or overnight for the flavors to blend and mature. Serve with croutons or on flatbread wedges or crackers.

Poached Mackerel with Hazelnut-Vinegar Sauce

✳✳

4 SERVINGS

[USKUMRU TARATORU]

HAZELNUT-VINEGAR SAUCE

1 cup lightly toasted
  hazelnuts, skins
  removed

1½ slices (about 1½
  ounces) firm
  sourdough French
  bread, crusts removed,
  crumbled

2 teaspoons crushed
  garlic (see page 286)

About 1 cup water

Salt

About 3 tablespoons wine
  vinegar

1 pound mackerel,
  cleaned

Court Bouillon (page 75)

Fine olive oil

Good paprika

½ cup lemon juice

The first printed Turkish cookbook, *Melce' üt-Tabbahin*, appeared in Istanbul in 1844. This recipe is an adaptation of a mackerel dish that appears in it under the title *uskumru taratoru*, meaning mackerel *tarator*. Here the hazelnut sauce, hazelnut *tarator,* which is very similar to almond sauce (page 75), is made with slightly toasted hazelnuts and flavored with garlic and vinegar. The dish is meant to be served cold or at room temperature as a salad or *meze* rather than as an entrée, and it is meant to be made with fresh and sweet-tasting hazelnuts, which grow abundantly in Turkey. Stale hazelnuts will not produce the desired result.

✳   ✳   ✳

Grind nuts finely in a food processor, add bread, garlic, and water. Process to a creamy sauce. Season with salt and vinegar. Transfer to a bowl, cover, and let mellow for several hours.

Poach fish in court bouillon about 8 minutes. Cool in the liquid. Drain fish on paper towels, remove bones, and cut fish into bite-size pieces. Place in a serving dish. The nut sauce thickens as it stands, so thin it with water to a creamy consistency and taste for salt and vinegar. Mash the fish with the sauce. Drizzle olive oil over it and sprinkle with paprika. Serve cold with lemon juice, passed separately. The finished dish will keep 2 days.

Stuffed Mussels

●●

10 SERVINGS

[MIDYE DOLMASI]

About 50 large mussels

FILLING

*5 cups finely chopped
onions*
3 tablespoons pine nuts
1 cup good olive oil
1 cup uncooked rice
*1 ripe tomato, peeled
and diced*
3 tablespoons currants
1 tablespoon sugar
Salt
*Freshly ground black
pepper*
*½ teaspoon ground
cinnamon*
*⅓ teaspoon ground
allspice*
Pinch of grated nutmeg
3 tablespoons lemon juice

*Olive oil to coat the
mussel shells*
Lemon wedges

The esthetic appeal of Turkish food is sometimes proclaimed from the display windows of restaurants, a far more effective device for luring customers inside than a simple menu! The eye is caught by a rich profusion of glistening swordfish, stately turbot, impressively large orange-tinted prawns, pink lamb chops sprinkled with wild thyme, all intermingled with tomatoes, long green peppers, and red onions, everything ready to be grilled. Then there are shiny blue-black mussel shells, half opened to disclose their treasure of mussels, rice, toasted pine nuts, and plump currants, simmered in olive oil and sharpened with lemon juice.

❋   ❋   ❋

Scrub and beard mussels. The easiest way to open them is to leave them in warm salted water for 5 minutes. Once they relax and open slightly, you need to open them a little more to stuff them. Do this taking care not to break the hinges that hold the shells together. Holding the mussel over a bowl to catch all the liquid, insert a paring knife between the shells along the flat edge until the shells are loosened but remain intact. Refrigerate the mussels while you make the filling. Strain the liquid through a cloth-lined sieve, add water to make 1½ cups, and reserve.

Cook onions and pine nuts in hot olive oil for about 15 minutes, until nuts are lightly toasted and onions are soft. Add rice and cook, stirring, 5 minutes. Add tomato and cook 2 or 3 minutes longer, stirring all the time. Stir in currants, sugar, salt, spices, lemon juice, and ¾ cup of the reserved liquid. Simmer gently over low heat, covered, until all the liquid is absorbed. Cool and mix gently.

With a small spoon, stuff mussels loosely with filling. Place them in a heavy, wide pan in layers; drape a piece of parchment over the top. Then invert a small plate over the paper to keep the mussels in place. Add remaining liquid, cover, and simmer 25 minutes until rice is cooked. Add a little water from time to time if needed. Cool in the pan.

Coat each mussel with a film of olive oil to give it a shine. Arrange on a platter with lemon wedges and serve cold.

Filo Cheese Rolls

❀❀❀❀❀❀❀❀❀❀❀❀❀❀❀❀❀❀❀❀❀❀❀❀❀❀❀❀❀❀❀❀❀

[BEYAZ PEYNİRLİ VE KAŞAR PEYNİRLİ SİGARA BÖREĞİ]

½ pound filo pastry
About 8 tablespoons (1 stick) unsalted butter, melted

These small golden crisp pastry rolls, filled with feta or kasseri cheese, are popular appetizers or snacks. Feta cheese outside Turkey or the Balkans is not always as creamy as it should be, and sometimes it is too salty. To balance the flavor and texture, I add some cream cheese to the filling. Kasseri is a sharp aged cheese, made with sheep's milk and a small amount of goat's milk, very popular in Turkey and the Balkans. I am glad to say it is widely available in California and now is even made locally.

❊   ❊   ❊

Preheat the oven to 350 degrees; grease a baking sheet. Place half of the stack of filo sheets under a slightly dampened towel; repack the remaining half and store for future use. Cut the stack crosswise into 3 equal parts, creating 3 stacks of pastry strips, measuring about 6 by 12 inches each. Cover them promptly with the towel.

Work with a single strip at a time. Put one on the surface, short side near you, and brush it lightly with butter. Place 1 heaping tablespoon of whichever filling you've chosen along the bottom edge of the strip; fold the edge over the filling to cover. Fold each long side of the strip ½ inch in toward the center and roll up tightly. Place the roll seam down on the baking sheet. Repeating with the remaining strips and filling. Brush the tops with butter. Bake for 15 or 20 minutes until golden brown. Serve hot.

Kasseri Cheese Filling

❀❀❀❀❀❀❀❀❀❀❀❀

¾ to 1 pound kasseri cheese, grated
2 small eggs, lightly beaten
⅓ cup chopped flat-leaf parsley

Thoroughly blend the kasseri cheese with the eggs and parsley.

Feta–Cream Cheese Filling

❋❋❋❋❋❋❋❋❋❋❋

8 or 9 ounces feta
 cheese, crumbled
6 ounces cream cheese
⅓ cup chopped flat-leaf
 parsley or fresh dill
2 tablespoons chopped
 chives
2 small eggs, lightly
 beaten

Mash the feta and cream cheese with a fork and blend thoroughly. Mix in the herbs and half of the eggs. Gradually add the remaining egg for a very moist but not watery mixture. If it begins to look too thin, hold back some of the egg.

Roasted Eggplant and Hot Pepper Salad

❋❋

4 SERVINGS

[IZGARA PATLICAN VE BİBER SALATASI]

1¼-pound eggplant
2 poblano chilies
1 or more jalapeños
2 tablespoons lemon juice
2 teaspoons crushed
 garlic (see page 286)
½ cup fine olive oil
Salt
2 or 3 tablespoons red
 wine vinegar
Chopped flat-leaf parsley

Roast the eggplant and chilies directly over a charcoal grill or gas flame, turning frequently, until the vegetables are charred all over and eggplant is thoroughly soft (see pages 279–82 for different ways of roasting and peeling eggplant and peppers). Put the peppers in a plastic bag to steam for 5 or 10 minutes. Cool the eggplant slightly and peel off the charred skin. Put the eggplant flesh in a bowl and sprinkle with lemon juice, letting it stand while you prepare the peppers.

Scrape the charred skin from the chilies with a knife, remove the tops and seeds, mince and reserve in a bowl.

Squeeze out all the moisture from the eggplant, mince, and put in the bowl with the chilies. Mix in the garlic. Stir in the olive oil last, a few tablespoons at a time. Season with salt and vinegar. Chill and serve sprinkled with parsley.

Roasted Eggplant and Peppers with Yogurt-Garlic Sauce

❋❋

[YOĞURTLU PATLICAN BİBER IZGARA]

YOGURT-GARLIC SAUCE

2 teaspoons crushed
   garlic (see page 286)
Salt
2 cups yogurt

1 pound eggplant
Olive oil
Salt
Chopped fresh thyme
   leaves
6 poblano chilies or
   sweet red peppers
4 or more jalapeños

On summer evenings, Turkish towns seemed imbued with the aroma of roasting eggplant and peppers and the unmistakable smell of garlic and yogurt.

❋   ❋   ❋

Beat the garlic and salt into the yogurt until smooth and creamy. Set aside.

Peel the eggplant lengthwise in a striped fashion (see pages 279–80). Cut into ¼-inch slices. Brush generously with olive oil on both sides. Sprinkle with some salt and thyme.

Roast the poblanos or red peppers and jalapeños on an outdoor grill until the skins are charred all over and the peppers are soft. Put them in a plastic bag and let them steam for 5 to 10 minutes. Scrape off the charred skins with a knife, quarter the poblanos or red peppers, remove the cores and seeds; leave the jalapeños whole (see page 282.) Wipe excess oil from eggplant slices and grill over a moderate fire until they are soft. (Alternatively, you can fry the eggplant slices and roast the peppers directly over a gas flame.)

Arrange the eggplant and peppers on a plate and pour the yogurt sauce over them. Serve at room temperature or cold.

Mussel *Plaki*

❋❋

4 SERVINGS

[MİDYE PİLAKİSİ]

About 4 pounds sweet
fresh mussels,
scrubbed and bearded
1½ cups finely chopped
onions
12 to 15 small garlic
cloves, peeled
½ cup fine olive oil
½ cup diced carrots
1 cup diced potatoes
¾ cup diced celery root
1 large tomato, peeled
and diced
1 teaspoon sugar
1 teaspoon flour
Salt
⅔ cup chopped flat-leaf
parsley
Lemon juice
Lemon wedges

At first sight, this is another typically colorful Mediterranean shell-fish stew. But it is deliciously distinctive, thanks to the whole garlic cloves stewed in olive oil, which become sweet and creamy. The addition of celery root, along with the other vegetables, gives this stew yet another dimension. The finished dish is garnished with parsley, given a slight tang with lemon juice, and served cold. Served with a generous piece of baguette, mussel plaki makes an excellent summer lunch.

❋   ❋   ❋

Soak the mussels for 5 minutes in warm salted water, open, and reserve their liquid. Discard the shells. Strain the mussel liquid in a cheese cloth-lined sieve and reserve; add water, if necessary, to make 1 cup.

Sauté the onions and garlic in the olive oil about 5 minutes. Do not let them brown. Add the carrots, potatoes, and celery root; cook, stirring, 5 minutes. Add the mussel liquid, cover, and simmer until the vegetables are tender, about 20 minutes. Add some water if necessary.

Stir in the tomato, sprinkle in the sugar, flour, and some salt. Stir once and cook until there is very little liquid left. Stir in the mussels and cook for 4 or 5 minutes, just until the mussels are done. Stir in ½ cup parsley, adjust with salt, and remove from heat. Serve cold or at room temperature, sprinkled with lemon juice and re-maining parsley, accompanied by lemon wedges.

FISH AND SEAFOOD

✸✸

S oon the demands of progress—and, it must be admitted, public safety—will claim as victim another monument of old Istanbul. The Galata Bridge, the pontoon bridge that since before World War I has linked the two halves of European Istanbul across the mouth of the Golden Horn, will be gone, replaced by a new structure the pillars of which now rise menacingly next to it out of the water. The new bridge will no doubt be safer and better able to carry the fearsome burden of Istanbul's traffic, but it is hard to imagine it acquiring, even in time, a fraction of the charm held by the old Galata Bridge.

The lower deck of the bridge is distinguished not only by one of the few teahouses in Istanbul that still provides waterpipes to its customers but also—and more important—by a whole row of fish restaurants that, nestled beneath the grinding traffic on the roadway above, face out at the confluence of the Golden Horn, the Sea of Marmara, and the Bosphorus. The view alone would justify taking dinner in one of these restaurants. It becomes particularly spectacular at dusk, when the lights on the Asiatic shore begin to define the horizon and the ferryboats gliding through the dark illuminate the gently heaving waters with their searchlights. The presence of history hangs distilled in the air, and the sight of the vessels passing back and forth brings to mind all those distant lands that were once bound to this great metropolis.

But let us not be too solemn. These restaurants are, after all, places of enjoyment, where for some reason a link has been established between the eating of fish on the one hand and the drinking of *rakı* and the consumption of *meze* on the other. Loud but rarely raucous conversation vies with the noise of the traffic and the sirens of the ships, while outside each restaurant waiters obstinately but with good humor accost passersby, especially tourists, with the invitation to step inside and favor their establishments.

It is customary for the waiter to make his recommendation depending on the day's catch and, of course, the amount you are willing to pay, some varieties being particularly expensive as they become rarer and rarer. Whatever your choice, you are almost certain to be pleased, for the quality of the fish is high and its taste is preserved through simple preparation, being grilled or panfried instead of masked by sauces and creams. It may however be dressed in olive oil and lemon juice and will commonly be accompanied by crusty fresh bread, salads, and a variety of appetizers, either savory or sour, that serve to set off the flavor of the fish.

Among the common choices are *barbunya*, small tasty red mullet, at its best when panfried; grilled *lüfer*, bluefish, light and no bigger than a herring; *levrek*, a milky fresh sea bass that can be either panfried or grilled; *kalkan*, creamy turbot that can also be sautéed or grilled; *kılıç*, swordfish, usually cooked kebab-style interspersed with bay leaves and lemon slices; mussels cooked on wooden skewers and served with *tarator* sauce; and crab, lobster, and langoustines.

❋ GRILLING FISH

Grilling is a favored way of cooking fish in Turkey. Mackerel, red mullet, bonito, swordfish, bluefish, fresh sardines, and anchovies are the most frequent choices. The fish is usually sprinkled with salt and allowed to stand for 20 or 30 minutes and then coated with a little olive oil and grilled, either whole or cut into steaks, over hot charcoal or on a stove-top grill. Occasionally, fish is marinated with olive oil seasoned with lemon juice and/or herbs and bay leaves. Cutting into cubes and grilling on skewers or grilling fish enveloped in fig leaves, vine leaves, or bay leaves are all popular methods.

GRILLING FISH ON A STOVE-TOP GRILL

In Europe, as in Turkey, where people live mostly in apartment houses, they frequently grill their fish, chops, and steaks on a stove-top grill. This is a simple and inexpensive utensil made of enamel or cast-iron with a long handle. It is called *izgara* in Turkey and is the same as the Italian *gratella*. The fish or meat is sprinkled with salt, brushed with a little olive oil, and quickly seared and cooked on the hot grill placed directly over the heat on a stove without any addition of fat. It imparts a surprisingly good grilled taste to food.

GRILLING FISH WRAPPED IN LEAVES

The practice of grilling fish wrapped in leaves or on a bed of leaves goes back to antiquity. Mary Taylor Simeti quotes Archestratus of Gela, writing in the fourth century B.C.:

Wrap it up in fig leaves with a little marjoram. No cheese, no nonsense! Just place it tenderly in fig leaves and tie them on top with a string: then push it under hot ashes, bethinking thee wisely of the time when it is done, and burn it not up.*

Today in those same lands where the Greeks grilled their fish wrapped in fig leaves, local people use the same method. One warm summer evening I watched some humble folk in the Aegean area, where matchless Smyrna figs grow, sprinkle their fish with salt and the thyme that grows wild on foothills throughout the region and is used in almost everything, and grill it wrapped in fig leaves. For them, this was not a matter of culinary practice; they little cared that the leaves impart a pleasant aroma and flavor to the fish. It was simply a way to protect the fish from the fire. Having been an observer of the California barbecue cult for years, I was filled with an inexplicable surge of affection watching these simple people grill their fish on a broken-down iron grid placed on a wood fire.

However the fish is grilled, it is almost always served with raw onions, cut paper-thin and mixed with chopped parsley (see Red Onion–Parsley Relish, page 154) or simply with cut-up onions, and always with plenty of crusty fresh bread. It is served very hot from the grill. Its only embellishment may be a drizzle of olive oil, olive oil mixed with lemon juice (Olive Oil–Lemon Dressing, page 72), or plain lemon juice. Occasionally Walnut *Tarator* (page 58) or a Garlic-Vinegar Sauce (page 55) may accompany it.

Other favorite accompaniments to grilled fish are salads made with greens such as garden lettuce and rocket, moistened with olive oil and a little lemon juice. White Bean Salad (page 147) is another good choice.

* *Pomp and Sustenance* (New York, 1989), 27.

❈ A WORD ON ANCHOVIES

As Alan Davidson (*Mediterranean Seafood*) puts it, "Turks are the greatest Mediterranean connoisseurs of the anchovy." In particular, the people of the Black Sea coast where anchovies are found in abundance take the anchovy seriously. To them it is more than a fish, it is a part of the folk culture: poetry, proverbs, songs, jokes, and, of course, cuisine. The people of the Black Sea boast of a seemingly infinite number of anchovy dishes, from soup to corn bread (the local bread of the Black Sea region) to omelets, pilafs, stews, and even—incredible as it may sound—anchovy baklava (this last one, I would rather pass!).

Olive Oil–Lemon Dressing

❈❈

MAKES ²/₃ CUP   [ZEYTİNYAĞI VE LİMON SALÇASI]

⅓ cup good olive oil
Salt to taste
2 or 3 tablespoons lemon
   juice
¼ cup minced fresh
   parsley

For about 2 pounds grilled, fried, or poached fish.

❈   ❈   ❈

Combine all ingredients in a bowl and mix with a fork.

Sea Bass Fillets Grilled on a Bed of Fig Leaves

4 SERVINGS

[LEVREK IZGARA]

4 sea bass fillets
Salt
⅓ cup olive oil
1 tablespoon chopped
fresh thyme
2 tablespoons chopped
flat-leaf parsley
Lemon wedges
Olive Oil–Lemon
Dressing (page 72)
(optional)
Fig leaves (grape or bay
leaves can be
substituted)

When I grill delicate fish fillets or small fish such as sardines and anchovies, I find using a double grill with a long handle very useful. Here I line the grill with fig leaves, place the fillets on them, cover the fillets with more leaves, and fold and secure the grill. Fragrant bay leaves are also very good used this way. The leaves impart a subtle and pleasant flavor and aroma to the fish.

❋   ❋   ❋

Sprinkle fillets with salt, brush with some of the olive oil, sprinkle with thyme and parsley, and let stand 30 minutes while you make the fire.

Line a double-hinged grill with fig leaves and brush them lightly with oil. Place fillets over leaves and cover with more leaves. Fold and secure the grill. Grill quickly over hot fire on both sides until fish is just done. Serve with lemon wedges and/or olive oil–lemon dressing. Be sure to serve fresh, crusty bread and a green salad.

Poached Sea Bass with Delicate Almond Sauce

4 SERVINGS

[BADEM TARATORLU LEVREK]

Nineteenth-century Turkish cookbooks include recipes for fish or shellfish served with creamy nut sauces (*tarator*) made with almonds, hazelnuts, or walnuts. The nuts are pounded and thinned to a creamy consistency and flavored with lemon juice or vinegar. The sauces may or may not include garlic.

The following recipe is adapted from the nineteenth-century Turkish cookbook compiled by Türabi Efendi, first published in London in 1864. In his recipe, Türabi Efendi serves a grilled salmon trout with almond sauce. Alan Davidson, in his renowned *Mediterranean Seafood*, gives a recipe for a similar sauce, which he serves on poached gurnard. I also prefer to use this delicate sauce with poached fish. In Turkey I choose milky sea bass; in North America I serve it on poached grouper, sea bass, or spring salmon. I like to serve the fish and the sauce at room temperature or cold.

One thing should be emphasized: the almond sauce is at its best several hours after it is made, for it really needs time for the full flavor to develop. In fact, it is very good the day immediately after it is prepared and it even keeps for several days more. So plan to make it ahead. Also, be sure to make it with sweet-tasting almonds, and blanch them yourself. The blanched almonds available on the market have long since lost their moisture and flavor.

The following recipe yields about 1½ cups sauce; you can increase the amount by doubling the recipe.

ALMOND SAUCE

1 cup freshly blanched
    almonds
1½ slices (about 1½
    ounces) firm
    sourdough French
    bread, crusts removed,
    crumbled coarsely
1 teaspoon crushed garlic
    (see page 286)
Salt
¾ to 1 cup water
2 to 2½ tablespoons
    lemon juice
¼ cup fine olive oil
Four 6-ounce steaks or
    fillets of sea bass,
    grouper, or salmon
Court Bouillon (recipe
    follows)
Lemon wedges and
    chervil for garnish

To make the sauce, first grind almonds finely in a food processor. Add bread, garlic, a little salt, ¾ cup water, and process. With motor running, add lemon juice and olive oil. Transfer to a bowl and adjust taste with salt and lemon juice. Add up to ¼ cup water if sauce seems too thick; cover and allow to sit at room temperature for several hours. (If I make the sauce a day ahead, I keep it in the refrigerator.) The sauce will thicken as it stands. Before you serve, thin with water to a creamy consistency.

Poach fish 3 or 4 minutes in court bouillon and cool in the cooking liquid; drain on paper towels.

Place a piece of fish on a plate and cover it with the almond sauce. Garnish with chervil, and serve at room temperature with lemon wedges.

Court Bouillon
❀❀❀❀❀❀❀❀❀❀❀❀

1 small onion, chopped
1 carrot, chopped
1 celery rib, chopped
1 bay leaf
2 sprigs flat-leaf parsley
2 sprigs fresh thyme
10 peppercorns
2 teaspoons salt
4 cups water

Simmer all ingredients together for 25 to 30 minutes. Taste for salt and strain.

Turkish Stuffed Mackerel

[USKUMRU DOLMASI]

Interesting and delectable as it is, Turkish stuffed mackerel, prepared in the original way, belongs to another era when it was cooked in the kitchens of stately homes, and elaborate culinary operations were carried out by a whole staff. Today, this old delicacy seems to have vanished from the home cook's repertoire. However, the only difficult thing about preparing this dish for cooking is the curious way the backbone, entrails, and flesh must be removed through the gills, without opening the belly and without cutting the skin. A rather simple but delicious filling, including the flesh, is stuffed back into the fish, again through the gills, restoring the original shape. It is then dipped in eggs and bread crumbs and fried in olive oil.

The subtly sweet and tangy filling is made with onions, pine nuts, currants, walnuts, herbs, and sweet spices. Its delicate flavors, combined with those of the fish, result in a delightful creation. In the following trout recipe, an adaptation of the classic Turkish Stuffed Mackerel, I make an almost identical filling with the exception of the flesh of the fish, and stuff it in a much more simple and conventional way. Where I live it is not easy to find the traditional rather large and superlatively fresh mackerel, so I use trout, which is consistently fresh and good.

Trout Stuffed with Pine Nuts, Currants, Herbs, and Sweet Spices

4 SERVINGS [USKUMRU DOLMASI USULÜYLE BALIK DOLMASI]

Four 12-ounce trout, gutted and cleaned
Salt

Cut fins off the fish; snap backbone close to the tail end and at the base of the head. With your fingertips gently remove the backbone and all the small bones. Sprinkle fish lightly with salt and prepare filling.

FILLING

1¼ cups finely chopped
    onions
6 tablespoons good olive
    oil
¼ cup pine nuts
1¼ cups fresh French
    bread crumbs
6 tablespoons ground
    walnuts
6 tablespoons currants
6 tablespoons chopped
    flat-leaf parsley
6 tablespoons chopped
    fresh dill
1 teaspoon ground
    cinnamon
½ teaspoon ground
    allspice
Pinch of ground cloves
Salt and freshly ground
    pepper
1 teaspoon sugar
2 tablespoons lemon juice

BATTER

1 cup flour
2 eggs, lightly beaten
2 cups fresh French
    bread crumbs

⅓ cup light olive oil
Vegetable oil (optional)
Lemon juice
Chopped flat-leaf parsley

Cook onions in oil for 2 minutes. Stir in pine nuts and cook over low heat, stirring frequently, until nuts turn golden and onions become soft. Stir in bread crumbs and walnuts and turn them a few seconds; turn off the heat. Stir in currants, herbs, and spices. Season to taste with salt and pepper, sugar, and lemon juice. Set aside to cool.

Stuff fish with filling and sew the stomach cavity. Coat fish with flour, dip in eggs, then coat with bread crumbs, pressing them onto the fish to make them adhere. Heat the olive oil (or a combination of half olive oil and half vegetable oil) until hot. Fry the fish on each side about 8 minutes until golden brown; regulate the heat frequently. Drain on paper towels and serve sprinkled generously with lemon juice and parsley. This fish can also be grilled instead of fried.

Bass in Paper

✼✼

4 SERVINGS

[KAĞITTA LEVREK]

Four 6- to 8-ounce bass,
   sea bass, or grouper
   steaks
Salt
Butter
5 tablespoons lemon juice
8 tablespoons (1 stick)
   unsalted firm butter,
   cut into 8 pats
4 bay leaves
4 teaspoons fresh thyme
4 sprigs flat-leaf parsley
½ cup chopped scallions
2 very good tomatoes,
   sliced

The fish is served in its paper case. As the package is opened it releases a bouquet of fragrances. It takes only a few minutes to prepare and about 20 minutes to cook, and the result is splendid. I cook it on a Mexican *comal* or a stove-top grill (see page 70) directly over a gas flame. The fish can be cooked over a charcoal fire or in a hot oven.

✼   ✼   ✼

Sprinkle both sides of fish steaks with salt. From a 15-inch-wide roll of parchment paper, make 8 squares. To prepare fish, use 2 squares together for each piece. Place parchment squares on work surface and coat inside with butter. Place one piece of fish in the center of each double square. Sprinkle fish with a little lemon juice. Place 2 pats of butter and 1 bay leaf on each fish steak. Then evenly distribute thyme, parsley sprigs, scallions, and tomato slices on each steak. Sprinkle each with 1 tablespoon of water and fold the paper around each piece as if making a package. Put a toothpick through the folds of paper on top to keep the packets closed.

Sprinkle packages with water and place them on a *comal* or any stove-top grill and bake 20 minutes over medium heat. Or cook them over a charcoal grill or in a 450-degree oven for 20 minutes. Serve hot in packages.

Swordfish with Red and Green Peppers

✻✻

4 SERVINGS [YEŞİL BİBERLİ KILIÇ]

Four 6-ounce swordfish
   steaks
Salt
1 medium onion, cut into
   paper-thin slices
6 large garlic cloves, cut
   into slivers
⅓ to ½ cup good olive
   oil
6 to 8 tender long green
   peppers, if available,
   or 2 green bell
   peppers, seeded and
   cut into strips
2 sweet red peppers,
   seeded and cut into
   strips
1 jalapeño pepper,
   seeded and cut into
   slivers
2 large tomatoes, peeled
   and chopped
Freshly ground pepper
⅔ cup chopped flat-leaf
   parsley
Lemon juice

Sprinkle fish steaks with salt and set aside.

Cook onion and garlic in olive oil for 3 or 4 minutes, stirring frequently. Add peppers and continue cooking a few minutes longer. Add tomatoes, season with salt and pepper, cover, and simmer over low heat 5 minutes. Add fish steaks, ½ cup parsley, and ¼ cup water. Cover and simmer for 10 minutes. Serve at room temperature or cold, sprinkled with remaining parsley and lemon juice.

Fried Fresh Anchovies

✱✱✱

4 SERVINGS

[HAMSI TAVASI]

*Fresh anchovies or
  smelts, deboned, tails
  intact*
Salt
Flour
Oil for frying
Lemon wedges
*Red Onion–Parsley Relish
  (page 154)*

Although fresh anchovies have a distinct flavor that cannot really be duplicated, in their absence smelts are very good cooked this way.

✱   ✱   ✱

Wash fish, drain, sprinkle with salt, and allow to sit 1 hour. Dust in flour and fry in hot oil until crispy on both sides. Serve hot with lemon wedges on a bed of red onion and parsley relish.

POULTRY

✸✸✸✸✸✸✸✸✸✸✸✸✸✸✸✸✸✸✸✸✸✸✸✸✸✸✸✸✸✸✸✸✸

⁂⁂

Turkish chickens are not, at first sight, impressive. Scrawny, they run around freely, pecking on whatever they find. Maybe, however, this is the way all chickens should spend their brief lives, for Turkish chickens are full of the flavor and aroma that chickens should have.

Home cooks commonly boil chickens, and the cooking liquid is used to make a pilav that is served with the chicken itself. This simple procedure is widely favored because of the delicious results. I recommend the use of free-range chickens for obtaining the best taste in the chicken recipes that follow.

Chicken with Bulgur, Tomatoes, Peppers, and Tarragon

4 SERVINGS

[DOMATESLI BULGURLU PİLİÇ]

1 chicken, cut into 8
  serving pieces (thighs,
  legs, breast,
  quartered)

CHICKEN STOCK

Chicken back, neck, and
  gizzard
1 cup chopped onions
½ cup chopped carrots
3 sprigs flat-leaf parsley
½ teaspoon black
  peppercorns

6 tablespoons unsalted
  butter
1¾ cups finely chopped
  onions
1 cup seeded and
  chopped tender long
  green peppers, or
  sweet red and green
  bell peppers, or
  combination of any
1 or 2 red jalapeños
  (green jalapeños are
  also all right)
3 tablespoons fresh
  tarragon leaves
2 ripe tomatoes, peeled
  and chopped
Salt and pepper
2 cups bulgur

Put all the stock ingredients in a pot with water to cover and simmer 1 hour. Strain, reduce to 3½ cups, and reserve.

Heat the butter in a heavy pan and cook the onions until they turn almost reddish brown. Remove onions from the pan, add the chicken pieces, and sauté until golden on all sides. Push the chicken to one side, add the peppers and tarragon and cook, stirring, for 1 minute. Stir in the tomatoes and return the onions to the pan. Season with salt and pepper; combine all the ingredients, cover, and simmer for 20 minutes. Wash and drain the bulgur.

Heat the reserved stock.

Remove the chicken pieces to a plate, stir in the bulgur, and toss it with the vegetables and sauce for 3 minutes until it is well coated with the sauce. Add the hot chicken stock, let boil 1 minute, replace the chicken pieces reserving the breasts, cover, and simmer over low heat for about 15 minutes until all the liquid is absorbed. Add the breast pieces to the pan, remove from heat, and keep covered in a warm spot for 10 minutes. Stir once and serve with a *cacık* (page 151) or another salad.

Lemony Chicken and Okra

✳✳

4 SERVINGS

[PILIÇLI BAMYA]

One small chicken, about 1½ to 2½ pounds, cut into serving pieces

Black peppercorns

1½ pounds okra

½ cup wine vinegar

Salt

4 tablespoons unsalted butter

1½ cups chopped onions

2 ripe tomatoes, peeled and sliced

3 tender long green peppers left whole, or 2 other semi-hot peppers, tops and seeds removed

½ teaspoon crushed red pepper flakes

4 small sprigs thyme

3 sprigs oregano

3 tablespoons lemon juice

Put the chicken back and neck in a pan with 2 cups water and a few peppercorns and simmer 45 minutes. Strain and reserve stock.

Pare around the conical tops of the okra. Place in a bowl with the vinegar, sprinkle with salt, and set aside for 30 minutes.

Meanwhile, heat the butter in a heavy pan large enough to accommodate the chicken and okra. Cook the onions until limp. Remove from the pan and sauté the chicken pieces until golden on all sides, about 4 minutes.

Place the cooked onions, okra, tomatoes, and green peppers over the chicken pieces. Sprinkle all with some salt and pepper and the red pepper flakes. Place the herb sprigs over the top, add 1½ cups reserved chicken stock and the lemon juice; cover and simmer 40 or 50 minutes, or until okra is tender. Adjust to taste with salt and pepper and serve hot.

Succulent Grilled Chicken Served with Roasted Vegetables

✳✳

4 SERVINGS

[KIRMA TAVUK KEBABI]

Two 3- to 3½-pound
  chickens
Salt and freshly ground
  black pepper
Ground cinnamon
1½ cups coarsely
  chopped onions
2 tomatoes, 2 red onions,
  4 green bell or/and
  sweet red peppers and
  a few chilies of choice
Olive oil to coat the
  vegetables
Melted unsalted butter to
  baste the chickens

Preparing chicken this way goes back at least to the eighteenth century, when we find it mentioned in an anonymous early Turkish treatise on food.

✳   ✳   ✳

Bone the chickens and split into halves. Make small cuts all over them to expose the flesh more evenly. Sprinkle with salt, pepper, and some cinnamon. Process the onions with 2 or 3 tablespoons water in a blender and strain its juice into a small bowl (about ⅔ cup juice). Saturate the chickens generously with the onion juice and let stand at least 8 hours.

Make a moderately hot charcoal fire.

Cut the tomatoes and onions into wedges, and sweet peppers into 1-inch squares.

Thread the chickens onto flat skewers. Coat the vegetables lightly with olive oil and thread on separate skewers. Heat the grill and brush with oil. Grill the chickens, turning and basting with butter frequently. Roast the vegetables over the cooler side of the grill until specks appear on the surface and they become slightly tender.

Roast Duck Stuffed with Rice, Pistachios, and Raisins

✳✳

4 SERVINGS

[ÖRDEK DOLMASI]

2 ducks, about 5 pounds
  each

Remove neck, feet, wing tips, and all loose fat from the duck. Put all the stock ingredients in a pot with water to cover and simmer about 1 or 1½ hours, skimming from time to time. Strain the stock and cool.

STOCK

*Duck heads, feet, and
  necks plus ½ pound
  leftover duck wings or
  chicken backs or wings*
1 small onion, chopped
1 carrot, chopped
5 sprigs flat-leaf parsley
Black peppercorns

RICE STUFFING

*2 cups uncooked basmati
  rice*
*4 tablespoons unsalted
  butter*
*3 tablespoons rendered
  duck fat or unsalted
  butter*
*⅓ cup unsalted
  pistachios*
*1¾ cups finely chopped
  onions*
2 cinnamon sticks
5 cloves
Salt
⅓ cup raisins
*¼ cup fresh mint leaves,
  cut into thin ribbons*
*½ teaspoon ground
  allspice*
*½ teaspoon ground
  cinnamon*
*Freshly ground black
  pepper*

Meanwhile, chop the duck fat into small pieces and simmer over low heat about 45 minutes until completely rendered. Remove from heat and reserve.

Wash and soak the rice in cold water to cover.

Remove all fat from the duck stock and reduce the stock slightly. You will need 2½ cups for the stuffing.

To make the stuffing, heat the butter and duck fat (if using) in a heavy pan, add the pistachios and stir-fry until lightly toasted and still green in color. Remove with a slotted spoon and reserve.

Stir the onions, cinnamon sticks, and cloves into the butter remaining in the pan and cook over low heat, stirring frequently, for 10 minutes. Drain the rice and stir into the pan. Cook, stirring, for 5 minutes, until it is well coated with the butter. Stir in 2½ cups hot duck stock; correct with salt. Stir in the raisins, mint leaves, allspice, cinnamon, and pepper. Cover and cook over low heat for about 15 minutes until all the liquid is absorbed. Remove from heat and allow to stand covered for 15 minutes and cool. Fold in the reserved pistachios.

To roast the ducks, preheat oven to 500 degrees. Salt and pepper them inside and out. Fill cavities loosely with the stuffing and sew the flaps closed. Place on racks in shallow roasting pan and roast for 1 hour.

To serve, remove ducks from oven and allow to stand for 10 minutes. Cut off the strings to open the cavity. With a large spoon remove the stuffing, taking care not to mash it. Put it on a large platter, cover, and keep warm while carving the ducks. Remove the legs and thighs. Slice the breast diagonally, leaving some skin on the slices. Place the meat over the stuffing and serve.

Quail Grilled on Fig Leaves

✳✳

2 SERVINGS

[BILDIRCIN IZGARA]

MARINADE

1 small onion
½ cup olive oil
3 bay leaves
10 peppercorns
2 tablespoons lemon juice
5 sprigs flat-leaf parsley
Salt

Four 5-ounce quails
Fig leaves (if not
    available, substitute
    grape leaves)

Mix the onion in a blender with a few tablespoons water; strain into large bowl. Stir in the olive oil and remaining marinade ingredients.

Split the quails down the back, removing the backbone. Remove the rib cage and with your fingers release the shoulder bones from the flesh and remove them, severing them from the wings.

Marinate the quails loosely covered in the refrigerator for several hours.

Rinse the fig leaves and pat dry. Make a medium hot charcoal fire.

Remove the quails from the marinade and sprinkle with salt. Place one on each leaf, skin side up. Cook on the hot grill for 3 minutes. With a long-handled spatula turn each quail over on its leaf, now skin side down, and cook about 5 minutes. Cut into breast to check; it should be very moist and pink. Serve immediately with or without the leaves.

LAMB

✺✺✺✺✺✺✺✺✺✺✺✺✺✺✺✺✺✺✺✺✺✺✺✺✺✺✺✺✺✺✺✺✺✺

KEBABS

KÖFTE

Here with a loaf of bread beneath the bough,
A flask of wine, a book of verse—and thou . . .

✿✿

So runs Edward Fitzgerald's translation of the first half of Omar Khayyam's celebrated quatrain. One line, however, does not match the Persian original. At the risk of disillusioning the Western lover of Khayyam, I must point out that the second line runs:

A flask of wine, a leg of lamb—and thou . . .

Despite the gargantuan appetites of his contemporaries, it seems that Fitzgerald did not regard a leg of lamb as worthy of poetic mention. In other words, he missed the point that in Persian, Turkish, and other Middle Eastern cultures the enjoyment of food is an important and legitimate aspect of esthetic and sensory experience. Thus a leg of lamb was quite in harmony with the scene Khayyam wished to depict.

But let us come to culinary matters. Lamb, particularly young lamb, holds a regal position in Turkish cookery, for it is without doubt the most favored of meats. I must immediately add, however, that lamb in Turkey is very tender, juicy, and flavorful. This is partly because lamb is slaughtered younger than in other countries, and partly because of the pasturelands where the lambs graze. Certain areas are particularly renowned for their lamb, such as Thrace. There, and elsewhere in Turkey, the mountain slopes are covered with wildflowers, grasses, and such flavorful herbs as oregano and purple-blossomed wild thyme. Lambs roam these hillsides lazily and graze naturally on all they find. As a result, the lamb is so flavorful that it needs no adornments or flavor enhancers beyond pepper and salt and perhaps a few herbs such as thyme.

Apart from what they eat, the weight of the lamb is also impor-tant. In Turkey, young lambs not more than one year old or preferably younger with a dressed weight of 30 to 35 pounds are commercially available as well as heavier and older lambs. In North America, lambs commercially available in the markets have a dressed weight of 50 to 65 pounds, although butchers tell me that younger and lighter-weight lambs can be ordered by restaurants from the suppliers.

In accordance with its general practice, Turkish cuisine takes care to preserve the distinctive natural flavor of lamb. For example, when a piece of lamb is roasted on charcoal, it is rarely marinated and it is never covered with sauce. Lamb chops are flattened, sprinkled with a little salt and pepper as well as a little thyme, and grilled on charcoal to remain juicy and pink inside; there are few things more flavorful. In some regional kebabs, however, morsels of grilled lamb or minced grilled lamb are served on flat bread, sometimes with some creamy yogurt and/or a sauce made with fresh tomatoes, and topped with frothy hot butter. Variations from south and southeastern Turkey provide an added element of spiciness and pungency in the lamb and the sauce.

Lamb Shanks Braised with Cinnamon-Glazed Quince

✱✱

4 SERVINGS

[AYVA YAHNİSİ]

3 or 4 lamb shanks (or about 2 pounds lamb shoulder)
2 tablespoons unsalted butter
1½ cups finely chopped onions
2 cinnamon sticks
3 cloves
½ teaspoon ground allspice
Salt and freshly ground pepper
1 cup pomegranate juice (see Glossary)
4 tablespoons sugar
4 quinces, unpeeled, quartered, cored, and cut into ⅓-inch thick segments
1 teaspoon ground cinnamon
1 to 2 tablespoons lemon juice

This recipe is inspired by one in Ayşe Fahriye Hanım's *Ev Kadını*, a cookbook published between 1882 and 1883. Meats braised with such fruits as apricots, quince, plums, and chestnuts and slightly sweetened with sugar or *pekmez* (grape syrup; see page 288) were evidently still known at that time, although now they have disappeared from the classic cuisine, surviving only in scattered regions of Anatolia. Very probably dishes such as these go back to Persian forebears.

✱   ✱   ✱

Ask the butcher to cut 1½ inches of bone off the ends of the shanks, trim off all the fat, and cut them into halves.

Heat a wide, heavy pan over a low fire and brown the shanks about 20 minutes on all sides. Pour out all the fat, stir in the butter and onions, and cook for 2 minutes. Add the cinnamon sticks, cloves, allspice, salt, pepper, pomegranate juice, 1 cup water, and 2 tablespoons sugar. Cover and simmer about 1½ hours, until the meat is tender. As the meat cooks, maintain the liquid level.

Stir in the quince and simmer about 40 minutes until they are very tender yet still firm enough to hold their shape. Remove the shanks and fruit to a plate and strain the cooking liquid. Bone the shanks if you wish and return the meat to the pan, discarding the bones.

Put ¾ cup of the cooking liquid into a nonstick sauté pan. Pour the remaining liquid back into the pan in which the meat cooked. There should be at least 1 cup; if there is not, add some water and keep it at a gentle simmer. Also taste for salt. Add ground cinnamon and 2 tablespoons sugar to the cooking liquid in the sauté pan. Bring the mixture to a boil, stir in the quince segments, and quickly glaze them on both sides. Add the quince to the meat with whatever sauce there is in the sauté pan. Stir in some lemon juice to taste (not more than 1 or 2 tablespoons). Arrange the lamb pieces on warmed plates, arrange the quince over the meat, and pour the sauce over everything. Serve immediately. Pilaf would go nicely with this dish.

Lamb Shanks Braised with *Haricots Lingots*

✹✹

4 SERVINGS

[KURU FASULYE]

4 lamb shanks (lamb neck or breast cut into chunks will also be good)

1 tablespoon olive oil

5 tablespoons butter

3 cups chopped onions

6 sprigs thyme

1 tablespoon tomato puree or Red Pepper Paste (page 156)

2½ cups chopped tomatoes (use good canned tomatoes in winter)

1 tablespoon paprika

Salt and freshly ground pepper

3½ cups meat stock or water

2 cups haricots lingots, soaked in cold water overnight

2 or more red or green jalapeños or dried red chili peppers

1 cup chopped flat-leaf parsley

Every now and then, especially in the cold and gloomy days of winter, Turks in exile are stricken with an urge to have a big bowl of haricot beans. They feel nostalgia for this hearty dish that warms you within and without. And sooner or later, no matter how young and ignorant of culinary matters they may be, they finally master the art of cooking haricot beans, if not another single dish. Endowed with a cuisine of such a wide range, why, I wonder, do Turks have this special feeling for haricot beans? It is not shish kebab or baklava, as Westerners might think Turks regularly crave, but a humble bowl of beans. One good reason is that at the first sign of winter this dish is cooked frequently in almost all Turkish homes, and a longing for them becomes a part of one's longing for home. Then again, some of us ate so much of it (terrible versions, I might add) in places such as boarding schools that missing it while abroad, again, merges with our yearning for home.

I make this dish with lamb shanks because I think they are one of the tastiest parts of the animal. But you can use almost any part of the lamb, or even beef or sausages. It is also delicious without any meat at all.

Haricots lingots are medium-size dried white beans with a fine flavor imported from France. They are available in specialty shops. If you must, substitute dried white beans.

Ask the butcher to cut off 1½ inches of the bone at the end of the shanks and trim off all the fat.

Heat the oil in a large heavy pan and brown the shanks over medium-low heat for about 20 minutes. Pour off all the fat. Add the butter and sauté the onions for 5 minutes, until soft. Add the thyme sprigs, tomato puree or pepper paste, and tomatoes; cook for 5 minutes. Stir in the paprika, some salt and pepper, and ½ cup meat stock or water. Simmer the shanks, covered, about 30 minutes.

Drain the beans and stir into the pan containing the shanks. Stir in the jalapeños or dried red peppers, some salt, and 3 cups stock or hot water; cover and simmer about 1½ hours or until the beans are soft. As they cook, maintain the liquid level with hot water to barely cover the beans. The finished dish should have plenty of sauce but not be watery. Remove the thyme sprigs. Stir in ½ cup of the parsley and simmer a minute. Remove from heat and correct the seasoning. Serve hot sprinkled with the remaining parsley. A plain pilaf or fresh crusty bread is most appropriate with this dish.

Morsels of Lamb Served on a Bed of Smoked Eggplant Cream

❋❋❋

4 SERVINGS

[HÜNKAR BEĞENDİ]

2 pounds lamb shoulder
  chops or boned lamb
  shoulder
3 tablespoons unsalted
  butter
1 cup finely chopped
  onions
1½ cups chopped
  tomatoes
5 sprigs parsley
5 sprigs thyme
1 bay leaf
2 cloves
Salt and pepper
About 1 cup meat stock
  or water

SMOKED EGGPLANT CREAM

2 eggplants (about 3
  pounds)
3 tablespoons lemon juice
5 tablespoons butter
6 tablespoons flour
2 cups light cream or
  milk, heated
Salt
½ cup grated kasseri
  cheese

The highly evocative name of this celebrated dish, literally "the sultan approved," refers to what is probably an apocryphal event: the sultan giving his approval to its first cooking. Putting ourselves in the spirit of the times, we can imagine the cook waiting with fearful anticipation for news of the royal reaction to his invention and learning of the sultan's approval with joyful relief. It is said that the sultan in question was Murad IV, a particularly irascible and arbitrary ruler who was known to execute his soldiers for smoking. Gaining his approval would, then, have been particularly important for the palace cook. An imperial figure of somewhat milder disposition, Empress Eugénie of France, also gave enthusiastic approval to this dish when it was served during her visit to Istanbul.

This is truly an imperial dish in its rich yet dignified combination of flavors, and also exemplifies the Turkish genius for bringing together the most diverse ingredients with thoroughly happy results.

❋   ❋   ❋

If you are using lamb chops, bone them and reserve the bones. Trim all fat from the lamb and cut the meat into ¾-inch cubes. Heat the butter in a heavy shallow pan over medium heat. Add the meat and the bones (if using lamb chops) and cook uncovered, stirring occasionally, about 10 minutes until the meat gradually loses all its moisture and turns reddish brown. Stir in the onions and cook until they begin to brown around the edges. Add the tomatoes, herbs, and spices and cook a minute or so. Add some salt and pepper and ½ cup stock or water. Cover and simmer over low heat for about 45 minutes, or until the meat is very tender. Stir occasionally and make sure there is enough liquid. The sauce should be thick and not watery. Taste and adjust the seasoning. Remove from heat.

Roast the eggplants over high heat. Roasting eggplant over charcoal or a gas burner gives it a very pronounced and distinct smoky taste. Place them directly over the gas burner and cook on all sides until the skin is black and charred and the pulp is soft.

After cooking the eggplants on the stove, remove them directly to the sink and let them cool enough to handle. Put 1 quart cold water into a bowl and mix in lemon juice. Peel the eggplants, removing all the black and charred skin and seeds (see page 280). Drop the flesh into the lemon water and leave for 20 minutes or a little longer if you need to. Take the eggplant out of the water, holding from the stem with one hand over the sink, and squeeze all the moisture out with the other hand. Remove the stems and shred the eggplant into pieces by hand.

Melt the butter in a saucepan. Add the flour and cook, stirring, 2 minutes. Add the eggplant pieces. Using a small whisk, cook the eggplant 2 or 3 minutes, whisking briskly until it becomes smooth. Gradually stir in the hot cream or milk and keep on whisking and cooking for 3 or 4 minutes more, until the texture becomes very smooth and creamy. Season with salt and stir in the cheese. Cook a second or so, remove from heat, and keep warm.

Remove the thyme and parsley sprigs, bones if you used lamb chops, bay leaf, and cloves (if you can find them) from the braised lamb. Reheat the lamb gently until very hot. Make sure the eggplant cream is also hot. Spread some eggplant cream over heated plates and place the lamb over the eggplant in the center. Serve immediately.

Braised Lamb Hidden under a Dome of Eggplant, Tomatoes, and Roasted Peppers

❋❋

4 SERVINGS

[İSLİM KEBABI]

8 Japanese eggplants
  (about 3 pounds)
Salt
3 or 4 lamb shanks or
  lamb shoulder, about
  2 pounds
2 tablespoons unsalted
  butter
1½ cups finely chopped
  onions
2 large tomatoes, peeled
  and chopped
5 sprigs thyme
8 sprigs parsley
2 sprigs marjoram
1 bay leaf
2 cloves
Salt and pepper
1 to 1½ cups meat stock
  or water
½ cup oil
2 tomatoes
4 roasted tender long
  green peppers, or 2
  roasted poblanos
  (seeded and stemmed),
  or peppers of choice
  (see instructions for
  stove-roasting peppers,
  page 282).

Peel the eggplants lengthwise in a striped fashion (pages 279–80), cut off the stems, and slice them lengthwise into ¼- to ⅓-inch-thick slices. You will need slices about 1½ inches wide and about 6 or 8 inches long to wrap around the meat to create four individual bundles. If you are using regular eggplant, cut accordingly. Put about 1½ quarts cold water in a bowl, mix in 3 tablespoons salt, and soak the eggplant in the mixture for at least 1 hour. Weight the slices to keep them submerged.

If using lamb shanks, ask the butcher to cut off 1½ inches of the bone at the end of the shanks and trim off all fat.

To cook the meat, heat a heavy pan over low heat, add the meat, and cook uncovered, turning occasionally, on all sides about 20 minutes until the meat gradually turns reddish brown.

Pour off all the fat, add the butter and onions, and cook about 5 minutes. Stir in the chopped tomatoes, herbs, bay leaf, and cloves. Season with salt and pepper, add meat stock or water, cover, and simmer 1½ hours, or until the meat is very tender. As the meat cooks maintain the liquid level. Remove from heat and let cool.

Drain the eggplant, rinse with cold water, and squeeze dry by hand. Heat the oil until hot and fry the slices lightly until golden brown on both sides. Set them aside.

Take the meat out of the pan and remove from the bones, trying also to get some marrow from the bones. Discard the bones and add the marrow to the cooking liquid in the pan. Cut the meat into bite-size pieces and divide into four equal portions. Also divide the eggplant into four portions. Arrange the slices from one portion of eggplant in a small bowl or ramekin in a crisscross fashion, their ends hanging over. Now put one portion of meat in the bowl lined with the eggplant and turn the ends of the slices in over the meat. Turn the bowl or ramekin upside down into a shallow heavy pan. You will have a neat domelike package. Repeat this with the remaining portions of meat and eggplant. Place a tomato half, cut side down, over the bundle and put a roasted pepper on top of the tomato. Secure the tomato and pepper with a toothpick. If you used poblanos use ½ pepper on each portion. Place the bundles in a heavy shallow pan side by side.

Taste sauce, adjust the seasoning with salt and pepper, and strain the cooking liquid over the eggplant packages, pressing against the onions and herbs to extract their flavor into the pan (you should have about 1½ cups sauce). Cover and simmer about 20 minutes over gentle heat. Carefully remove one portion at a time to a warmed plate, pour over some sauce, and serve hot.

Spring Lamb Chops with New Potatoes, Fresh Peas, and Thyme in Paper

4 SERVINGS

[PİRZOLAYLA KAĞIT KEBABI]

4 spring lamb rib chops
Salt and pepper
4 to 6 tablespoons olive oil
1¼ cups diced new potatoes
2 or 3 tablespoons unsalted butter
½ cup chopped shallots
2 garlic cloves, minced
1 cup chopped ripe tomatoes
1¼ cups shelled fresh spring peas
1 teaspoon chopped fresh thyme
½ cup chopped flat-leaf parsley
Thyme sprigs

Trim all the fat from the chops, sprinkle with a little salt and pepper, brush lightly with olive oil, and brown over high heat about 1 minute on each side. Place the chops on a plate and set aside.

Cook the potatoes in a little olive oil until golden on all sides and set aside. Heat the butter in a pan and simmer the shallots and garlic 2 minutes, add the tomatoes and simmer 1 or 2 minutes. Stir in the potatoes, peas, chopped thyme, parsley, and a little salt and pepper. Cover, and simmer about 15 minutes or until the vegetables are tender. As they cook, sprinkle with some water if necessary. Vegetables should be very moist but not watery. Remove from heat and mix well.

Preheat the oven to 450 degrees.

Cut the parchment paper into four 16-inch lengths. Fold each piece in half and brush lightly with butter. Place one chop on the center of each piece of paper, cover with an equal portion of the cooked vegetables, and put a sprig of thyme on top. Fold 2 opposite sides of each piece of paper over the chop and vegetables, then fold over the two remaining sides to make a package. Secure the top with a toothpick. Place the packages on a baking sheet, sprinkle the tops with water, and bake about 8 minutes. Serve immediately with packages intact.

Lamb Chops with Molasses-Glazed Chestnuts

4 SERVINGS

[KESTANELİ YAHNİ]

1½ pounds chestnuts
4 shoulder lamb chops,
    trimmed of fat
4 tablespoons unsalted
    butter
1 onion, finely chopped
5 or 6 cloves
1 teaspoon ground
    cinnamon
6 sprigs flat-leaf parsley
Salt and freshly ground
    pepper
¼ cup molasses

GLAZE

2 tablespoons unsalted
    butter
2 tablespoons molasses

Like Lamb Shanks Braised with Cinnamon-Glazed Quince, this recipe is inspired by a recipe in a nineteenth-century cookbook by Ayşe Fahriye Hanım. Here molasses is substituted for *pekmez* (grape syrup; see page 288).

❋   ❋   ❋

Boil the chestnuts about 30 minutes and drain. Remove the shells and inner skin and set aside.

In a heavy pan, brown the chops in the butter on both sides. Add the onion and cook a few minutes. Add the spices, parsley, salt and pepper, molasses, and 1 cup of water; cover and simmer about 20 minutes or until the chops are half done. Add the chestnuts and ½ cup water and simmer about 20 minutes until the chestnuts are tender and the meat is cooked. As the meat and chestnuts cook, maintain the liquid level.

Remove the chops and chestnuts to a plate and keep warm. Strain the sauce and keep it at a gentle simmer to reduce and thicken. Adjust the sauce with salt.

Meanwhile make the glaze. Melt the butter in a skillet, stir in the molasses and let caramelize slightly. Glaze the chestnuts in this mixture on all sides and remove from heat.

Return the meat and the chestnuts to the simmering sauce; make sure all is hot. Arrange the chops with the chestnuts on warmed plates, pour the sauce over, and serve immediately.

Lamb Tripe and Chick-peas with Garlic-and-Vinegar Sauce

❋❋❋

4 SERVINGS

[NOHUTLU İŞKEMBE]

1 pound lamb tripe (or
  substitute beef tripe)
1 small onion, coarsely
  chopped
5 garlic cloves
4 cloves
Salt
Juice of ½ lemon
1 cup chick-peas, soaked
  in water overnight
1 onion, chopped
¼ cup chopped flat-leaf
  parsley
3 tablespoons unsalted
  butter
2 sprigs thyme

GARLIC-AND-VINEGAR
SAUCE

3 large garlic cloves,
  chopped
2 red jalapeños, topped,
  seeded, and chopped
Salt
½ cup wine vinegar

Tripe can be delicious and this recipe is a good example of this fact. I would like to point out for those who do not like hot peppers that the dish is good with or without the sauce.

❋   ❋   ❋

Wash the tripe several times, put it in a pot with the onion, 3 whole garlic cloves, cloves, a little salt, and lemon juice. Cover and simmer 1 hour, or until the tripe is tender. Remove from the pot, let it cool slightly, dice, and reserve. Reserve also the cooking liquid, removing all the fat on the surface.

Drain the chick-peas and put them in a pan with some tripe-cooking liquid to cover, and simmer covered about 1 hour, or until they are very tender.

Cook the onion, 2 minced garlic cloves, and parsley in the butter 5 minutes, add the thyme sprigs, chick-peas, and tripe. Stir in enough tripe-cooking liquid to cover, adjust with salt, cover, and simmer 30 minutes until the tripe and chick-peas are meltingly tender. As it cooks, add more liquid if necessary. The finished dish should have plenty of liquid but not quite as much as a soup. You can serve it sprinkled with chopped parsley without the sauce if you wish. If serving with sauce, put the tripe and peas in serving bowls, stir in 1 or 2 teaspoons of sauce, and pass the remaining sauce separately.

To make the sauce, pound the garlic and jalapeños using a mortar and pestle with a little salt until the mixture is reduced to a paste. Add the vinegar, mix with a spoon, and transfer to a small serving bowl.

KEBABS

* *

Every visitor to Turkey is bound sooner or later to find himself in a kebab shop. An unpretentious place, generally patronized, especially at midday, by working men and merchants who can find in a kebab shop a satisfying and tasty meal without grossly disrupting their tight monthly budgets. But if an occasional tourist happens on one of these shops, he will be welcomed into their friendly and informal ambiance.

The many charms of the kebab shop lure the passerby inside: the familiar smell of roasting meat and globules of fat dripping onto a wood fire; the enticing and colorful spectacle of red pepper and parsley-studded meat threaded with tomatoes, long green peppers, and eggplants on skewers—all artfully arranged against a background of long golden ovals of freshly baked flat bread.

The repertoire of the kebab shop is firmly set and well known to all its regular customers. First comes—for those who want it—a slightly pungent lentil soup known as *ezo gelin çorbası*. Then a range of kebabs, many of which bear the names of the cities where they originate. They all have in common a robust boldness in taste and appearance, though the spices and herbs vary. A delicious mixed salad known as *çoban salatası* may be ordered to accompany the kebab. Finally, for those who want to end their meal with a contrasting taste, comes *tel kadayıf* or *künefe*, a pastry sweetened with syrup.

The kebab shop is a long-standing and familiar institution, just as indispensable for even the smallest of Turkish towns as its bakery, pharmacy, post office, and sweet shop. Thoroughly unpretentious and informal in the provinces, some kebab shops in Istanbul and Ankara show signs of sophistication. Uniformed waiters hand the customers a printed menu, some of whom find it necessary to show their refinement by attacking the *lahmacun* (see page 194) with knife and fork. The relatively high prices that are charged are to a degree justified by the lean meat that goes into the kebabs, but the taste suffers, and so does the atmosphere.

The first two kebab recipes I provide here (pages 104 and 106) were acquired by spending several days—pleasant days, I might add—in the kitchens of traditional kebab shops. I believe they capture the essential taste of kebab.

A principal element in the unique good taste of Turkish kebab is the manner in which the lamb is prepared. Instead of being ground, it is minced with two knives. Fat is then added, together with some spices, and the meat is cooked on a wood fire. The kebab is served on wonderfully soft and silky flat bread called *pide* (page 186), baked on the premises only a few seconds before the meat is put on it. The bread soaks up some of the meat juices and fat. The delicious trimmings of roasted tomatoes, pungent peppers, and paper-thin onion slices all play their part in the creation of kebabs.

In Turkey, kebabs are rarely made at home due to the proliferation of all the kebab shops. Though complete authenticity is difficult to achieve at home, you can come acceptably close by using carefully chosen cuts of lamb, good tomatoes and peppers, and keeping a vigilant eye on the fire.

Minced Lamb Kebabs on a Bed of Roasted Eggplant Served with Roasted Tomato and Poblano Sauce

4 SERVINGS

[DOMATES SOSLU KEBAP]

MEAT MIXTURE

1 pound minced lamb
  from the shoulder
1 pound minced lamb
  from the breast,
  including some fat
1½ cups very finely
  chopped onions
3 teaspoons minced
  garlic
¾ cup minced flat-leaf
  parsley
2 teaspoons freshly
  ground black pepper
About 1 teaspoon
  crushed red pepper
  flakes
Salt

This recipe is adapted from the spicy and delicious kebabs of south-eastern Turkey.

❋   ❋   ❋

Combine all the ingredients for the meat mixture and knead with one hand to a paste. Set aside.

To make the sauce, you need to roast the tomatoes and peppers. To simplify the procedure, it is best to roast them in advance on a stovetop using a *comal*, griddle, or a cast-iron pan (see page 283). Roast the tomatoes until they have dark spots and blisters all over them. Roast the poblanos until the skins are charred and black and they are soft. Keep them sealed in a plastic bag for 10 or 15 minutes; peel, seed, and chop finely. Peel and chop the tomatoes and cook them about 5 minutes in a saucepan, mashing them down with a fork until they form a puree. Stir in the garlic, roasted peppers, and red pepper flakes, and season with salt and a splash of vinegar. Remove from fire and set aside.

ROASTED TOMATO AND POBLANO SAUCE

4 or 5 ripe tomatoes

2 small poblanos

3 teaspoons minced garlic

Pinch of crushed red pepper flakes (optional)

Salt

Dash of vinegar

6 Italian or Japanese eggplants

Olive oil

Thyme leaves

4 tender long green peppers, 2 poblanos, or peppers of choice

8 tablespoons (1 stick) unsalted butter

Cut the eggplants into ¼-inch slices. Brush with olive oil, sprinkle with salt and thyme, and set aside.

Divide the meat mixture into 16 or 20 equal pieces. Shape each piece into a flat kebab 1½ inches wide and 8 inches long.

Make a fire and after a while add some wood sticks or chips to it. Just before you grill the kebabs, throw on some dried herb stalks if you have any. Grill the peppers first, and if using poblanos peel and seed them and cut into halves. Wipe the excess oil from the eggplant slices and grill them over the cooler part of the grill until they are soft; keep them warm wrapped in foil. Now grill the kebabs only 2 inches above the fire on a hot grill, maybe 2 or 3 minutes on each side. While they are cooking, warm the plates and the sauce. Place the eggplant slices on the plates and pour a little sauce over them. Put the kebabs over the eggplant; sprinkle with thyme, and top with hot sauce. Place the roasted peppers on top. Heat the butter until foaming and spoon some over the kebabs; serve immediately with fresh *pide* (page 186) or warm pita bread.

Minced Lamb Brochettes with Roasted Tomatoes and Peppers Served on a Bed of Flat Bread

✤✤✤

2 SERVINGS

[ADANA KEBABI]

MEAT MIXTURE

½ pound ground lamb
from the shoulder
½ pound ground lamb
from the breast (or 1
pound ground lamb
from the shoulder,
mixed with ⅙ pound
ground lamb fat)
1 cup very finely
chopped onions
½ cup chopped flat-leaf
parsley
1½ teaspoons minced
garlic
1 teaspoon freshly
ground pepper
½ teaspoon crushed red
pepper flakes
Salt

Oil
8 tender long green
peppers, or 1 or 2
poblanos or peppers of
choice
Melted butter
4 small tomatoes, halved
Flat bread (or 4 warm
pita breads)
Onion-Sumac Relish
(recipe follows)

This spicy kebab comes from the province of Adana. The kebab is served on a soft flat bread called *pide* (see page 186). You can use similar flat bread bought from Middle Eastern markets or, failing that, use pita bread. Make sure you warm and refresh the bread before serving the kebab. Paper-thin onion slices flavored with pleasantly tart and peppery sumac are always served with such kebabs.

You will need flat, sword-shaped skewers. I did once use the regular skewers to make this kebab and although they worked I had great difficulty molding the meat on them and having it adhere to them. The flat skewers are at least 1½ inches wide and easier to mold ground meat on; they are available at Middle Eastern markets.

✤   ✤   ✤

Combine the ingredients for the meat mixture in a bowl; mix well and knead with one hand to a paste. Divide it into 4 equal portions and mold each on a flat skewer, firmly creating flat sausagelike forms. Hold the skewer upright with your left hand. With your right hand, dampened a little, start at the lower end and gently squeeze the meat against the skewer. Then open your fingers and let the hand slide up to the next section, squeezing and letting go with a continuous quick motion until your hand reaches the top end of the molded meat. I will admit that securing the meat on the skewers takes a little practice, but after five minutes' concentration you will master the technique.

Make a charcoal fire and when it is almost ready put some chips or wood on it and wait until the whole thing is covered with a thin layer of ash. If you happen to have some dried herb stalks such as thyme or rosemary, put them on the fire. Place the grill only 2 inches away from the fire and let it get hot. Brush with a little oil. Start roasting the peppers. If you are using poblanos, you will need to peel, seed, and halve them. Tender green peppers can be left whole.

Heat the flat bread or pita until warm but not crisp; cut into cubes and keep warm wrapped in foil.

Grill the brochettes 2 minutes on each side, basting with butter once or twice. Simultaneously, roast the tomatoes. Put some bread cubes on warm plates and spoon some hot butter over them. Remove the meat from the skewers and place 2 brochettes over the bread cubes on each plate. Placed the roasted tomatoes and peppers on top; spoon a little foaming hot butter over the kebabs and serve immediately accompanied by onion-sumac relish.

Onion-Sumac Relish

❋❋❋❋❋❋❋❋❋❋❋❋❋

*1 onion, cut into
paper-thin slices*
*1 tablespoon sumac (see
Glossary)*

Toss the onion slices with sumac. Relish will keep well for several hours.

Roasted Lamb Cubes with Yogurt, Roasted Tomato Sauce, Peppers, and Frothy Butter

* *

4 SERVINGS

[YOĞURTLU KEBAP]

1½ to 2 pounds lamb
   sirloin (preferably) or
   boned lamb from the
   leg or shoulder, free of
   fat and sinew, cut into
   ¾-inch cubes

MARINADE

1 cup light olive oil
¼ cup yogurt
2 tablespoons onion
   liquid (see page 86)
1 tablespoon lemon juice
1 tablespoon thyme
Salt and freshly ground
   black pepper

½ recipe pide (page
   186), or store-bought
   flat bread or pita

In this dish the tender juicy morsels of charcoal-grilled lamb are served on pieces of lightly toasted flat bread that is smothered first with creamy yogurt and then with a roasted tomato sauce, flavored with green peppers, garlic, and thyme. The whole is topped with a roasted pepper and hot frothy butter. Against the white and mellow creaminess of yogurt the contrasting flavors, textures, and colors of the ingredients stand out vividly and distinctly while creating a harmonious whole. In fact, the dish is highly evocative of Turkish embroidery, which similarly depicts every nuance of color and texture.

At the elegant Divan Hotel in Istanbul this dish is served in a traditional copper *sahan*, which calls to mind the bygone splendor of the empire. Made of two parts, a tin-lined copper dish to contain the food and a dome-shaped copper lid with a tiny bronze knob on top, the *sahan* keeps food hot.

The actual cooking of the dish is not at all difficult. However, in order to coordinate the various procedures and to keep everything warm while doing different things, one must be well organized.

Pide, the flat bread you need, is the only thing that takes time. You could make it several hours ahead of time, according to the recipe on page 186, and keep it wrapped; alternatively you could buy similar bread at Middle Eastern markets. Failing all else, you could substitute warmed pita bread.

❋ ❋ ❋

Mix all the ingredients for the marinade and marinate the lamb overnight in the refrigerator or for 3 or 4 hours at room temperature. If marinating in the refrigerator, be sure to leave it at room temperature 3 hours before cooking it.

If you decide to make your own bread, bake it in the morning and keep it wrapped.

ROASTED TOMATO SAUCE

2 or 3 large tomatoes
*2 tender long green
  peppers, Hungarian
  green peppers, or 1
  poblano*
1 tablespoon olive oil
2 sprigs thyme
*2 teaspoons minced
  garlic*
*Pinch of crushed red
  pepper flakes*
Splash of vinegar
A few parsley leaves
Salt

*2 cups Yogurt Cream
  (page 275) or regular
  plain yogurt, at room
  temperature*
Salt
*8 tablespoons (1 stick)
  unsalted butter*
Pepper
*4 tender long green
  peppers, or 2 poblanos*

You can also make the tomato sauce ahead of time. The tomatoes should be roasted first, which imparts a very good flavor to them. Put the tomatoes in a hot dry cast-iron skillet over medium heat and roast on all sides until light brown blisters appear on the skin. Peel, chop, and put in a bowl.

Roast the peppers directly over a gas burner until black and charred (see page 282). Top and seed them, chop finely, and set aside in a bowl (poblanos must be peeled).

Heat oil in a saucepan; stir in tomatoes, thyme, and peppers; cook, mashing tomatoes with a fork until they form a sauce. Stir in garlic, pepper flakes, splash of vinegar, parsley, and salt. Taste and adjust with salt and/or vinegar and set aside.

Beat yogurt cream or yogurt with a wooden spoon, adding a little salt, until it is smooth and creamy. Keep it on a warm spot on the stove, if possible, for a couple of hours before serving.

Make a charcoal fire. Thread the lamb on skewers. Just before cooking the lamb, toast the bread so that it is only barely crisp. Cut it into bite-size pieces and keep warm, wrapped in foil, in a low oven. Warm the dinner plates in the oven at the same time. Make sure the tomato sauce is ready to be heated quickly. Put the butter in a small saucepan and also keep it warm, ready to be heated until frothy. If you are using poblanos, they need to be roasted before grilling the lamb so that they can be peeled, seeded, and halved. If using other peppers, top and seed them and cut into halves. When everything is ready, sprinkle the lamb cubes lightly with salt and pepper and grill them 2 or 3 inches above the fire only a few minutes on each side while also grilling the peppers. The meat will not take more than 2 or 3 minutes. You can remove a piece from a skewer and taste it to be sure. In any case, please do not overcook them. Meanwhile, it would be nice if you had someone to put the bread cubes on the plates and reheat the sauce. If you are not so lucky, put the lamb cubes in a bowl and place them in a warm oven. Reheat the tomato sauce until hot, place the bread cubes on the warm dinner plates, and spread the yogurt over the bread cubes. Then spoon the hot sauce over the yogurt, leaving yogurt visible around the edges. Put the cubes of meat over the sauce and put the peppers on top of the kebabs. Heat the butter until frothy, pour it over everything and serve immediately.

Spicy Shish Kebab Marinated with Peppers and Herbs

✳✳✳

4 SERVINGS

[GÜNEYDOĞU ANADOLU USULÜ ŞİŞ KEBABI]

2 pounds boneless leg of lamb or shoulder

MARINADE

1 onion, thinly sliced
⅓ cup light olive oil
3 teaspoons minced garlic
1 tablespoon good paprika
2 teaspoons freshly ground cumin seeds (see page 285)
1 tablespoon fresh thyme
½ teaspoon crushed red pepper flakes
½ cup chopped flat-leaf parsley
½ cup chopped mint
Salt and freshly ground pepper

Olive oil
4 tomatoes and 2 red onions, quartered
4 sweet red peppers, seeded and quartered
A few jalapeños (optional)

There is a special association between the Turks and kebab; in fact, in the West shish kebab is probably the best known of all Turkish dishes. The legend that shish kebab was a relatively late battlefield invention of the Ottoman armies must be discarded, for the eleventh-century lexicographer Mahmud al-Kashghari already records the expression *et siska takturdi*—"He threaded the meat on the skewer."

The Persians also loved kebab, even introducing it into their poetry as a fanciful device for describing the torments of the lover. His suffering liver (the liver being the seat of the emotions, as in Elizabethan English) is pierced by the glances of the beloved, each as sharp as a skewer, and then roasted like kebab on the fire of love. Since the Turk was often regarded as the ideal of beauty, it is often a Turk who is pictured threading the liver of her admirers onto the skewers of her glances.

The classic shish kebab is well known in the West. Here I give a spicy version of it—from southeast Turkey.

✳　　✳　　✳

Trim most, but not all, the fat from the lamb and cut the meat into 1-inch cubes. Mix all the ingredients for the marinade and marinate the meat in the refrigerator overnight. The next day, let it sit 3 or 4 hours at room temperature before cooking it.

Brush the vegetables with any leftover marinade, or with a little olive oil. Put the lamb on skewers. Do the same with the vegetables, threading the tomatoes on separate skewers since they take less time to cook.

Make a hot fire on the grill and brush the grill lightly with oil. Cook the kebabs 2 inches above the fire, turning on all sides about 4 or 5 minutes. Do not overcook. Cook the vegetables on the cooler parts of the grill until brown specks appear on their surfaces. Serve immediately with crusty bread and/or a pilaf.

KÖFTE

*K*öfte are made with ground or minced meat and flavored with different spices and herbs. Some *köfte* mixtures may include rice, bulgur, or fresh bread crumbs. Their size and shape vary: Some are formed into large balls and stuffed; others are shaped into tiny balls or may be thumb-shaped. Still others are threaded onto skewers (see page 106). They may be grilled, fried, or simmered in some sort of broth or sauce.

The following *köfte* dishes are adapted from the famed and spicy cuisine of Gaziantep, an ancient city in the southeastern part of Turkey.

Köfte Simmered with Roasted Eggplant and Pomegranate-Tomato Sauce

✽✽✽

4 SERVINGS

[NAR EKŞİLİ PATLICANLI KÖFTE]

KÖFTE MIXTURE

2 slices French bread,
   crusts removed
1 pound twice-ground
   lamb (beef can be
   substituted)
½ onion, grated
1½ teaspoons freshly
   ground cumin seeds
   (see page 285)
½ teaspoon ground
   allspice
¼ to ½ teaspoon crushed
   red pepper flakes
2 tablespoons olive oil
½ cup chopped flat-leaf
   parsley
Salt and freshly ground
   black pepper

4 tender long green
   peppers, Hungarian
   peppers, or 2 poblanos
4 or 5 Japanese
   eggplants

If pomegranate syrup is not available, use pomegranate juice sharpened with lemon juice, or a fruity vinegar.

✽   ✽   ✽

To make the *köfte,* put bread in small bowl with water to cover and let soak until soft. Squeeze dry by hand and put in bowl with lamb, onion, spices, olive oil, and parsley. Season with salt and pepper and knead by hand to a paste. Shape into small *köfte* and pan grill them in a hot cast-iron skillet brushed lightly with oil. Place the *köfte* in a heavy shallow pan in one layer, and set aside. Roast the peppers directly over a gas burner until light brown blisters appear on their surface (see page 282). If you are using poblanos, they will take a little longer to become soft and you will need to peel and halve them.

   Roast the eggplants directly on the gas burner until black and charred. Cool, peel, and cut off the stems (see page 280). Then cut them into ⅓-inch-thick rounds and place them over the *köfte* in the pan.

POMEGRANATE-TOMATO SAUCE

4 large ripe tomatoes,
  peeled and chopped
2 tablespoons olive oil
5 scallions, white and
  green parts, chopped
Pinch of crushed red
  pepper flakes
Salt and freshly ground
  pepper
1 tablespoon
  pomegranate syrup
Chopped flat-leaf parsley

To make the sauce, cook the tomatoes in the olive oil, mashing down with a fork 4 or 5 minutes. Stir in the scallions and pepper flakes and cook until the mixture forms a watery sauce. Season with salt and pepper and stir in the pomegranate syrup or whatever substitute you have. Stir in a handful of parsley and pour the sauce over the eggplant and *köfte*. Cover and simmer, adding ¼ cup water, over low heat about 20 minutes, until the eggplant is soft and *köfte* are hot. Serve sprinkled with parsley.

Spicy *Köfte* Simmered with Eggplant, Tomatoes, and Roasted Poblanos

4 SERVINGS

[GAZİANTEP'TEN PATLICANLI KÖFTE]

KÖFTE MIXTURE

1 pound medium-fat
   ground lamb
½ onion, minced
2 teaspoons freshly
   ground cumin seeds
   (see page 285)
½ teaspoon crushed red
   pepper flakes
½ cup chopped flat-leaf
   parsley
Salt and freshly ground
   pepper

8 small Japanese
   eggplants
2 large poblanos or 4
   Hungarian green
   peppers or tender long
   green peppers
2 or 3 tablespoons olive
   oil
1½ cups finely chopped
   onions
4 ripe tomatoes, peeled
   and chopped
2 teaspoons minced
   garlic
½ cup chopped flat-leaf
   parsley
Salt and pepper
Splash of vinegar

Combine the lamb, onion, cumin, pepper flakes, and parsley in a bowl. Mix thoroughly and season with salt and pepper. Divide into 8 equal portions. Shape each into flat *köfte*, 6 inches long and ¼-inch thick and set aside.

Top the eggplants. Beginning at the stem end, cut each one through the center lengthwise, stopping 1 inch from the other end. Place one *köfte* in each eggplant between the two separated halves. Place the eggplants side by side in a large shallow pan.

Meanwhile, roast the peppers directly over a gas burner or on a range-top grill or in a cast-iron skillet until brown blisters appear on all sides (see page 282). If you use poblanos, you will need to peel them, so put them in a plastic bag and let stand 20 minutes. Peel the peppers, top, seed, and halve them. If you use Hungarian peppers, or tender long green peppers, leave them whole.

Heat the olive oil in a saucepan and cook the onions 8 minutes until they begin to brown around the edges. Stir in the tomatoes and garlic and simmer them, mashing down with a fork until they form a sauce, about 5 minutes or so. Remove from heat and add the parsley, season with salt, pepper, and a splash of vinegar. The sauce should have a slight tang. Pour this sauce over the eggplants along with ¼ cup water. Place the peppers on top, cover, and simmer about 35 to 40 minutes until the eggplants are very tender. Check occasionally and add a little water if necessary. Serve hot.

Grilled Bulgur *Köfte* with Herbs and Chilies

[IZGARA BULGURLU KÖFTE]

½ cup fine-grained
   bulgur
1 pound medium-fat
   ground lamb
1 cup minced onions
1 jalapeño, seeded and
   minced
1 small sweet red
   pepper, seeded and
   minced
2 teaspoons crushed
   garlic (see page 286)
½ teaspoon crushed red
   pepper flakes
1½ teaspoons freshly
   ground cumin
½ cup chopped flat-leaf
   parsley
½ cup chopped fresh
   mint leaves
Salt and freshly ground
   pepper
2 tablespoons olive oil

Bulgur gives these spicy *köfte* a nutty flavor.

❋   ❋   ❋

Wash bulgur, put it in a bowl, sprinkle generously with enough water to moisten, and let stand 30 minutes. Add all the remaining ingredients, season with salt and pepper, and knead to blend. Mix to a paste in food processor. Shape egg-sized pieces in ¼-inch-thick oval patties (*köfte*). Grill on both sides until golden and crisp. Or you can cook them in a cast-iron skillet heated very hot and coated lightly with oil.

VEGETABLES

PICKLES AND RELISHES

VEGETABLE PASTES

VEGETABLES AND MEATLESS DOLMAS COOKED IN OLIVE OIL

. . . lit from a blessed olive tree, neither of the east nor the west; its oil almost gives light before the fire touches it.

—Qur'an, 24:35

And the dove came in to him in the evening; and, lo, in her mouth was an olive leaf pluckt off; so Noah knew that the waters were abated from off the earth.

—Genesis, 8:11

As one drives along the roads that link the towns of the Aegean together, closely following the contours of the coastline, olive groves are one's constant companions. Every now and then, as the road meanders away from the coast, the sea is lost to view, but the olive trees remain uniformly and obstinately visible. They seem to display an almost contemptuous indifference to the dazzling and stifling heat and the harshness of the terrain. Olive trees tend to be small, with crooked trunks and gnarled branches, and strangely rigid grayish green leaves.

There is something inherently classical about the olive tree, and Pliny remarked that "there is no plant which bears a fruit of as great an importance as the olive."

On the culinary plane, I must stress that olive oil for me is not at all a cooking medium, but a culinary ingredient that imparts a unique and irreplaceable flavor to everything with which it is cooked or combined. Turks are careful not to adulterate the precious flavor of olive oil, and have a whole family of dishes called, quite simply, "olive oil dishes" (*zeytinyağlılar*) in which no meat is used; these make up some of the most interesting dishes in Turkish cuisine, and have a special place reserved for them in the menu; they are enjoyed separately and in their own right, accompanied only by bread. Some people even enjoy dipping a piece of crusty, fresh bread in greenish, fruity olive oil.

Served cold or at room temperature, these dishes can be kept in the refrigerator for 3 or 4 days.

In my experience, the best olive oil comes from the Aegean. It tastes distinctly of olives, is full-bodied, and more green than gold. I always bring back from my annual trip to Turkey my allotted share of the family supply of olive oil, provided by a local merchant from the hand-pressed oil produced from his own olive groves. It has become a standard joke with my sons that whereas other women fill their carry-on luggage with toiletries and cosmetics, I fill mine with cans of olive oil!

To me, the best olive oil is that obtained from the first pressing of fine-quality olives; this oil is full-bodied, fruity and green. Unadulterated oil from the second pressing of good olives can also be quite good. The only way to find an oil to one's liking is by experimentation. For your salads, use extra-virgin olive oil, but to use it for frying would be extravagant; a less expensive one would be adequate. I do not use my own supply of oil from the Aegean for frying. And if that supply is exhausted before I have a chance to replenish it, I tend to favor olive oil from Sicily.

Small Eggplants Stuffed with Garlic Cloves, Tomatoes, and Parsley

❁❁❁

4 SERVINGS

[İMAM BAYILDI]

1½ pounds Japanese eggplants
Salt
2 to 3 tablespoons fine olive oil

This is a renowned dish whose origins are lost in apocryphal stories. The anonymous imam (prayer leader) after whom the dish is named is said to have fainted on first being confronted with this concoction, for two quite different reasons. The first is that his palate was so overwhelmed with pleasure that he lost consciousness and the sec-

FILLING

1 large onion (about 1½ cups sliced paper-thin)
18 small garlic cloves, peeled and left whole
¼ cup plus 2 to 3 tablespoons olive oil
1 cup chopped fresh tomatoes
¾ teaspoon sugar
1 cup chopped flat-leaf parsley
Salt

Chopped parsley
Lemon juice

ond is that his sense of economy was outraged when he learned how much olive oil had been required to produce it. While sympathetic to the legendary imam's desire for frugality, we prefer to believe the first explanation, for this dish, when properly made, can indeed take away the senses of the dedicated gourmet!

As with so many other Turkish dishes, the quality of ingredients is crucial to success when preparing *imam bayıldı*. Be sure to use good olive oil and select the eggplants carefully.

❋   ❋   ❋

Peel eggplants lengthwise in a striped fashion. Peel around the stem, sprinkle generously with salt, and allow to sit 45 minutes. Rinse with water and squeeze dry. Fry in olive oil over medium-low heat, turning on all sides. The eggplants should have a rich golden color all over. Set aside.

For the filling, cook onions and garlic in ¼ cup olive oil over medium-low heat about 10 minutes, stirring frequently, until onions are very soft. Do not allow them to brown. Add tomatoes and cook 5 minutes. Stir in sugar, ½ cup parsley, and season with salt. Remove from heat and let stand, covered, 30 minutes.

Preheat the oven to 375 degrees.

Place eggplants in a heavy-bottomed shallow baking dish in one layer, side by side. Slit each eggplant open lengthwise, creating a cavity. Take care not to cut through. Enlarge the cavities with your fingers, pulling the sides gently in opposite directions so they will hold as much of the filling as possible. Stuff generously with the filling and sprinkle with remaining oil. Add 1 cup hot water, cover, and bake for about 1 hour or until the eggplants are very tender when pierced with a fork. Check the water content during cooking and add hot water as needed. The finished dish should have only a few tablespoons of liquid. If there is more liquid, boil rapidly a few minutes to reduce. Alternatively, you can cook this dish on a stovetop. Remove from oven and cool.

Arrange on a platter, cover with plastic wrap, and refrigerate until ready to serve. It will keep 2 or 3 days. Serve cold or at room temperature, sprinkled with parsley and a little lemon juice, accompanied by crusty bread.

Celery Root and Potatoes in Olive Oil

[ZEYTİNYAĞLI KEREVİZ]

4 SERVINGS

1½ cups finely chopped
    onions
10 garlic cloves, peeled
    and left whole
⅓ cup olive oil
2 cups peeled and diced
    celery root
2 cups water
Salt
1¾ cups peeled and
    diced Finnish yellow
    or red-skinned
    potatoes
2 peeled and diced
    carrots
½ teaspoon flour
1½ teaspoons sugar
½ cup lemon juice
½ cup chopped flat-leaf
    parsley

Cook onions and garlic cloves in olive oil for 5 minutes until soft. Stir in celery root and cook, stirring, for 1 to 2 minutes. Add the water and a little salt, cover, and simmer about 20 minutes. Stir in potatoes and carrots, cover, and simmer 30 minutes, until all the vegetables are tender. Add water if necessary as it cooks. Sprinkle flour over vegetables, stir in sugar and 3 tablespoons lemon juice, cover, and simmer just until the liquid thickens to a sauce. Adjust with salt, stir in ⅓ cup parsley, remove from heat, and cool covered. Serve cold or at room temperature, sprinkled with the remaining parsley and lemon juice. The dish will keep 2 or 3 days, covered, in the refrigerator.

Artichoke Hearts Cooked with Dill

[ENGİNAR ZEYTİNYAĞLI]

4 SERVINGS

4 large artichokes
Salt
Lemon halves
⅓ cup lemon juice

Remove the outer leaves of the artichokes. Cut off the stems. Slice off the inner leaves almost down to the heart. Pare the artichokes as if paring an apple, removing green parts down to the white heart. Scoop out the fur of the chokes. Rub the artichoke hearts with salt

1 tablespoon flour
3 large shallots, finely
  chopped
1 cup water
6 tablespoons fine olive
  oil
1 teaspoon sugar
2 teaspoons flour
¾ cup chopped fresh dill

and lemon halves to prevent them from discoloring. Drop into a saucepan of water with 2 tablespoons lemon juice and flour. When all are prepared, simmer for 5 minutes. Remove from the liquid and arrange the hearts side by side in a heavy shallow pan. Put an equal amount of shallots in the center of each artichoke heart. Mix 1 cup water with the olive oil, some salt, sugar, and 2 tablespoons lemon juice, and pour over the artichokes. Cover and simmer about 30 minutes, until the vegetables are very tender. As they cook, add small amounts of water if necessary to retain the original liquid level. Sprinkle with ½ cup dill and cook a few minutes longer. Let cool. Serve cold sprinkled with remaining dill and lemon juice.

Jerusalem Artichokes Stewed in Olive Oil

✹✹

4 SERVINGS

[ZEYTİNYAĞLI YERELMASI]

¾ cup finely chopped
  onions
¼ cup fine olive oil
1½ pounds Jerusalem
  artichokes, peeled and
  cubed
2 tablespoons uncooked
  rice
1½ cups water
Salt
2 teaspoons sugar
3 tablespoons chopped
  fresh dill
Lemon juice
Lemon wedges

Sauté onions in olive oil a few minutes until soft. Add artichokes and turn them for a few minutes. Add rice and water mixed with a little salt and the sugar. Cover and simmer 30 to 35 minutes, until vegetables are tender. Add a little water as it cooks if mixture seems too dry. Add 2 tablespoons dill and cook 1 minute longer. Season with salt and lemon juice to taste. Refrigerate and serve cold or at room temperature with lemon wedges and the remaining dill. The artichokes will keep 2 or 3 days, covered, in the refrigerator.

Puree of Fava Beans with Olive Oil–Lemon-Dill Sauce

❀❀❀❀❀❀❀❀❀❀❀❀❀❀❀❀❀❀❀❀❀❀❀❀❀❀❀❀❀❀❀❀❀❀❀❀

[ZEYTİNYAĞLI BAKLA EZMESİ]

2 cups dried fava beans,
   soaked overnight in
   water to cover
1½ cups chopped onions
½ cup fine olive oil
1 tablespoon plus 1
   teaspoon sugar
Salt
3 cups water
¼ cup chopped fresh dill
1 tablespoon lemon juice

Remove skins from fava beans. Cook onions in the olive oil until limp. Add the beans, sugar, a little salt, and the water; cover and simmer about 50 minutes, until the beans are very soft. Adjust for salt, add the dill and lemon juice; cook a minute longer and remove from heat.

    Put the fava beans through a sieve, arrange in a 1-quart mold or bowl, and chill.

Olive Oil–Lemon-Dill Sauce

❀❀❀❀❀❀❀❀❀❀❀

4 tablespoons fine olive
   oil
2 tablespoons lemon juice
¼ cup chopped fresh dill
Salt

Chopped dill
Black olives
Lemon wedges

To make the sauce, mix the olive oil with lemon juice and dill and adjust with salt. Invert the puree onto a serving plate and pour the sauce over it. Garnish with dill, olives, and lemon wedges.

Eggplant with
Garlic-Jalapeño-Vinegar Sauce

❋❋

4 TO 6 SERVINGS

[PATLICAN PAÇASI]

1 pound Japanese
    eggplants, peeled
Lemon halves
1½ cups minced
    tomatoes
¼ cup plus 1 tablespoon
    olive oil
Salt
2 roasted poblanos,
    seeded and halved (see
    page 282)
½ cup water

This recipe is adapted from the nineteenth-century cookbook by Türabi Efendi.

❋   ❋   ❋

Rub eggplants with lemon halves and cut into halves. Place in a heavy shallow pan and top with tomatoes and olive oil. Sprinkle with a little salt and arrange poblano halves on top. Add water, cover, and simmer 50 or 60 minutes until eggplant is very tender.

Garlic-Jalapeño-Vinegar Sauce

❋❋❋❋❋❋❋❋❋❋❋

3 large garlic cloves
Salt
½ jalapeño, seeded and
    chopped
⅓ cup wine vinegar

Mash garlic with a little salt in a mortar, add jalapeño, and pound to a paste; mix in vinegar. Pour the sauce over the eggplant; boil for a few seconds and remove from heat. Serve cold or at room temperature.

White Beans Stewed with Garlic Cloves and Olive Oil

✴✴✴✴✴✴✴✴✴✴✴✴✴✴✴✴✴✴✴✴✴✴✴✴✴✴✴✴✴✴✴✴

[ZEYTİNYAĞLI FASULYE]

2 cups haricot lingots or
    dried white beans
3 cups finely chopped
    onions
18 small garlic cloves,
    peeled and left whole
4 small carrots, peeled
    and cut into ¼-inch
    slices
½ cup plus 2 to 4
    tablespoons fine olive
    oil
2 cups chopped tomatoes
3 tablespoons sugar
Salt
2½ cups water
1½ cups chopped
    flat-leaf parsley
Lemon juice

Soak beans overnight in cold water to cover.

In a large heavy pan cook onions, garlic, and carrots in olive oil over medium-low heat, stirring frequently, until onions are limp, about 15 minutes. Do not let onions and garlic brown. Add tomatoes and cook about 5 minutes until they are soft. Drain beans and add to the pan. Stir in sugar, a little salt, and the water; cover and simmer 1½ to 2 hours, until beans are very tender. As beans cook, maintain water almost at the same level as the beans. Add half of the parsley, adjust for salt, cook a minute or so longer, and remove from heat. Let cool, transfer to a serving bowl, and refrigerate until cold. Serve cold or at room temperature with lemon juice and remaining parsley. It is good with crusty bread. The beans will keep 3 days in the refrigerator.

Eggplant *Börek*

✴✴✴✴✴✴✴✴✴✴✴✴✴✴✴✴✴✴✴✴✴✴✴✴✴✴✴✴✴✴✴✴

[PATLICAN BÖREGİ]

1 pound Japanese
    eggplants
Salt
¼ cup olive oil

Deep-fried eggplant or zucchini slices sandwiched together with a cheese and herb filling appears in all Turkish cookbooks. I traced the origin to a recipe in Mehmed Kamil's nineteenth-century cookbook. There the dish is simply named *peynirli kabak*, zucchini with cheese.

✴   ✴   ✴

FILLING

1 cup (¼ pound)
  crumbled feta cheese
¾ cup (¼ pound) grated
  mozzarella cheese
1 egg, lightly beaten
¼ cup chopped parsley
1 tablespoon chopped
  fresh dill

1 or 2 eggs, lightly
  beaten
About 1 cup flour
2 cups fresh bread
  crumbs

Peanut oil

Peel eggplants in a striped fashion (pages 279–80) and cut into ⅓-inch-thick slices. Sprinkle generously with salt and let stand at least 1 hour. Rinse with water and squeeze dry. Heat the olive oil and sauté eggplant lightly on both sides. Drain on paper towels.

Mix all filling ingredients in a bowl until thoroughly blended. Spread a thin layer of filling on one slice of eggplant and place another slice on top of the filling. Press together. Continue in this manner until all the eggplant has been used.

Put flour and bread crumbs on separate plates. Dip sandwiches first in flour, then in egg, and then in bread crumbs, pressing gently to be sure the crumbs adhere to the slices. Place on a rack and allow to stand in the refrigerator at least 30 minutes.

Just before serving, deep-fry them in hot oil until golden brown; drain on paper towels and serve immediately.

Fresh Fava Beans in Dill

✺✺

2 TO 3 SERVINGS   [ZEYTİNYAĞLI TAZE İÇ BAKLA]

1½ pounds fresh fava
  beans in pods (½
  pound shelled)
3 tablespoons finely
  chopped onion
¼ cup fine olive oil
¾ cup water
1 teaspoon sugar
Salt
6 tablespoons chopped
  fresh dill

Shell beans and remove inner skins.

Cook onion in the olive oil for 2 to 3 minutes. Add beans and turn them for 2 minutes. Add water and sugar; season with salt; cover and simmer until beans are tender. The cooking time will vary according to the tenderness of the beans. In the spring, fresh and tender fava beans take only 15 to 20 minutes to cook, but other times they may need as long as 40 to 45 minutes. As the beans cook, add water to maintain the liquid level a little under the level of the beans. Stir in 3 tablespoons dill, cover, and remove from heat. Let cool. Serve cold or at room temperature, sprinkled with remaining dill. The beans will keep 2 or 3 days, covered, in the refrigerator.

Variation: This dish is also delicious served with garlic-yogurt sauce. Mix 1 cup yogurt with a little salt and crushed garlic until smooth; pour over the fava beans. Sprinkle fresh dill on top.

Green Beans

[YEŞİL FASULYE ZEYTİNYAĞLI]

1 pound tender green
  beans
1 cup finely chopped
  onions
Salt
½ cup plus 2 tablespoons
  fine olive oil
1 cup peeled and
  chopped tomatoes
1 cup warm water
1 tablespoon sugar

Top and tail the beans; string if necessary. Wash, drain, and cut each in half.

Put onions in a pan, sprinkle with salt, and rub with hands to soften a little. Add the olive oil, tomatoes, and beans; toss well. Cover and cook over medium heat for about 10 minutes, until beans turn pale green and no liquid remains. Stir the beans, add the warm water and the sugar. Cover and simmer about 1 hour or until beans are very tender. Check the liquid level from time to time and add a little water if necessary. At the end of cooking there should be no more than ⅓ cup liquid in the pan. Adjust for salt. Let cool; serve cold or at room temperature. The beans will keep 3 days in the refrigerator.

Red Peppers Stuffed with Rice, Pine Nuts, and Currants

ABOUT 8 SERVINGS

[BIBER DOLMASI ZEYTİNYAĞLI]

RICE, PINE NUT, AND CURRANT FILLING
¾ cup fine olive oil
5 cups finely chopped
  onions
3 tablespoons pine nuts
1 cup uncooked rice
½ cup minced fresh
  tomatoes
3 tablespoons chopped
  fresh mint leaves, or
  crushed dried mint
  leaves

To make filling, heat olive oil in a heavy pan. Cook onions and pine nuts about 18 minutes, stirring frequently. Add rice and turn for 5 minutes. Stir in tomatoes and cook a few minutes longer. Reduce heat to low and stir in herbs, sugar, spices, and currants. Add the hot water and lemon juice, adjust for salt, cover, and simmer for about 10 minutes, until all the liquid is absorbed. Let cool.

Stir the filling once and stuff the peppers loosely. Arrange the stuffed vegetables upright in a shallow, heavy pan. Mix 1 cup hot water with about ¼ cup olive oil, a little salt, and 2 tablespoons lemon juice; pour into the pan. Place a sheet of parchment paper over the vegetables and cover with an inverted plate to keep them in place. Cover and cook over low heat for 45 to 55 minutes or until rice is cooked. As the vegetables cook, add more hot water in very

1 tablespoon chopped
   fresh dill
3 to 4 teaspoons sugar
¾ teaspoon ground
   cinnamon
¼ teaspoon ground
   allspice
¼ teaspoon freshly
   grated nutmeg
⅛ teaspoon ground
   cloves
3 tablespoons currants
¾ cup hot water
3 tablespoons lemon juice
Salt

About 8 small sweet red
   peppers, seeded
1 cup hot water
¼ cup fine olive oil
Salt
⅓ cup lemon juice
Lemon wedges
Lemon juice

small quantities (3 to 4 tablespoons) if needed. Let cool. Sprinkle with remaining lemon juice and serve cold or at room temperature, together with lemon wedges and lemon juice. The dolmas will keep 3 days in the refrigerator.

Zucchini with Yogurt

✻✻✻

4 SERVINGS

[YOĞURTLU KABAK]

1 pound zucchini,
   coarsely grated
Salt
3 to 4 tablespoons fine
   olive oil
1½ cups yogurt
3 garlic cloves, crushed
   (see page 286)

Put zucchini in a bowl, sprinkle with salt, and let stand for 30 minutes. Squeeze with hands to press out as much liquid as possible. Heat oil in a wok or large skillet and sauté zucchini, stirring, for about 6 or 7 minutes. Cool.

Beat yogurt with garlic until smooth, season with salt. Put zucchini in a bowl, mix well with yogurt, and serve at room temperature.

Zucchini Cakes with Green Onions, Cheese, and Herbs

✳✳

6 TO 8 SERVINGS [KABAK MÜCVERİ]

*1½ pounds zucchini,
  coarsely grated*
Salt
5 scallions, chopped
⅓ cup chopped fresh dill
*⅓ cup chopped flat-leaf
  parsley*
*2 tablespoons grated
  onion*
*⅓ cup grated kasseri
  cheese*
3 eggs, lightly beaten
3 tablespoons flour
Freshly ground pepper
*Light olive oil or peanut
  oil for frying*

Sprinkle zucchini with salt and allow to sit in a colander at least 20 minutes. Squeeze dry and mix in a bowl with the remaining ingredients except the oil. Season with salt and pepper.

Heat ¼ cup oil in a nonstick frying pan, drop tablespoonfuls of the mixture into the hot oil, and cook until golden brown on both sides. Drain on paper towels and serve hot or cold.

Leek Fritters

✳✳

4 SERVINGS [PEYNİRLİ PRASA]

4 medium leeks
2 tablespoons olive oil
Salt
*1 cup crumbled feta
  cheese*

Trim leeks, removing roots, tough outer leaves, and coarse greens. Wash well and drain. Quarter lengthwise and chop; you should have 4 cups.

Cook in olive oil a few minutes over medium heat with a little salt. Sprinkle with a few tablespoons of water, cover, and simmer

Small handful chopped
  fresh herbs such as
  flat-leaf parsley, dill,
  basil, mint
4 eggs, separated
Freshly ground black
  pepper
3 to 4 tablespoons flour
Oil for frying

until leeks are tender. At the end of cooking, if there is any liquid left in the pan, boil rapidly for a minute to dry the mixture. Put in a bowl, cool slightly. Stir in cheese and herbs. Beat egg yolks lightly and add; season with salt and pepper. Stir in enough flour to make a thick batter (a little thicker than pancake batter). Beat egg whites to firm peaks and gently fold into batter.

Heat a little oil in a heavy frying pan, reduce heat to medium, drop batter by spoonfuls, and fry until golden brown on both sides. Take care not to dry them; they should remain moist inside. Serve immediately.

Leeks Braised in Olive Oil and Lemon Juice

❋❋

4 SERVINGS

[PRASA ZEYTİNYAĞLI]

2½ pounds leeks
3 small carrots
6 tablespoons fine olive
  oil
3 tablespoons uncooked
  rice
Salt
1½ cups water
½ tablespoon sugar
3 tablespoons lemon juice
Lemon juice

Remove coarse outer leaves and tough green leaves from leeks. Trim off roots. Slice into ½-inch pieces and wash well to remove all traces of soil. Drain.

Put leeks in a heavy saucepan with carrots and olive oil, cover, and let sweat over medium-low heat for 20 minutes, stirring occasionally. Sprinkle in rice, some salt, add the water and sugar; cover and simmer 30 or 40 minutes until vegetables are soft.

Stir in the lemon juice, adjust with salt, and remove from heat. Let cool. As the leeks cook, add a few tablespoons of water as needed. The finished dish should have plenty of sauce but not be soupy. Serve cold or at room temperature, with lemon juice. The leeks will keep 3 days in the refrigerator.

Squash Blossom Dolmas

****

[KIBRISIN ÇIÇEK DOLMASI]

Squash blossoms
½ recipe Rice, Pine Nut,
*   and Currant Filling*
*   (page 130), using ½*
*   cup water*
½ cup water
2 tablespoons fine olive
*   oil*
Salt
⅓ cup lemon juice
Lemon wedges

This is a specialty from Cyprus. Squash blossoms are also used in different parts of Anatolia to make dolmas.

❊   ❊   ❊

Wash squash blossoms very gently. Stuff them loosely with the filling and place them upright in layers in a heavy shallow pan. Mix water and olive oil, a little salt and 2 tablespoons lemon juice and pour over the dolmas. Cover and simmer over gentle heat for 15 minutes, or until rice is cooked. Add a little water as they cook, if necessary. Cool and transfer to a serving plate. Serve cold or at room temperature, sprinkled generously with remaining lemon juice and accompanied by lemon wedges.

MEAT DOLMAS

****

Meat dolmas are quintessentially Turkish, an expression of the Turkish love for stuffing not only vegetables, but also various types of pastas. The technique employed is the same as in the case of meatless dolmas made with olive oil, but the taste and use are very different. Meat dolmas are never used as *meze*; they are substantial, colorful, and healthy dishes, eaten as entrées.

Quince Dolmas with Cinnamon Sauce

✾✾

4 SERVINGS

[AYVA DOLMASI]

8 quinces, about 6
  ounces each
Water
½ cup sugar
3 cinnamon sticks
Mint leaves

MEAT STUFFING

¾ cup finely chopped
  onions
2 tablespoons unsalted
  butter
¼ cup uncooked rice
1 cup hot water
½ pound ground lamb
  shoulder
½ cup chopped mint
  leaves
¼ cup chopped flat-leaf
  parsley
1 teaspoon ground
  cinnamon
½ teaspoon ground
  allspice
½ teaspoon freshly
  grated nutmeg
Salt and freshly ground
  pepper
2 to 3 tablespoons lemon
  juice

Wash and dry the quinces. Cut off the tops and remove the cores. Using a small paring knife, remove part of the pulp, leaving a ½-inch-thick shell. Put the pulp and seeds in a saucepan with 4 cups water, the sugar, cinnamon sticks, and a few mint leaves; cover and simmer 1 hour. Strain the liquid into a bowl and reserve. You should have 2 cups; if you have less, add enough water to make this amount.

In the meantime, cook the onions in the butter until they begin to turn golden around the edges. Add hot water and the rice. Cover and simmer until the rice is cooked, about 20 minutes. Let it cool.

Preheat the oven to 350 degrees.

Put the rice, meat, herbs, and spices in a bowl, season with salt and pepper, and mix by hand thoroughly. Stuff the quinces with this mixture. Place a sheet of parchment paper in a heavy shallow pan, and arrange the dolmas side by side on it. Pour the reserved quince liquid in the pan. Place another sheet of parchment paper over the dolmas, cover, and bake for 1¼ hours, or until the quinces are very tender. As they cook maintain the liquid level. At the end of cooking you should have more than 1 cup of cooking liquid remaining in the pan. Remove the cooked dolmas to a serving dish. Taste the sauce in the pan and adjust with salt and lemon juice. Pour over the dolmas and serve hot.

Swiss Chard Dolmas with Yogurt-Mint Sauce

✻✻✻✻✻✻✻✻✻✻✻✻✻✻✻✻✻✻✻✻✻✻✻✻✻✻✻✻✻✻✻✻✻✻✻✻✻✻✻

4 SERVINGS

[PANCAR DOLMASI]

10 to 12 leaves red or
  green chard
2 cups finely chopped
  onions
Salt
1 pound medium-fat
  ground lamb shoulder
  or breast
6 tablespoons uncooked
  rice
1 cup chopped ripe
  tomatoes
½ cup chopped parsley
½ cup chopped fresh
  mint leaves
¼ cup chopped fresh dill
1 tablespoon fresh thyme
  leaves
Freshly ground pepper
1 teaspoon freshly
  ground cumin
½ teaspoon ground
  allspice
Unsalted butter
  (optional)
1 to 1½ cups seasoned
  meat stock or water
Yogurt-Mint Sauce
  (recipe follows)

To blanch the chard, hold each leaf by the stem and dip into boiling water for 1 second; refresh under cold water. Drain the blanched leaves and reserve.

Sprinkle the onions with salt and rub with one hand to soften. Put the onions, meat, rice, tomatoes, herbs, and spices in a bowl. Season with additional salt and some pepper and mix thoroughly with one hand.

Put a chard leaf on the work surface, cut off the stem and the hard lower part of the artery that runs through the center of the leaf. Press down on any hard part of the leaf to make it pliable. With the smooth, shiny side down, stem end facing you, put some filling along the short edge of each leaf near you. Put in enough so that the finished rolled dolmas will be about ¾ inch in diameter. Fold over the two sides to seal the filling. Fold the stem edge to cover the filling and roll the whole thing toward the pointed edge like a jelly roll. Repeat this until all the filling is used.

Place any unused leaves and the stems on the bottom of a shallow heavy pan. Place the dolmas seam sides down in layers. Dot with butter, if desired. Place a piece of parchment paper over to cover and an inverted plate to keep everything in place. Add meat stock or water and simmer, covered, for 30 minutes, or until the rice is cooked. Check liquid level to make sure there is enough. The finished dish should not have more than ½ cup liquid. Serve hot with Yogurt-Mint Sauce and crusty bread.

Variation: Use grape or cabbage leaves in place of chard.

Yogurt-Mint Sauce

✹✹✹✹✹✹✹✹✹✹✹

2 cups yogurt
2 teaspoons crushed
    garlic (see page 286)
2 tablespoons minced
    fresh mint leaves
Salt

Mix all ingredients in a bowl until smooth and creamy.

Basil-Perfumed Tomato Dolmas

✹✹✹

4 SERVINGS

[DOMATES DOLMASI]

6 to 8 very firm summer
    tomatoes (about 4
    pounds)
2 tablespoons butter
1 cup chopped onions
1 cup hot water
5 tablespoons uncooked
    rice
¾ pound medium-fat
    ground lamb shoulder
    or breast, or ground
    chuck
1 cup loosely packed
    chopped basil
½ teaspoon ground
    allspice
½ teaspoon freshly
    ground cumin
Salt and freshly ground
    pepper
4 tablespoons unsalted
    butter (optional)
¾ cup meat stock or
    water
Basil leaves

Cut off the stem ends of tomatoes, wash and drain. Remove the pulp, making a case of the shell. Reserve both the tomato shells and pulp.

Heat the butter in a saucepan and cook the onions until soft. Add hot water and rice; cover and simmer until the rice is cooked, about 20 minutes. Set aside to cool.

Put the rice, meat, basil, spices, and tomato pulp in a bowl. Season with salt and pepper and mix thoroughly by hand. Stuff the tomatoes with the mixture. Place the dolmas in a heavy shallow pan. Dot with butter, if desired, and add the meat stock or water, cover, and simmer 20 to 30 minutes until the meat filling is done. As the dolmas cook, add some water if necessary. Serve hot, garnished with basil leaves cut into ribbons and fresh, crusty bread.

Sweet Red and Green Pepper Dolmas

2 TO 3 SERVINGS

[KIRMIZI VE YEŞIL BIBER DOLMASI]

4 to 6 sweet red and
  green bell peppers
  (about 1 pound)
1 cup finely chopped
  onions
Salt
¾ pound medium-fat
  ground lamb shoulder
  or breast, or ground
  chuck
5 tablespoons uncooked
  rice
1 cup chopped ripe
  tomatoes
¾ cup chopped flat-leaf
  parsley
½ cup chopped fresh dill
½ cup chopped mint
  leaves
1 tablespoon fresh thyme
  leaves, or ½ teaspoon
  dried
½ teaspoon freshly
  ground cumin
½ teaspoon ground
  allspice
Salt and pepper
¾ cup water
Unsalted butter
  (optional)
¾ cup meat stock or
  water

Cut a slice off each end of the peppers; reserve the tops. Remove the seeds and cores, wash and drain.

Sprinkle onions with salt and rub with hands to soften. Put onions, meat, rice, tomatoes, herbs, and spices in a bowl. Season with additional salt and some pepper, add water, and mix thoroughly by hand. Let the mixture stand 30 minutes.

Stuff peppers loosely with the meat filling. Arrange the dolmas side by side in a heavy shallow pan. Place pepper tops over the dolmas. Dot with butter, if desired. Add the meat stock or water, cover, and simmer 35 or 45 minutes, or until the peppers are tender. Add small amounts of hot water during cooking if necessary. Serve hot with fresh, crusty bread.

Celery Root Dolmas in Lemon-Dill Sauce

✽✽✽

3 TO 4 SERVINGS

[ETLİ KEREVİZ DOLMASI]

4 to 6 celery roots
   (about 3 pounds)
3 tablespoons lemon juice
½ cup chopped onion
2 tablespoons unsalted
   butter
¾ cup hot water
¼ cup uncooked rice
½ pound medium-fat
   ground lamb shoulder
   or breast, or ground
   chuck
½ cup chopped fresh dill
½ cup chopped flat-leaf
   parsley
½ teaspoon ground
   allspice
Salt and freshly ground
   pepper
Unsalted butter
   (optional)
2 cups meat stock or
   water

LEMON-DILL SAUCE

2 egg yolks
1½ tablespoons lemon
   juice
1 to 2 tablespoons
   chopped fresh dill

Wash the celery roots well, cut a slice off the top and the bottom. Peel the roots and cut them in half. Put 1 quart water in a pot, mix in lemon juice and bring to a boil. Add the roots to the pot and cook for 20 minutes, then drain.

Using a small spoon scoop out the centers, creating cavities and leaving shells about ½ inch thick. Discard the pulp and reserve the shells.

Cook the onion in the butter until it begins to turn golden brown around the edges. Add the hot water and rice. Cover and simmer until almost all the water is absorbed. Cool the rice and put it in a bowl with the meat, herbs, and allspice. Season with salt and pepper and mix by hand thoroughly. Heap the celery roots with this mixture.

Spread a sheet of parchment paper in a shallow, heavy pan. Arrange the dolmas side by side in the pan over the paper; dot with butter, if desired. Place another sheet of parchment over the dolmas, stir in the meat stock or water, cover, and simmer 1 hour, or until the celery roots are tender. As they cook, maintain the liquid level; at the end of cooking there should be at least 1½ cups cooking liquid in the pan. Remove the dolmas to a serving dish and keep warm while you make the sauce.

Mix the egg yolks and lemon juice in a small bowl. Bring the cooking liquid in the pan to a simmer. Mix a little of the cooking liquid into the eggs. Then slowly pour the whole thing back into the pan. Adjust seasoning with salt and additional lemon juice. Stir in dill. Cook until the sauce thickens slightly. Pour the sauce over the dolmas and serve immediately with fresh, crusty bread.

VEGETABLE STEWS AND CASSEROLES

Cabbage Stew with Lamb and Jalapeños

✸✸

4 SERVINGS

[KAPUSKA]

1 pound lamb neck cut into 2-by-4-inch chunks

3 to 4 tablespoons unsalted butter

3 cups chopped onions

½ teaspoon crushed red pepper flakes

1 tablespoon Hungarian paprika

1 tablespoon Red Pepper Paste (see page 156; optional)

2 cups chopped tomatoes

1½ cups meat stock or water

Salt and freshly ground pepper

1 medium cabbage

3 or 4 red or green jalapeños, or dried hot red peppers

This stew is a hot and spicy winter dish. If you prefer a mild version, use milder peppers.

✸   ✸   ✸

Heat a wide heavy pan over medium heat. Add the meat and butter and cook, uncovered, stirring occasionally, about 10 minutes, until the meat gradually loses all its moisture and turns reddish brown. Stir in the onions and cook them about 5 minutes, or until they begin to brown around the edges. Stir in the pepper flakes, paprika, pepper paste (if desired), and the tomatoes; cook 1 or 2 minutes. Add ¾ cup meat stock or water, season with salt and pepper, cover, and simmer about 1 to 1½ hours, until the meat is tender.

In the meantime, wash, quarter, and core the cabbage. Shred it coarsely. When the meat is cooked, stir in the cabbage and jalapeños, cover, and cook 5 minutes or until the cabbage is wilted somewhat. Stir in remaining stock or water, cover, and simmer 35 minutes, or until the cabbage is cooked. As it cooks, check the liquid level and add small amounts of liquid if necessary. The dish should not be watery but should have an ample amount of sauce. Serve hot with crusty bread.

Small Eggplants Stuffed with Lamb, Tomatoes, Peppers, and Herbs

✽✽

4 SERVINGS

[KARNIYARIK]

1½ pounds Italian or
  Japanese eggplants
¼ cup olive oil
2 tablespoons unsalted
  butter
¾ cup chopped onions
¼ pound medium-fat
  ground lamb shoulder
  (or ground beef)
¾ cup chopped tomatoes
2 tender long green
  peppers, topped,
  seeded, and chopped,
  or ½ small sweet
  pepper and 1 small
  jalapeño, seeded and
  chopped
1 cup chopped flat-leaf
  parsley
Salt and freshly ground
  pepper
1 cup meat stock or
  water

4 or 5 tender long green
  peppers, if available,
  or 2 small green
  peppers, cut into
  ½-inch-wide strips

This dish is a perfect illustration of the principle that it is the imaginative combination of carefully cooked ingredients, however humble they may be, that creates good taste. I have observed that in the West ground meat is somehow neglected and looked down upon, unless it comes in the form of a sausage or a hamburger. Properly made, with carefully selected Italian or Japanese eggplants, this dish surpasses many that are made with expensive cuts of meat.

✽   ✽   ✽

Peel the eggplants lengthwise, giving the effect of stripes, and peel around the stem. Heat the oil in a frying pan and fry the eggplants over medium-low heat until they are uniformly golden brown on all sides, about 10 minutes. Remove from heat; set aside.

Heat the butter in a saucepan and cook the onions until limp. Stir in the meat and brown. Add the tomatoes and peppers; cook a minute or so. Stir in the parsley, salt, and pepper and remove from heat.

Cut each eggplant lengthwise along one side, taking care not to cut through all the way. Enlarge the cavity with fingertips. Stuff an equal amount of the filling into each eggplant. Arrange the eggplants side by side in one layer in a heavy shallow pan. Place the pepper strips over the filling in each eggplant. Add meat stock or water, cover, and cook gently over medium-low heat for about 40 to 50 minutes, until the eggplants are very tender when pierced with a fork. You must check the water level from time to time and add hot water as needed. The finished dish should not have more than ¼ cup of liquid in the pan. If there is more liquid, boil rapidly to reduce. Serve hot with a pilaf or crusty bread.

Eggplant with Lamb

✳✳

4 SERVINGS

[PATLICANLI KEBAP]

2 pounds eggplant

2 pounds boned lamb
   shoulder

2 tablespoons unsalted
   butter

1½ cups finely chopped
   onions

2 tomatoes, peeled and
   chopped

5 sprigs thyme

5 sprigs parsley

1¼ cups meat stock or
   water

Salt and freshly ground
   pepper

½ cup peanut oil

1 large sweet red pepper
   or, if not available,
   green bell pepper,
   seeded and cut into
   1-inch squares

Peel the eggplant in a striped fashion lengthwise and cut into 1-inch cubes. Soak in salted water for at least 1 hour (see instructions on pages 279–80).

Remove and discard all fat and sinew from the lamb and cut into 1-inch cubes.

Heat a large heavy pan over medium heat. Add the meat and butter and cook, uncovered, stirring occasionally, about 10 minutes, until the meat gradually turns reddish brown. Stir in the onions and cook until they begin to brown around the edges, about 5 minutes. Add the tomatoes and herbs and cook a few minutes longer. Add ¾ cup meat stock or water, season with salt and pepper, cover, and simmer over low heat about 1 to 1½ hours, until the meat is very tender. As the meat cooks, add small amounts of hot liquid if the mixture looks dry.

While the meat is cooking, drain the eggplant and rinse with cold water. Squeeze dry by handfuls. Heat the oil in a wok or a similar utensil and fry the eggplant in batches, turning, until eggplant turns a uniform golden brown. Drain on paper towels.

When the meat is cooked, remove the herb sprigs and add the eggplant and pepper. Stir in ½ cup stock or water, cover, and simmer about 20 minutes until the eggplant is soft. If it needs more liquid, add in small quantities. The finished dish should have about ¾ to 1 cup sauce. Adjust seasoning with salt and pepper and serve hot with a pilaf. You can cook this dish ahead of time, even a day before you need to serve it. In fact, the taste matures and is even better the next day.

Potatoes Baked with Tomatoes, Peppers, and Herbs

✳✳

4 SERVINGS

[PATATES OTURTMASI]

3 pounds red-skinned
   potatoes or yellow
   (Finnish) potatoes
3 tablespoons peanut oil
3 tablespoons unsalted
   butter or oil
2 cups chopped onions
½ pound ground lamb
   or beef
1 sweet red pepper,
   chopped
1 or 2 tender long green
   peppers, or any
   semihot peppers,
   seeded and chopped
1 or 2 red or green
   jalapeños, seeded and
   finely chopped
2 ripe tomatoes, peeled
   and chopped
2 sprigs thyme
2 sprigs marjoram
Salt and freshly ground
   pepper
¾ cup chopped flat-leaf
   parsley
Tomato slices
3 or 4 tender long green
   peppers, or 1 green
   bell pepper, cut into
   rings
1 cup water
Chopped parsley

This is a perfect example of everyday home cooking in which the most common and humble ingredients are transformed into a dish that sparkles with flavor. The generous use of a variety of fresh peppers and herbs plays its role in this transformation.

✳   ✳   ✳

Wash the potatoes, peel, and cut into ½-inch-thick rounds. Fry them in the peanut oil on both sides until reddish brown. Set aside.

Heat the butter or oil in a large sauté pan and cook the onions until they begin to brown around the edges. Stir in the meat and brown. Add the peppers, cook 1 minute; then add the tomatoes, thyme, marjoram, salt, and pepper; simmer until the tomatoes are soft. Stir in the parsley, adjust for salt and pepper, remove the herb sprigs, and remove from heat.

Preheat the oven to 350 degrees.

Layer half of the potatoes in an ovenproof casserole and sprinkle with salt and pepper. Spread half the meat mixture over the potatoes. Place the remaining potatoes over the meat and sprinkle with a little salt and pepper. Spread the remaining meat mixture over the potatoes. Place the tomato slices and pepper rings on top. Add water, cover, and cook in the oven for 40 to 50 minutes, until the potatoes are tender. Serve hot, sprinkled with parsley.

Caramelized Onions with Eggs

✳✳

4 SERVINGS

[SOĞANLI YUMURTA]

2 large red onions
4 tablespoons unsalted
   butter
Salt
Water
½ teaspoon mild vinegar,
   such as balsamic
⅛ teaspoon ground
   allspice
¼ teaspoon ground
   cinnamon
Freshly ground black
   pepper
½ teaspoon sugar

4 eggs
Salt and pepper

Again an unlikely combination of simple ingredients resulting in a surprisingly rich and colorful dish. Yellow and white rounds of eggs are nestled in caramelized red onions. The creaminess of the eggs contrasts with the slight crunchiness of the onions.

This modest dish was customarily eaten by the Ottoman sultans on the fifteenth day of Ramadan when they returned to Topkapı Palace after solemnly visiting a cloak kept in Istanbul that allegedly had been worn by the Prophet. If the sultans approved of the way in which these eggs had been prepared—evidently a demanding task— they would often appoint the cook who was responsible for its preparation to be head of the royal pantry.

✳   ✳   ✳

Quarter the onions and slice paper-thin. Heat butter in a heavy skillet and add onions. Sprinkle with salt and cook over very low heat, stirring occasionally, for at least 40 or 50 minutes, until onions turn reddish brown and become slightly crispy. Take care not to burn them. As onions cook and become dry, sprinkle in some water. When onions are caramelized, sprinkle with vinegar, spices, pepper, and sugar, and mix thoroughly.

Make 3 or 4 depressions in the onions and break an egg into each. Sprinkle with a little salt and pepper, cover, and cook gently until eggs are covered with a thin transparent film. Serve immediately.

Purslane Stew Served with Yogurt-and-Garlic Sauce

4 SERVINGS

[YOĞURTLU SEMİZOTU]

2 pounds purslane or
  spinach leaves
3 tablespoons unsalted
  butter
1 cup chopped onions
¼ pound ground lamb or
  beef
1 tomato, peeled and
  chopped
1 cup meat stock or
  water
¼ cup uncooked rice
Salt and freshly ground
  pepper

This ancient vegetable still grows throughout Anatolia and is frequently prepared in homes in much the same way as spinach. It is also used in salads, dressed simply in olive oil and lemon juice.

The green leaves have a delicate lemony flavor and are fleshier than spinach leaves.

＊　　＊　　＊

Cut off purslane roots, wash in plenty of water, and drain.

Heat butter in a large heavy pan and cook onions about 8 minutes. Add meat and cook, stirring frequently, until it browns. Add tomato and cook a minute longer. Add purslane and cook, covered, 10 minutes, until the leaves become wilted. Stir in the stock or water, bring to a boil, and stir in the rice. Adjust with salt and pepper, cover, and cook gently until rice is cooked, about 20 minutes. Add more liquid as necessary. The finished dish should have a little liquid but not be watery. Serve as is or with Yogurt-and-Garlic-Sauce and bread. Pass the sauce separately.

Yogurt-and-Garlic Sauce

2 cups yogurt
2 teaspoons crushed
  garlic (see page 286)
Salt

For the sauce, blend all the ingredients together with a wooden spoon until the mixture is smooth and creamy.

Cauliflower Stew

✻✻

3 TO 4 SERVINGS

[KARNIBAHAR MUSAKKA]

1 cauliflower (2 pounds)
3 tablespoons unsalted
  butter
1 cup chopped onions
⅓ pound ground lamb
  or beef sirloin
3 sprigs thyme
3 sprigs marjoram
1½ cups meat stock or
  water
Salt and freshly ground
  pepper
Flat-leaf parsley

Remove the stalk and leaves from the cauliflower. Blanch it in boiling salted water just a few minutes. Refresh with cold water and set aside.

Heat the butter in a heavy pan and cook the onions until they begin to brown around the edges. Add the meat and cook, stirring until it browns. Divide the cauliflower into florets and stir into the pan. Add herbs, meat stock or water, salt, and pepper; cover and cook gently for 30 to 40 minutes, until the cauliflower is tender. Five minutes before the cooking is finished, stir in a handful of parsley. During cooking check for liquid and add some if necessary. Adjust seasoning, take out the herb sprigs, and serve hot.

SALADS

Turks eat salads in plentiful amounts; almost every meal features one, especially in summer. The hot meat dish will typically be accompanied by a simple garden salad made with various greens or tomatoes, cucumbers, scallions, and radishes. Such a salad is dressed in fruity olive oil flavored with lemon juice or vinegar. More substantial salads, such as white bean salad or various eggplant salads, are treated as side dishes.

White Bean Salad

4 TO 6 SERVINGS [FASULYE PİYAZI]

1 cup dried white beans, soaked in water to cover overnight
1 large red onion cut into paper-thin slices
Salt
½ cup fine olive oil
5 tablespoons (or more) red wine vinegar
1¼ cups chopped flat-leaf parsley
2 hard-boiled eggs, cut into wedges
Black olives

Drain the beans. Bring a large pot of water to a boil, add the beans, and cook until tender. Drain and put in a bowl with the onions. Season with salt, olive oil, and vinegar. Stir in 1 cup parsley and let stand at least 1 hour. This salad will keep for 2 or 3 days in the refrigerator. Just before serving, place in a bowl, sprinkle with remaining parsley, and decorate with egg wedges and olives. Serve at room temperature or cold.

Chick-pea Salad with
Garlic-Cumin Vinaigrette

✻✻

4 SERVINGS

[NOHUT SALATASI]

*1 cup dried chick-peas,
soaked overnight, or
2½ cups drained
canned chick-peas*
*1½ cups finely diced red
onion*

Drain chick-peas and cook in water to cover until tender, about 2 hours or a little longer. Plunge them into cold water, then rub them between fingers to remove the skins. Rinse and drain. Toss in a bowl with onions.

Garlic-Cumin Vinaigrette

✻✻✻✻✻✻✻✻✻✻✻✻

*About 6 tablespoons fine
olive oil*
*4 garlic cloves, crushed
(page 286)*
1 red jalapeño, minced
*3 tablespoons finely
chopped mixed herbs:
cilantro, thyme, mint,
tarragon, parsley*
*2 tablespoons red wine
vinegar or lemon juice*
*1½ teaspoons coarsely
crushed cumin seeds*
*Salt and freshly ground
pepper*

For the vinaigrette, whisk olive oil with garlic, jalapeño, herbs, vinegar or lemon juice, cumin, salt, and pepper. Pour over the salad and mix thoroughly. Adjust with salt and vinegar, let stand 30 minutes or longer, and serve at room temperature.

Green Olive, Walnut, and Pomegranate Salad

✿✿✿

4 SERVINGS

[GAZIANTEP'TEN ZEYTIN, CEVIZ VE NAR SALATASI]

1½ cups large meaty
   Sicilian olives, pitted
1 cup pomegranate seeds
   (see Glossary)
1 cup chopped scallions,
   including tender green
   parts
1 cup coarsely chopped
   walnuts
Fine olive oil
Pomegranate syrup to
   taste (see Glossary; or
   substitute lemon juice)
Salt
Crushed red pepper
   flakes to taste

I ate this delicious sweet-and-sour salad in Gaziantep, an ancient city in the southeastern part of Turkey where the food is hot and spicy. The recipe, along with others, was kindly given to me by a dear college friend, Gülümay Özbay, on a recent visit to Ankara. She had prepared several dishes from Gaziantep and I took notes as she described them to me while we sampled them. Back in California, as I test and write up the recipes, I relive that happy day.

✻   ✻   ✻

Chop olives coarsely and toss in a bowl with pomegranate seeds, scallions, and walnuts. Dress with a little olive oil and pomegranate syrup or lemon juice whisked together; season with salt and a pinch of red pepper flakes. Mix thoroughly; let stand 10 or 15 minutes for the flavors to blend before serving.

Beet Salad

✿✿✿

4 SERVINGS

[SIRKELI SARMISAKLI PANCAR SALATASI]

1 pound cooked beets
1 cup red wine vinegar
2 large garlic cloves,
   crushed (page 286)
Salt

Slice beets into thin rounds. Put them in a bowl with vinegar, garlic, and salt to taste and let stand at least 2 hours. Serve arranged in a serving bowl with the vinegar sauce.

Beet Salad with Yogurt

[YOĞURTLU PANCAR SALATASI]

2 cups cooked beets,
  coarsely grated
1½ cups yogurt
1 to 2 teaspoons crushed
  garlic (page 286)
2 tablespoons olive oil
2 tablespoons wine
  vinegar
Salt

Put beets in a bowl. Mix yogurt with garlic and olive oil until smooth. Combine beets with the yogurt sauce, mix thoroughly, and season with vinegar and salt. Serve at room temperature.

Roasted Eggplant Salad

4 SERVINGS

[PATLICAN SALATASI]

1¼-pound eggplant
6 tablespoons lemon juice
2 to 3 large garlic cloves,
  crushed (page 286)
Salt
6 tablespoons fine olive
  oil
Chopped cilantro or
  flat-leaf parsley

Roast eggplant directly over charcoal grill or gas flame until all the skin is black and charred and eggplant is soft. Cool slightly and peel off all the burned skin, wiping with wet hands, and remove seeds (see page 280). Place in a colander, sprinkle with 3 tablespoons lemon juice, and let stand for 20 minutes.

Squeeze out all the moisture and put eggplant in a bowl. Divide into several parts and pound in a mortar with the garlic and some salt or mix in a blender or food processor. Gradually add olive oil and remaining lemon juice to taste while pounding or blending. Adjust salt and serve sprinkled with cilantro or parsley.

Note: See also Roasted Eggplant and Hot Pepper Salad on page 63.

Cucumber Salad with Yogurt and Mint Sauce

✺✺✺✺✺✺✺✺✺✺✺✺✺✺✺✺✺✺✺✺✺✺✺✺✺✺✺✺✺✺✺✺✺✺✺✺

4 SERVINGS

[CACIK]

1 English (or regular)
  cucumber
2 cups yogurt, preferably
  tangy yogurt cream
  (see page 275)
1 to 2 teaspoons crushed
  garlic (page 286)
2 tablespoons olive oil
2 tablespoons crushed
  dried mint leaves
Salt
Fresh mint leaves for
  garnish

This simple yet very refreshing salad is especially welcome on hot summer days. *Cacık* should have a slight edge to it—a subtle tang or sharpness. Therefore tangy yogurt cream is preferable. Regular yogurt will work if it is not particularly sweet. In hot weather, *cacık* is also good served with a few ice cubes in it.

✺   ✺   ✺

Grate the cucumber coarsely into a colander, sprinkle with salt, and let stand 15 to 20 minutes. If using regular cucumber, be sure to remove the seeds.

In a bowl, beat yogurt with garlic, olive oil, dried mint, salt, and a little water until smooth and creamy. If you are using yogurt cream, you will need to add a little more water to bring it to a thick sauce consistency. Mix cucumber with the yogurt and mint sauce until thoroughly blended. Chill and serve garnished with fresh mint leaves.

Potato Salad with Cumin Vinaigrette

✳✳✳

4 SERVINGS   [PATATES SALATASI]

*1 pound red-skinned
   potatoes*
*About 5 tablespoons fine
   olive oil*
*2 tablespoons or more of
   red wine vinegar*
*1½ teaspoons coarsely
   crushed cumin seeds*
*Salt and freshly ground
   black pepper*
*1 large red onion cut
   into paper-thin slices*
Black olives
*2 hard-boiled eggs, cut
   into wedges*
Chopped flat-leaf parsley

Cook potatoes until tender. Peel and cut into thin rounds. In a serving bowl, whisk olive oil with vinegar and cumin, season with salt and pepper. Add potatoes and onion slices. Mix thoroughly, adjust to taste with salt and vinegar. Garnish with olives, eggs, and a large handful of parsley.

Smoked Eggplant Salad with Walnuts, Jalapeños, and Yogurt

✳✳✳

4 SERVINGS   [YOĞURTLU PATLICAN SALATASI]

1½-pound eggplant
3 tablespoons lemon juice
2 jalapeños
1 large green bell pepper
*2 teaspoons crushed
   garlic (page 286)*
Salt

Roast eggplant directly on a gas burner, turning frequently, until skin is charred and eggplant is soft. Cool briefly and peel, removing all black skin and seeds (see page 280). Place in a bowl of water to cover and stir in the lemon juice. Let stand 30 minutes.

    Roast peppers the same way; when they become charred and limp, seal in a bag for 10 minutes and then peel. Remove the stems and seeds and chop finely.

2 or more tablespoons
  olive oil
5 tablespoons ground
  walnuts
½ cup yogurt
1 tablespoon wine
  vinegar
Olives
Chopped parsley

Remove eggplant from water and squeeze dry. Pound to a paste in a mortar with the peppers, garlic, and salt. Stir in 2 tablespoons olive oil, walnuts, and yogurt. Season with vinegar and adjust with salt, olive oil, and/or vinegar if necessary. Let stand 2 or 3 hours for flavors to blend and serve at room temperature, garnished with olives and parsley.

Lentil and Bulgur Salad

❋❋

6 SERVINGS

[BULGURLU MERCİMEKLİ KÖFTE]

1 cup red lentils, picked
  over and washed
3 cups water
1½ cups finely chopped
  onions
3 to 4 tablespoons fine
  olive oil
¾ cup fine-grain bulgur,
  washed and drained
1 cup finely chopped
  scallions, including
  tender green parts
1 cup chopped flat-leaf
  parsley
2 teaspoons freshly
  ground cumin seeds
  (see page 285)
¾ to 1 teaspoon crushed
  red pepper flakes
Salt
Lettuce leaves

Cook lentils in water for about 30 minutes, until soft and all the water is absorbed.

Cook onions in oil until they begin to turn golden brown around the edges; set aside.

Pour cooked hot lentils over bulgur, mix thoroughly, cover, and let stand until the bulgur becomes soft. Stir remaining ingredients except lettuce leaves into the lentil-bulgur mixture, including onions and oil in which they were cooked, season with salt and knead until the mixture becomes a paste. Shape small pieces into thumb-sized *köfte*. Place on lettuce leaves arranged on a plate. Serve at room temperature.

Grated Carrot Salad in Yogurt and Dill

4 SERVINGS

[YOĞURTLU HAVUÇ SALATASI]

5 cups peeled and
   coarsely grated carrots
2 tablespoons fine olive
   oil
1 to 1½ cups yogurt
2 garlic cloves, crushed
   (page 286)
½ cup chopped fresh dill
Salt

Swish carrots in hot olive oil for a few minutes until slightly wilted. Put in a bowl. With a wooden spoon, beat yogurt and garlic with ¼ cup dill and a little salt until smooth. Mix carrots with yogurt sauce until thoroughly blended. Adjust with salt and let stand 20 minutes or so. Serve sprinkled with remaining dill.

PICKLES AND RELISHES

Red Onion–Parsley Relish

4 TO 6 SERVINGS

[SOĞAN PİYAZI]

2 large red onions
¾ teaspoon salt
2 cups chopped flat-leaf
   parsley

Quarter the onions and slice paper-thin; you should have about 4 cups. Sprinkle with salt and let stand 10 minutes. Rub very lightly with hands, rinse, and squeeze dry. Toss with the parsley and serve as accompaniment to grilled meats and fish.

Small Eggplant Pickles Stuffed with Garlic Cloves and Herbs

8 PICKLES

[PATLICAN TURŞUSU]

8 Japanese eggplants
2 quarts boiling water

FILLING

1 cup finely shredded
  cabbage
1 sweet red pepper, diced
1 cup peeled small garlic
  cloves
¾ cup chopped fresh dill

Dill sprigs
Red wine vinegar
Salt
Fresh dill

Cook eggplants in boiling water about 8 minutes, until tender but still firm. Drain and leave under a heavy object overnight to remove maximum moisture. Cut open lengthwise, being careful not to cut all the way through.

Toss all filling ingredients together and stuff eggplants with the mixture. Tie each eggplant closed with dill sprigs. Arrange in a large clean jar.

Mix vinegar with salt (8 teaspoons salt for each quart of vinegar) and pour over the eggplants to cover. Cover jar with airtight lid and keep at room temperature for 3 weeks. Once open, keep refrigerated.

VEGETABLE PASTES

Red Pepper Paste

⚜ ⚜

MAKES 1 ½ POUNDS

[BİBER SALÇASI]

5 pounds sweet red
peppers and/or
pimientos
Red jalapeños (optional)
Salt (2 tablespoons for
each 5 pounds of
peppers)

This is an essential ingredient in the spicy cuisine of southeast Turkey. On hot summer days the picturesque rooftops of sleepy towns seem clad in bright red with pots of red pepper paste and strings of peppers of various shapes in a wide range of red shades, all drying under the blazing sun. Red pepper paste adds a wonderful flavor and color to winter stews and some sauces. Use sweet red peppers, pimientos, and red jalapeños. The proportion of jalapeños to sweet peppers can vary to taste, from a slight heat using only a few jalapeños to a hotter paste with a larger amount of them. Three sweet red peppers to one jalapeño will yield a mild pepper paste.

⚜   ⚜   ⚜

Remove tops, ribs, and seeds from peppers (for a very hot paste, leave jalapeño seeds), and chop them with a meat grinder or food processor. Simmer for 15 minutes with just enough water to keep them from burning. Mix in the salt and put the pepper pulp in large shallow noncorroding trays or containers, cover with cheesecloth to keep out insects and dirt, and set in direct sunlight for several days until reduced to a paste, stirring every day. Spoon into clean jars, cover with a film of olive oil, tie cheesecloth over jars, and store. The pepper paste will keep several months at room temperature.

Sun-Cooked Tomato Paste

MAKES 3 POUNDS
[DOMATES SALÇASI]

14 or 15 pounds ripe
summer tomatoes
2 ounces salt

Wash tomatoes, cut in half, place in large shallow noncorroding dishes or trays, sprinkle with salt, and set in direct sunlight for a few days, covered with cheesecloth to keep out insects and dust. Tomatoes will thicken slightly. Put them through a small-holed colander set over a bowl, pressing against the tomatoes until only the seeds and skins remain in the colander. (A food mill may be used instead of a colander, but only if the tomato skins remain inside it.) Put this creamy pulp into noncorroding trays again and place in sunlight covered with cheesecloth. Stir every day for several days until the pulp is reduced to a paste. Pour into clean jars, cover with a film of olive oil, and tie a piece of cheesecloth over the mouth of each jar. The paste will keep for several months, all throughout the winter, at room temperature.

PILAF

✳✳✳✳✳✳✳✳✳✳✳✳✳✳✳✳✳✳✳✳✳✳✳✳✳✳✳✳✳✳✳✳✳✳✳✳✳

Is there anything better, for instance, than a genuine Turkish pilaff?
Norman Douglas, *South Wind* (1917)

✽✽

Centuries old and imbued with the mystery of faraway places, pilaf seems magically fresh and contemporary in our culinary world. Its basic ingredient is rice, a legendary grain, one of the oldest known to mankind. Far Eastern tradition fancifully depicts rice as a beautiful, delicate, and vulnerable girl-child. In India, rice is the symbol of fertility, an ever nurturing mother. This explicitly female character of rice in Far Eastern tradition finds its echo in Turkey where rice is handled with the utmost care and cooked meticulously so that each grain retains and exhibits its independent shape and beauty. Couched in a silver platter, it is adorned fancifully, tinted here and there with saffron, perfumed with rose water, and veiled mysteriously with a fragile sheet of silver tissue.

The word *pilaf* is of Persian origin and passed into Western usage via Turkish. The word designates a whole variety of dishes made primarily with rice and one or more other ingredients. In the sixth century, Persians knew rice and secured its westward transmission and cultivation in the Middle East. The Arabs in turn took it to Spain and planted it in Andalusia in the eighth or ninth century, and from Spain it passed to Italy.

The early cultivation and use of rice in the Islamic Middle East was, however, relatively restricted. In the coastal areas where rice grew, such as southern Iraq and the southern shores of the Caspian Sea, it typically served as a substitute for wheat and barley in making bread, and accompanied the fish that were plentiful in those areas. Elsewhere, rice was generally regarded as a food for the poor, although it was sometimes used in making desserts and various beneficial effects were attributed to it. What is certain is that independent dishes of rice—what we know as pilaf—were not part of the region's cuisine before Turkish influence began to make itself felt.

161

The period in which pilaf made its first appearance cannot be fixed exactly. It must have been consolidating its supremacy on the culinary scene in the fifteenth century, because it is then we find the Persian gastronomic poet Bushaq of Shiraz imaginatively celebrating its triumph over *bughra* (an old Turkish noodle dish) to become the monarch of foods, symbolically crowned with saffron. In the same century, Sultan Mehmed Fatih was being served pilaf dishes in his newly conquered capital of Istanbul, and the Ottoman fondness for pilaf soon became legendary.

To the classic pilafs made with butter, meats, nuts, dried fruits, and aromatics, Turks added elements: shellfish, olive oil, eggplant, and other unconventional ingredients. Along the Black Sea coast of Turkey, a particularly delicious pilaf is made with fresh anchovies, which is indeed a local specialty.

The Persians have also excelled in the cultivation of pilaf. Jean Chardin, a French traveler who visited Iran in the seventeenth century, describes pilafs made with meats, game, whole spices, mulberries, cherries, pomegranates, and tamarind. A Persian cookbook for the same period lists no fewer than seventy-five recipes for pilaf. It is noteworthy, however, that the names of almost all of them are Turkish.

Pilaf also found its way to India with the Moghul dynasty, which was established by Turks from Central Asia. In India, with the addition of local spices, glorious, elaborate, and distinctively Indian pilafs were created.

Unlike the Persians and Indians, Turks often seem to favor short-grain rice for pilaf; it is similar to Italian Arborio rice. They also use other grains such as bulgur and couscous.

✳ HOW TO WASH AND SOAK RICE

When rice is bought in bulk or in Hessian sacks, it must be picked and cleaned of small pieces of stones and other foreign particles. To wash rice, put it in a large bowl with plenty of cold water. Run fingers through the grains gently, then tip the bowl and pour off most of the milky water. Repeat this until the water is clear. Soak basmati rice in cold water for 30 minutes. Soak other kinds of long-grain or short-grain rice in hot water mixed with salt (½ tablespoon to 1 quart water) for at least 1 hour. Drain 20 minutes.

Pilaf with Eggplant and Pine Nuts

4 SERVINGS

[FISTIKLI PATLICANLI PİLAV]

1 cup uncooked Arborio
 rice
¾ pound (about 3 small)
 Japanese eggplants
Salt
Olive oil
1½ cups onions, chopped
2 tablespoons pine nuts
4 tablespoons fine olive
 oil
1 medium tomato, peeled
 and chopped
½ teaspoon ground
 allspice
½ teaspoon freshly
 ground pepper
½ teaspoon ground
 cinnamon
½ teaspoon sugar
1½ cups beef stock
½ cup chopped fresh dill

Wash, soak, and drain the rice according to directions on page 162.

Top the eggplants, quarter lengthwise, and cut into cubes. Sprinkle with salt and let stand at least 30 minutes. Rinse with water and squeeze dry. In a wok, quickly stir-fry eggplant in olive oil in two batches. Set aside.

In a heavy pan, cook onions and pine nuts in olive oil until they turn golden brown. Add tomato and cook 2 to 3 minutes until soft. Add spices and sugar and cook, stirring, a second or two. Stir in rice and cook, stirring, 5 minutes. Add stock and eggplant and ⅓ cup dill; cover and simmer over medium-low heat about 15 minutes, until all the liquid is absorbed. Reduce heat to very low and raise pan on a wok ring. Drape a folded kitchen towel over pan, cover with lid, and let rice steam about 15 minutes longer. Remove from heat and let stand covered on a warm surface at least another 15 minutes. Stir gently and serve sprinkled with remaining dill.

Pilaf with Spring Fava Beans and Fresh Dill

4 SERVINGS

[TAZE BAKLALI DEREOTULU PİLAV]

1 cup uncooked basmati
rice
1 pound fresh fava beans
4 to 5 tablespoons
unsalted butter
Salt
¼ cup water
About 1½ cups
full-flavored chicken
stock
¼ cup chopped fresh dill

Make this pilaf in the spring when fava beans are tender and most flavorful.

* * *

Wash, soak, and drain rice according to directions on page 162.

Shell fava beans and remove skins. Sauté them in half the butter for 2 minutes, sprinkle with salt, add water, cover, and simmer for about 8 minutes. If there is any liquid left in the pan, strain it into a bowl; reserve the fava beans and liquid.

To make the pilaf, heat remaining butter in a heavy pan and sauté rice, stirring gently, for 3 minutes. Measure the cooking liquid from the beans, add enough stock to make 1½ cups, and heat. Stir stock into rice, add beans, season with salt, and cook over medium-low heat until almost all the liquid is absorbed, about 10 minutes. Reduce heat to very low, raise pan over the flame on a wok ring, and stir in half the dill. Drape a folded kitchen towel over pan, cover with lid, and let it steam for 15 minutes. Uncover quickly to sprinkle with the remaining dill, cover again with the towel and lid, and let stand over a warm spot for another 15 or 20 minutes. Stir gently and serve.

Saffron Pilaf

✳✳✳

4 SERVINGS

[SAFRANLI PİLAV]

2 cups uncooked basmati
rice
¾ teaspoon saffron
threads
2 tablespoons hot water
3 quarts water
3 tablespoons salt
6 to 8 tablespoons melted
unsalted butter

Wash, soak, and drain rice according to directions on page 162.

Crumble saffron with fingertips and soak in the hot water.

Fill a large pot with 3 quarts water mixed with 3 tablespoons salt. Bring to a rolling boil. Gradually sprinkle in rice. Stir gently to prevent rice from sinking to the bottom. Bring water back to a rapid boil; time carefully and boil rice for only 5 minutes. After 4 minutes bite into a few grains. The rice has cooked long enough when the grains are barely tender.

As soon as rice is cooked, empty it into a large sieve. Run lukewarm water over it for a few seconds, then let it drain 5 minutes. Shake sieve to remove excess water.

Cover bottom of the dry cooking pan with 2 tablespoons of the butter. Sprinkle rice into pan, letting it fall from a large spoon into a heaping conical pile. Pour remaining butter over it. Drape a towel over pan and cover tightly with lid. Raise pan over a wok ring and steam over lowest heat for 30 or 40 minutes until steaming hot. Move pan to a warm place and let it rest 10 minutes.

Just before serving, mix 2 large tablespoons of the cooked rice with the saffron water in a small bowl. Stirring gently, place the pilaf on a platter and garnish with the saffron rice, sprinkling it all over the top. Serve immediately.

Bulgur Pilaf with Lentils, Tomato, Jalapeños, and Mint

4 SERVINGS

[BİBERLİ, MERCİMEKLİ, NANELİ BULGUR PİLAVI]

⅓ cup lentils, soaked in
  water overnight
1½ cups water
5 tablespoons unsalted
  butter
1 or 2 jalapeños, seeded
  and chopped
1 tomato, peeled and
  chopped
½ teaspoon freshly
  ground pepper
½ teaspoon ground
  allspice
1 cup coarse-grained
  bulgur, washed and
  drained
1¾ cups beef broth
  (may be canned) or
  full-flavored, seasoned
  chicken or turkey stock
Salt
1½ cups chopped onions
⅓ cup chopped fresh
  mint leaves, or ¼ cup
  dried

Drain lentils and put in a saucepan with the water; cover and simmer until they are soft and all the water is absorbed. Set aside. Heat 1 tablespoon of the butter in a heavy pan, add jalapeños and tomato and cook over medium heat until tomato is soft and all the liquid is evaporated. Stir in spices and cook a few seconds. Add bulgur and cook, stirring 3 or 4 minutes. Add broth and lentils, adjust with salt, cover, and simmer 15 minutes over low heat. Reduce heat to very low, raise pan over a wok ring and simmer, covered, about another 10 to 15 minutes. Remove pan from flame and let stand over a warm spot. Meanwhile, heat remaining butter in a sauté pan and cook onions until reddish brown. Stir in mint and cook a few seconds; pour over the pilaf. Stir gently and serve hot.

Bulgur Pilaf with Chick-peas

✴✴

6 TO 8 SERVINGS   [HİNDİ SUYUYLA NOHUTLU BULGUR PİLAVI]

6 tablespoons unsalted
  butter
1½ cups finely chopped
  onions
2 cups coarse-grained
  bulgur, washed and
  drained
2 cups cooked chick-peas
3½ cups full-flavored
  turkey or chicken stock
  (canned chicken or
  beef broth can be
  substituted)
Salt and freshly ground
  pepper
Chopped cilantro

Heat butter in a heavy pan and cook onions over medium heat until they begin to brown around the edges. Stir in the bulgur and turn it with the onions for 3 minutes or so. Stir in chick-peas and stock, season with salt and pepper, cover, and cook over low heat for about 15 minutes. Raise pan over a wok ring and let cook 15 minutes. Move pan to a warm spot and let pilaf rest for at least 15 minutes. Stir gently and serve piping hot garnished with cilantro.

Tomato Pilaf

✴✴

4 SERVINGS   [DOMATESLİ PİLAV]

1 cup uncooked Arborio
  rice
4 tablespoons butter
½ cup minced fresh
  ripe tomatoes or
  good-quality canned
1½ cups chicken stock or
  water
Salt
Freshly ground pepper

Wash, soak, and drain rice according to directions on page 162.
     Melt butter in a heavy pan. Add tomatoes and simmer until they become soft and reach the consistency of a sauce. Add rice and sauté, stirring gently, for 5 minutes.
     Heat stock or water and add to rice. Season to taste with salt. Cook over medium-low heat, uncovered, for about 10 minutes until almost all the liquid is absorbed. Reduce heat to very low and raise pan over a wok ring. Drape a folded kitchen towel over the pan, cover with lid, and let rice steam for 15 minutes. Remove from heat and let stand on a warm surface, covered, for at least another 15 minutes. Stir gently and serve sprinkled with pepper.

Turkistani Pilaf

4 TO 6 SERVINGS

[TURKİSTAN PİLAVI]

4 shoulder lamb chops
   (1½ to 2 pounds)
¾ pound carrots
2 cups uncooked basmati
   rice
½ cup vegetable oil
2 cups chopped onions
1 teaspoon cumin seeds
1 teaspoon salt
Freshly ground pepper
3 cups beef broth
Toasted blanched
   almonds

Trim the chops of fat and cut into halves. Peel and cut carrots into matchstick pieces. Wash, soak, and drain rice according to directions on page 162.

In a heavy pan, heat oil and cook onions until they begin to turn brown. Crush cumin seeds slightly, add to hot oil and onions and cook a few seconds until they release their fragrance. Push onions to one side, add meat and brown over medium-low heat about 10 minutes. Cover pan and simmer over low heat for about 15 minutes. As the meat cooks, sprinkle with water as needed.

Push meat to side of pan, add carrots, and cook, stirring frequently, for 5 minutes. Sprinkle with salt and pepper, stir everything once, cover, and simmer for 25 minutes, until meat and carrots are very tender. As it cooks, sprinkle some water if necessary. Add rice and cook, stirring, 2 minutes. Add broth and let it cook over medium flame for about 10 minutes until almost all the liquid is absorbed. Cover pan and raise it over a wok ring; let it steam over very low heat for 15 minutes. Remove from heat and let stand, covered, on a warm spot for another 15 minutes. Stir gently and serve decorated with the almonds.

Pilaf with Fresh Anchovies from the Black Sea Region

❋❋❋

4 SERVINGS

[HAMSİLİ PİLAV]

1 cup uncooked Arborio
    rice
½ pound fresh anchovies,
    cleaned, boned, heads
    removed
1½ cups chopped onions
2 tablespoons pine nuts
6 tablespoons fine olive
    oil
2 tablespoons currants
¾ teaspoon sugar
½ teaspoon ground
    allspice
½ teaspoon ground
    cinnamon
Salt and freshly ground
    pepper
1½ cups hot water
Chopped fresh dill

A specialty of the Black Sea region where the best anchovies are abundant and are part of the folk culture, appearing in poetry, songs, jokes, stories, and every possible dish.

❋　❋　❋

Wash, soak, and drain rice according to directions on page 162.

Be sure all the small bones are removed from the anchovies.

Cook onions and pine nuts in olive oil over medium heat for 5 to 10 minutes until they are golden. Add rice and stir with the onions for a minute or two until it is well coated with oil. Stir in currants, sugar, spices, a little salt and pepper, and the hot water. Cook over medium-low heat for 10 minutes until almost all the liquid is absorbed. Cover tightly, raise pan over a wok ring, and cook over lowest heat for 15 minutes longer. Remove from heat and let rest for 10 minutes.

Preheat oven to 350 degrees.

Coat a casserole lightly with butter. Spread half of the pilaf in the casserole. Arrange half of the anchovies over the rice. Spread remaining rice over the fish and arrange the remaining anchovies on top. Sprinkle some fresh dill over the pilaf, cover with a sheet of parchment paper first, then with the lid. Bake for 30 minutes. Gently arrange on a serving dish and serve piping hot sprinkled with pepper and dill.

Pilaf with Mussels and Fresh Dill

[MİDYELİ PİLAV]

2 cups uncooked Arborio
   rice
18 large mussels,
   scrubbed and bearded
Light chicken stock (may
   be canned)
1½ cups finely chopped
   onions
½ cup good olive oil
¾ cup chopped fresh dill
Freshly ground pepper

Wash, soak, and drain rice according to directions on page 162.

Soak mussels in salted warm water for 5 minutes. Open with a paring knife (see directions on page 61), holding them over a bowl to catch all the liquid. Strain liquid through a cloth-lined sieve, measure, and add enough stock to make 3 cups. Reserve mussels and liquid.

Sauté onions in hot olive oil in a heavy pan until they become soft and start turning golden around the edges. Add rice and cook, stirring, over medium heat for 5 minutes. Heat stock and mussel liquid and stir into rice. Cook over medium-low heat, uncovered, for 10 minutes, until almost all the liquid is absorbed. Reduce heat to low, raise the pan over a wok ring, and stir in mussels, dill, and the mussel liquid accumulated in the bowl (the liquid should not exceed ¼ cup). Drape a folded kitchen towel over pan, cover with lid, and steam 10 minutes. Let it rest for 10 minutes on a warm surface, stir gently, and serve piping hot sprinkled with pepper.

MANTI AND OTHER PASTA DISHES

✽✽✽✽✽✽✽✽✽✽✽✽✽✽✽✽✽✽✽✽✽✽✽✽✽✽✽✽✽✽✽✽✽✽✽✽✽✽

✱✱

It is often hazardous to pinpoint a single origin for a certain dish, and almost always so in the case of a particular class of food. Nonetheless, persistent legends seek to discover the genesis of noodles in either China or Italy, or, failing that, to link together these two centers of the primordial noodle through the travels of Marco Polo. The picturesque notion of the Venetian traveler carefully carrying his noodles westward along the Silk Route is, however, fatally undermined by our knowledge that flat noodles (*laganum*) existed in Roman Italy. The origin of vermicelli is sometimes traced to the period of Arab rule in Sicily; the first mention of vermicelli being commercially produced is contained in the writings of a twelfth-century Arab Sicilian geographer, al-Idrisi. The word he uses to describe vermicelli, *itriya*, has moreover survived in Sicilian dialect as *tria* down to the present, as Mary Taylor Simeti informs us in her delightful book on Sicilian food, *Pomp and Sustenance*.* However, the word *itriya* is itself of Greek origin, as Charles Perry, that master of culinary etymology, points out, so that the ultimate origin of the Western noodle retreats into an inaccessible past.

Persia also has a claim to be regarded as one of the homelands from which noodles spread. The Persian word *lakhsha*, meaning either noodles as such or a dish using noodles, seems to be the origin of both the Russian *lapsha* and the Malay *laksa*, although the route of transmission is not yet fully established (there must have been Turkish, probably Tatar, involvement in the Russian case). The word *rishta*, which gradually came to supplant *lakhsha*, was also known to the Arabs during the period they owed fealty to Persian culinary models.

It would be unwise to insert into this tangled web of evidence a claim for the Turkish origin of noodles. It is nonetheless certain that

* New York, 1989, 144.

Turks have prepared noodle dishes throughout their recorded history, and with one or two exceptions, these dishes cannot be ascribed to outside influences. The *oklava*, a special rolling pin used for the preparation of some kinds of noodle, existed in quite ancient times, and as the historian Bahaeddin Ögel enthusiastically writes of this word, "Its root is Turkish, its ending is Turkish, and its sound is Turkish" (*Türk Kültür Tarihine Giriş*).

The Central Asian Turks apparently borrowed from the Persians a dish known as *jushpara*—boiled pasta with a meat filling. But they more than repaid the debt by bestowing on the cuisine of the Islamic Middle East the dish known as *tutmaç*, celebrated in its heyday by the Persian poet Shams ad-Din Shastkulah as "the sultan of the realm of appetite." A charming folk etymology for *tutmaç* connects its origin with Zu'l-Qarnayn, the Qur'anic figure sometimes identified with Alexander the Great. It is said in the *Divan Lugat at-Türk* that when-he and his followers emerged from the lands of darkness on the edge of the inhabited world, they turned to him in their weakness and hunger, imploring, "Do not keep us hungry" (*Bizi tutma aç*). Consulting with his attendant sages, Zu'l-Qarnayn invented a dish consisting of dough boiled in water to which fried meat, mint, garlic, yogurt, and clarified butter were added; in memory of the occasion, it was ever after known as *tutmaç*, a contraction of *tutma aç*! The etymology is untenable, since the names of numerous Turkish dishes end in the suffix *-aç*, but it is fairly clear that no one could possibly remain hungry after eating a good portion of *tutmaç*! *Tutmaç* has also been held to strengthen the body and give a healthy glow to the cheeks.

Tutmaç was part of the courtly cuisine of the Seljuqs, and was even employed by the great mystic poet Celal ed-Din Rumi as one element in the rich and varied symbolism he deployed. It retained its high standing until at least the fifteenth century; Sultan Mehmed the Conqueror had it served to his pashas on the days he granted them audience, and an Arabic cookbook of the same period still grants it prominent mention. But *tutmaç* was not ultimately incorporated into the classical Ottoman cuisine that had its highest expression at the court, although it has survived in the folk cuisine of Anatolia down to the present. Even in the ancestral homeland of the Turks in Central Asia, *tutmaç* lost its pride of place to the upstart *pilav*. This change in preferences may be reflected, as Charles Perry has suggested, in a Turkistani story that attributes to Alexander the invention not of *tutmaç* but of *pilav*.

Other noodle dishes of Central Asian origin that found their way to both Anatolia and the Arab lands were *salma*, small noodles varyingly described as coin-shaped and shell-shaped, and *umaç* (or *ovmaç*), small round noodles also used in soups.

Yet another noodle dish, *mantı*, differs from those mentioned so far both in its long record of uninterrupted popularity and in its non-Turkish origin. The etymological evidence is clear: *mantı* is derived from the Chinese *mantou*. *Mantı* is, however, rather different from *mantou*, which appears to mean stuffed sheep intestines, comparable to the Bukharan *gipa*. Despite some local variations, *mantı* has been basically uniform throughout the Turkic world; the Hungarian traveler and Turcologist Arminius Vambéry reported that the *mantı* he ate in Bukhara in 1863 was identical to that he was accustomed to enjoying in Istanbul.

Mantı was eaten at the Ottoman court. Thanks to the precision of the official records, we know for example that Sultan Mehmed the Conqueror had *mantı* to eat on 21 February 1474! *Mantı* has also been part of the people's cuisine down to the present, although the frequency with which it is prepared may now be decreasing because of the labor involved in making all the small packages needed to satisfy a hungry family.

So it may be claimed on behalf of Turkish noodle dishes that at least in certain places and periods they have greatly advanced the status of the class to which they belong. The work of the fifteenth-century Persian poet and gastronome, Bushaq of Shiraz, is replete with Turkic names for noodle dishes, too numerous and obscure to be mentioned here, that demonstrate the central position of noodles in the Persian cuisine of his time. Some authorities go so far as to suggest a Turkish origin for Russian *pel'meni*, a plausible theory although the etymological evidence is shaky and involves reference to Udmurt, a non-Turkish language.

Although the rank of noodle dishes in general is somewhat reduced in the Turkish cuisine of today, *mantı* alone, with its quintessentially Turkish combination of pasta, yogurt, garlic, and mint, may count as a worthy echo of the days of noodle supremacy.

Mantı à la Tatare

❋❋

4 SERVINGS

[TATAR BÖREĞİ]

DOUGH

2 cups unbleached
  all-purpose flour
¼ teaspoon salt
1 egg
½ cup water

VEAL FILLING

6 ounces ground veal
¾ cup finely chopped
  onions
Salt
Freshly ground pepper
2 tablespoons chopped
  basil leaves

YOGURT-GARLIC SAUCE

3 cups yogurt, at room
  temperature
2 teaspoons crushed
  garlic (see page 286)
Salt

BUTTER-PAPRIKA TOPPING

5 tablespoons butter
¾ teaspoon Hungarian
  paprika
Pinch of cayenne

Basil or mint leaves,
  cut into ribbons for
  garnish

For the dough, put the flour on the work surface, make a well in the center, and put in the salt, egg, and water. Mix the ingredients in the center first and gradually work in the flour to make a stiff dough. Knead the dough on a lightly floured work surface 10 or 15 minutes until it is smooth and elastic. Put in a buttered bowl, cover with plastic wrap, and let rest 1 hour.

Put all the ingredients for the filling in a bowl, mix thoroughly, and set aside.

Beat the yogurt, garlic, and salt with a wooden spoon until the mixture is very creamy and smooth. Set aside in a warm spot.

Knead the noodle dough on a lightly floured surface and divide in half. Roll each half into a tight ball, cover with a slightly damp towel, and let rest 20 more minutes. Following the instructions for rolling thin pastry for *börek* by hand (page 205), roll out one piece of pastry until it is stretched in a 19- or 20-inch circle. After stuffing and shaping the pasta into *mantı* (instructions follow), roll out the other piece and shape into *mantı*.

If you use a pasta machine to roll out the pasta, you should divide the dough into 4 pieces and roll them out following instructions on page 206.

Cut the rolled pastry into 1-inch strips, then cut them into 1-inch squares. Place a hazelnut-sized bit of veal filling in the center of each square, bring the four corners up together, and pinch to seal. Place the *mantı* on a lightly floured large dish in one layer. Repeat with the second piece of dough.

Bring a large kettle of salted water to a rolling boil and drop in half of the *mantı*. They will come up to the surface, cooked, within 1 or 1½ minutes. Remove the *mantı* to a large serving bowl or into individual bowls, adding a little of the cooking liquid, and keep warm while cooking the other half.

Pour most of the yogurt sauce over the *mantı*. Quickly heat the butter in a small saucepan until frothy. Stir in the paprika and cayenne, wait a second or so, and drizzle the butter over the yogurt sauce. Sprinkle some basil or mint leaves on top and serve very hot. Pass the remaining yogurt sauce separately.

Mantı with Chick-peas and Yogurt Sauce

[NOHUTLU MANTI]

CHICK-PEAS

*1 cup dried chick-peas,
soaked in water over-
night, or 2½ cups
drained canned
chick-peas*

*2 tomatoes, peeled and
chopped*

*1 red or green jalapeño,
seeded and chopped*

2 to 3 tablespoons butter

2 cups or more meat stock

*¼ cup chopped fresh
mint leaves*

*Salt and freshly ground
pepper*

*1 recipe pasta dough
(page 176)*

*Yogurt-Garlic Sauce
(page 176)*

MEAT FILLING

*5 ounces ground lamb or
veal*

*1 small onion, finely
chopped*

*2 tablespoons chopped
fresh mint leaves*

Salt

Freshly ground pepper

BUTTER-MINT TOPPING

5 tablespoons butter

*¼ cup crumbled dried
mint*

For the chick-peas, cook the tomatoes and jalapeño in the butter until soft. Add the drained chick-peas, stock, and mint; cover and simmer for 1 to 1½ hours, until the chick-peas are very tender. As they cook, maintain the liquid level by adding hot stock. Season with salt and pepper and set aside. If using canned chick-peas, cook them 30 minutes.

Make the pasta dough. Place in a buttered bowl, cover with plastic wrap, and let stand for 1 hour. Make the yogurt-garlic sauce and place it on a slightly warm spot on the stove.

Mix all the meat filling ingredients in a bowl until thoroughly blended and set aside.

Roll out the pasta and stuff the *mantı* according to the instructions for *börek* on pages 205–06.

Bring a large kettle of salted water to a rolling boil and cook the *mantı* in two batches for 1 or 2 minutes. If they have dried a little, they will take longer to cook. Reheat the chick-peas until hot. Drain the pasta, reserving some liquid, and add to the chick-peas. Chick-peas should have at least ¾ cup of cooking liquid. If not, add a little of the pasta cooking liquid. Make sure the whole dish is very hot. Put the *mantı* and chick-peas in a serving bowl. Pour the yogurt-garlic sauce over them.

Heat the butter until foamy. Stir in the mint and let it sizzle. Pour this over the yogurt sauce and serve immediately.

Baked *Mantı*

✱✱✱

4 SERVINGS

[MANTI]

FILLING

5 ounces ground lamb or
   veal
¾ cup finely chopped
   onions
Salt and freshly ground
   black pepper
2 tablespoons chopped
   mint leaves

Yogurt-Garlic Sauce
   (page 176)
7 ounces won ton skins
About 3 cups good
   chicken broth, heated
Butter-Paprika Topping
   (page 176)
Fresh mint leaves, cut
   into ribbons for
   garnish

In this version of *mantı*, the stuffed pasta is lightly browned in the oven and then cooked in broth, resulting in a different texture. In this recipe I use won ton skins for pasta so that those who do not have time to make pasta can also have a taste of this interesting dish. Won ton skins do not duplicate the exact taste or texture of home-made (especially hand-rolled) pasta, but they are very good. I must also mention that won ton skins sold at Chinese groceries are superior to those found in supermarkets; they are thinner and more delicate. If you prefer making your own pasta, follow the recipe for *Mantı* à la Tatare (page 176) to make the dough and to shape the *mantı*, and then turn to this recipe for cooking the pasta.

✱   ✱   ✱

Make the filling by thoroughly mixing all the ingredients in a bowl and set aside. Prepare the yogurt-garlic sauce and set aside on a slightly warm spot.

Put the stack of won ton skins on a work surface. Using a sharp knife, slice the whole stack through the center, first lengthwise and then crosswise. You will have 4 piles, each containing small squares of won ton skins.

Working with one pile at a time, spread each square on the work surface and place a chick-pea-sized bit of mixture in the center of each square. Dampen the edges of the squares with a little water, bring all four corners up together and pinch to seal. As you make the *mantı*, place them on a lightly buttered baking sheet in one layer. You will probably need more than one baking sheet.

Preheat oven to 375 degrees.

When all the squares are filled and shaped, bake them for 15 to 20 minutes, until the tops turn golden brown. Remove them from the oven and put in a large baking pan with 2-inch sides. Reduce oven to 350 degrees; pour the hot chicken broth over the *mantı* and bake for 15 minutes. Taste to see if they are done; if they need to cook a little longer, add a little more broth and cook 5 minutes or so, until they are tender.

Remove from the oven and transfer to a serving bowl or individual bowls with whatever liquid remains in the pan. Pour the yogurt-garlic sauce over the *mantı*.

Make the paprika topping and pour over the yogurt sauce and serve immediately, sprinkled with mint leaves.

Spaghetti with Eggplant, Roasted Red Peppers, and Poblano Chilies

4 SERVINGS

[PATLICANLI MAKARNA]

4 small Japanese eggplants
Salt
2 sweet red peppers
2 poblano chilies
Olive oil
1 medium red onion, finely chopped
2 or 3 garlic cloves, minced
2 ripe tomatoes, peeled and chopped
2 sprigs thyme
Handful of chopped flat-leaf parsley
Splash of wine vinegar
1 pound spaghetti

Cut the eggplants into ¼-inch-thick round slices, sprinkle with salt, and let stand 40 minutes.

Meanwhile roast, seed, peel, and cut the peppers and chilies into ¼-inch-wide strips. Rinse the eggplant, squeeze dry, and fry in olive oil until brown on all sides. Discard oil.

Heat 2 to 3 tablespoons olive oil in a large pan and cook the onion and garlic until soft. Stir in the tomatoes and thyme sprigs and cook until they become soft and form a sauce. Stir in the peppers and eggplant, cover, and simmer briefly to make sure that the vegetables are soft. Stir in parsley, season with salt, and add a splash of vinegar to taste. Remove from heat, remove the thyme sprigs, and keep warm.

Cook the pasta, drain thoroughly, toss with the sauce in the pan, and serve hot.

Pasta with Meat and Yogurt-Mint Sauce

❋❋❋

4 SERVINGS

[YOĞURTLU MAKARNA]

MEAT SAUCE

3 tablespoons olive oil
¾ cup chopped onions
½ pound ground meat or
  sausage
1 or 2 jalapeños, seeded
  and finely chopped
2 sprigs thyme
Handful of chopped
  flat-leaf parsley
Salt and freshly ground
  pepper

YOGURT-MINT SAUCE

3 cups yogurt, at room
  temperature
2 or 3 teaspoons crushed
  garlic (see page 286)
2 teaspoons minced fresh
  mint leaves
Salt

1 pound penne or
  rigatoni

BUTTER-PAPRIKA
TOPPING

5 tablespoons butter
¾ teaspoon Hungarian
  paprika
Pinch of cayenne

Fresh mint leaves for
  garnish

In Anatolia, people continue to make various kinds of noodles at home, the best known being *erişte,* an egg pasta rolled and cut by hand into fettucine or tagliatelli-shaped noodles. They are cooked fresh or dried and kept for later use. In large cities, however, various shapes and styles of Italian-type pasta are sold in stores and it is to these that people have recourse, making frequent use of them as a change from rice, This ready-made pasta is cooked and usually prepared very simply by coating it with butter or olive oil, and frequently it is combined with fresh tomatoes and herbs, different cheeses, and other ingredients.

This we might call mock *mantı,* in that it uses some of the same ingredients and has a similar taste though not as much work is required.

❋   ❋   ❋

To make the meat sauce, cook the onions in olive oil until soft. Add meat, jalapeños, thyme, and parsley and brown the meat. Stir in a few tablespoons water, season with salt and pepper, cover, and simmer 10 minutes, adding more water if necessary. If you use sausage meat, brown it separately, pour off the fat, and stir it into the cooked onions with thyme, jalapeños, and parsley and simmer as described.

To make the yogurt-mint sauce, put all ingredients in a bowl and beat with a wooden spoon until the mixture is very creamy. Set aside on a warm spot on the stove.

Cook and strain the pasta, and reheat the meat sauce. Toss the pasta with the hot meat sauce and place in a serving bowl. Pour the yogurt-mint sauce over it.

For the topping, heat the butter until frothy, add the paprika and cayenne, wait one second, and drizzle it over the yogurt-mint sauce. Sprinkle the top with mint leaves and cut into ribbons and serve hot.

BREADS, ROLLS, AND *BÖREK*

BÖREK

Most of us instinctively feel that if ever humanity had a single primordial food, it must surely have been bread. Certainly the bakers' guilds in Ottoman Turkey regarded Adam as their patron saint; they believed that the archangel Gabriel had taught him how to make dough and bake bread after his expulsion from the Garden of Eden.

The Turks began cultivating wheat early in areas of Central Asia where they had a settled existence, developing many different kinds of bread and dough products and various techniques for preparing them. Most of these breads and methods of preparation have accompanied the Turks wherever they went and survive to the present day.

Central Asian Turks of the eleventh century knew both flat breads and loaves, and at least one variety, known as *kevşek,* was leavened. White bread made from well-sifted wheat flour was highly prized, although the thin bread known as *lavaş* (a word of Persian origin) was probably more widespread. Breads stuffed with minced meat, onions, and other substances go back to ancient times; do we have here, maybe, a Central Asian Turkish origin for the stuffed parathas familiar to us from Indian cuisine? This is possible: Babur, founder of the Moghul dynasty, migrated across the Pamirs to India.

Bread was sometimes fried on a *sac,* a round, concave griddle, and sometimes baked in embers. Bread is still baked in embers in Anatolia; it is known as *kümeç.* Sometimes as much as fifty kilograms of dough are placed in the embers to make a large bread for weddings. Bread was also baked in clay ovens known as *tandır.* This is definitely a Turkish word, despite its similarity to the Persian *tannura,* and we can therefore confidently claim a Turkish origin for the Indian tandoori style of cooking.

Numerous kinds of bread were developed during Ottoman times, many of them tied to special seasons and days. There were different kinds of white and black bread, flat breads, ringed breads and loaves, stuffed breads, and toasted breads. The palace—eager even in this sphere to emphasize its separate and exalted rank—baked its own special bread called *fodla*. According to Evliya Çelebi, author of a celebrated seventeenth-century travelogue, no fewer than 10,000 people were professionally engaged in Istanbul in the baking of bread; 999 shops sold the different basic varieties of bread, and 2,000 sold various kinds of *çörek* (special, savory or slightly sweetened rich bread). To take Evliya Çelebi at his word, Istanbul must have been permanently suffused with the scent of baking bread! Particularly interesting among the traditional breads of the Ottoman period that are still eaten today are *gözleme* (griddled and buttered bread), *poğaça* (turnovers), *peksimet* (toasted, slightly sweet bread), *kurabiye* (butter cookies), *simit* (sesame rings sold stacked up on sticks or piled in a pyramid on trays), and different kinds of *pide* (small flat breads) and *çörek* decorated with almonds, poppy seeds, aniseed, and nigella, and glazed with saffron and eggs.

But perhaps the clearest evidence for the Turkish devotion to dough is furnished by *börek,* a word that serves as a desgination for a whole family of foods. The genus *börek* embraces dishes made from a flour dough first rolled into very thin sheets of pastry and then layered or shaped in various ways before being filled with sweet or savory substances and fried or baked. (It should be stressed that *börek* is much thinner than pasta and depends on skillful rolling.)

The genealogy of *börek* is not entirely clear. It seems that two lines of evolution, one in the meaning of the word, the other in culinary technique, ultimately converged to produce the *börek* we know today. The word *börek* was originally synonymous with *buğra,* a dumplinglike dish the invention of which is credited to Bugra Khan, ruler of Eastern Turkistan. This had in common with *börek* as we now know it the placing of a filling in dough.

The thin sheets of pastry from which *börek* is made are known as *yufka.* Now *yufka* is defined by eleventh-century lexicographer Mahmud Kashghari as "folded bread." In order for the bread to be folded it must clearly have been made from flattened, thin dough, and one of the meanings *yufka* still has in present-day Turkish is "very thin flat bread." One variety of *yufka* recorded by Kashghari, *katma yufka,* was not only folded but also cooked in butter, a technique still employed in the preparation of *börek.* Add to this the fact that rolling pins were common and diversified enough to be called by different names, and we can see that most elements involved in the making of *börek* were already present in the eleventh century. Also relevant is the fact that most Turkic languages of Central Asia have words denoting rolled flat bread, quite often layered with butter; some including fillings and thus border on pastry.

In view of all this, it seems only logical that *börek* should have been the final outcome of a process in which the custom of flattening dough for one's daily bread led to the production of very thin sheets of pastry, which were then filled according to Central Asian precedent.

In any event, *börek* was an established part of Ottoman cuisine by the time of the conquest of Istanbul in 1453. We know that at least two varieties of it were prepared for Sultan Mehmed the Conqueror. The position of chief *börek* maker in the palace kitchens was always an important one. Numerous apprentices labored under his watchful eye rolling out the dough on huge marble slabs. As for the popular consumption of *börek,* Evliya Çelebi tells us that Istanbul in his time had no fewer than 4,000 *börek* shops—interestingly enough, a figure four times higher than he gives for bakers' shops.

Börek remains central to the popular cuisine of Anatolia, and it would hardly be an exaggeration to say that Anatolia feeds itself primarily on different varieties of dough! Indispensable utensils for every Anatolian housewife are the *oklava*—a rolling pin about 32 inches long and ½ to ¾ inch thick—and the *hamur tahtası*—a special round table used only for rolling dough, about 10 inches off the ground and 25 inches in diameter. The sight of a woman, often tired from her work in the fields, sitting before her *hamur tahtası* rolling the dough is an endearing and poignant reminder of how heavily family life depends on her versatile and self-sacrificing labors.

The broad and lasting popularity of *börek* would be impossible without the great diversity that is concealed by the uniform name of this food. There is great variety in the techniques of preparing and layering the doughs, in the fillings that are used, in the shapes that are given to the final product, and in the methods of cooking that are used; some of these variations are regional in nature.

No doubt other cuisines have had roughly comparable dishes— the spring rolls of the Chinese, the *lumpia* of the Malays and Indonesians, the *sanbusa* of the Iranians (now surviving only in India in the form of *samosa*). But no other cuisine can boast of a whole family of dishes akin to *börek,* an Ottoman legacy found not only in Turkey but also in the Balkans and North Africa. Even the Russian *pirog* (more familiar in its diminutive form, *pirozhki*) may be derived from *börek,* according to the Finnish scholar Georg Ramstedt.

FLAT BREADS AND FILLED *PIDE*

Flat Bread

✸✸

2 *PIDE* [PİDE]

With the arrival of Ramadan, alluring flat breads appear in the windows of bread bakeries. The bakeries continue throughout the month to make the regular round or loaf breads, but now they add round or oval golden *pide,* glazed with eggs, and shaped by hand with a border and crisscrossing grooves in the center. These *pide* have a soft crust and chewy interior, and sometimes are sprinkled with sesame or nigella seeds.

As dusk gathers and the mosques are illuminated just before *iftar* (the time for breaking the fast), the streets become lively with men and children hurrying home with stacks of *pide.* There are also small bakeries that specialize in baking different varieties of *pide* at all times of the year. *Kebap* shops also make a variety of *pide,* plain or filled, and they serve almost all kebabs on a bed of *pide.*

For the best results, I like to bake *pide* directly on heated quarry tiles. It is very simple to line the oven shelf with the tiles and heat them at least 30 or 40 minutes before baking the *pide.*

SPONGE

4 teaspoons active dry
 yeast
½ teaspoon sugar
½ cup warm water
½ cup unbleached
 all-purpose flour

DOUGH

3½ cups bread flour
1 teaspoon salt
3 tablespoons olive oil
1 cup plus 1 tablespoon
 lukewarm water

GLAZE

2 eggs, lightly beaten

TOPPING

Nigella seeds (see
 Glossary) and/or
 sesame seeds

Dissolve the yeast and sugar in warm water and let stand in a warm place 10 minutes, until frothy. Stir in the flour, cover with plastic wrap, and let rise 30 minutes.

To finish the dough, put the flour in a large bowl, make a well in the center, and put in the sponge, salt, olive oil, and lukewarm water. Gradually work in the flour to make a soft and sticky dough. Knead the dough on a floured surface for 15 minutes. The dough will be very sticky at first, but as you knead, it will gradually cease to stick to your hands. You should have a damp and very springy dough that will offer no resistance to kneading.

Put the dough in a buttered bowl, cover with plastic wrap, and let rise 1 hour, until well swollen. You can refrigerate the dough at this point until you are ready to use it.

To shape the *pide,* divide the dough into 2 pieces and shape each into a ball. Cover with a towel and let rest 30 minutes.

Preheat the oven to 550 degrees, and heat the quarry tiles 30 minutes before baking.

Flatten one piece of dough slightly. Wet your hands, press and enlarge the dough outward into a circle. Stretch out the circle, pressing hard, particularly with the sides of your hands. When the dough is stretched to a 10-inch circle, paint it generously with egg. Using the sides of your hands, mark a border 1 inch wide all around the edge.

Dip your fingertips in egg; holding your hands above the circle, 4 fingertips pointing down, mark 4 horizontal rows of indentations parallel to each other with your fingertips, staying within the border. Rotate the circle halfway (180 degrees) and mark 4 rows of indentations parallel to each other and perpendicular to the previous rows. Let your fingertips go down deep, stopping short of piercing the dough.

Sprinkle a wooden paddle with some flour. Lift the *pide,* holding it at both ends, and stretch it into an oval shape while placing it over the paddle. Now it should measure approximately 9 by 15 inches. Make sure it is well brushed with egg and sprinkle it with some nigella seeds or sesame seeds. Slide it gently onto the hot tiles and bake 6 to 8 minutes. As it comes out of the oven keep it in the folds of a towel. Repeat with the remaining dough. *Pide* will be at its best fresh from the oven, but it can be reheated in foil if necessary.

Peasant Flat Bread Baked on a Griddle

[YUFKA EKMEK VEYA LAVAŞ]

2 LARGE BREADS
(OR 6 MEDIUM OR
13 SMALL BREADS)

This rolled bread is so thin that it can be folded. Favored now chiefly by villagers who do not have a bakery and therefore must make their own bread, *yufka* is usually oval or round. It is an ancient bread, first cooked by the Turks more than 900 years ago, known then as *yufka* and now, additionally, as *lavaş*, depending on the region. Another variation by region relates to the method of cooking: either on a large *sac* (convex griddle) or in a *tandır* (clay-lined pit). When this bread is fresh, it is silky soft. In villages, however, these flat breads are cooked in large batches and stored on a board suspended by all four corners from the ceiling. The bread becomes dry, so it is lightly sprinkled with water and reheated to restore its softness and freshness.

2½ teaspoons active dry
    yeast
½ cup warm water
2½ cups unbleached
    all-purpose flour
½ cup whole wheat flour
1 teaspoon salt
1 cup lukewarm water

Dissolve the yeast in ½ cup warm water and let stand 10 minutes in a warm place until frothy. Combine the all-purpose flour and the whole wheat flour in a large bowl. Make a well in the center and add the salt and dissolved yeast. As you mix with one hand, gradually work in the lukewarm water. Once the dough comes together, clean your hands, rub them with a little oil, and knead this very soft dough on a work surface for at least 15 minutes, until it feels smooth and springy. Put the dough in a buttered bowl, cover with plastic wrap, and let stand 1 hour.

If you have a very large griddle (professional stoves have 12-by-24-inch griddles), divide the dough into 2 equal pieces and shape each one into a tight ball. If you have a small *sac,* divide the dough into 13 pieces and shape each one into a ball. With a regular-size griddle, you can divide the dough into 6 pieces. Place the balls on a floured surface and let stand 30 minutes under a slightly damp towel.

If you divide the dough into 2 pieces, put one ball on a generously floured surface and flatten it first. Sprinkle its surface with flour and roll it with a rolling pin until it is an oval measuring 12 by 24 inches. (If you divide the dough into 13 pieces, each rolled-out bread should measure 9 inches in diameter; if you divide it into 6 pieces, each bread should measure 12 by 14 inches.) As you roll out the dough, sprinkle the work surface and the surface of the dough with flour as needed so that the dough will not stick to the surface or the rolling pin and it will roll out easily and smoothly without being stretched by the rolling pin.

To bake the bread, heat the griddle and oil lightly. Stretch the dough over the griddle and cook about 15 seconds on each side until pale brown blisters appear on the surface. After you stretch the dough, tap the surface gently with your fingertips to discourage it from rising. Cook the bread as soon as you roll it out. Let it cool only a few seconds and cover it to keep it soft. Then roll out another piece. If you make the large breads, carry them to the griddle draped over the rolling pin.

Flaky Griddle Bread with Tahini

✺✺

[TAHİNLİ KATMER]

DOUGH

2 cups unbleached
   all-purpose flour
¼ teaspoon salt
2 tablespoons unsalted
   butter, at room
   temperature
¾ cup milk

6 or 7 tablespoons tahini
   (sesame paste)
4 tablespoons unsalted
   butter, at room
   temperature
Oil (optional)
Clarified butter

Combine the flour and salt in a bowl. Add the butter in small pieces and rub into the flour with fingertips until the flour is evenly coated with butter. Make a well in the center, pour in the milk, and make a soft dough. Put the dough on a lightly floured work surface, knead for 5 minutes until it is very smooth. Put in a buttered bowl, cover with plastic wrap, and let rest 1 hour.

Put the dough on the lightly floured work surface, shape it into a log, and divide into 8 equal pieces. Roll each piece into a tight ball, place on a floured surface, and let rest 20 minutes under a slightly damp towel.

With a wooden spoon, cream together 4 tablespoons tahini and the butter; set aside. Roll each of 4 pieces of dough into a 7-inch circle. Coat the surface of 3 circles with some of the sesame-butter mixture and stack. Place the fourth circle on top; do not coat this one with the mixture. Press the edges together to seal and put the dough under a towel. Repeat this with the 4 remaining circles. Let them rest 20 minutes.

Put one of the stacks of layered dough on a lightly floured work surface. Press it gently, sprinkle with a little flour, and roll it out into a large circle, ¼ inch thick. Spread half of the remaining tahini over the circle and roll it up tightly as if rolling a jelly roll. Cut the roll into 4 equal pieces and place under the towel. Repeat with the remaining stack and let the pieces rest 15 minutes.

Press out each piece of dough, fold in half, then roll it into a 6-inch square. Heat the griddle over medium heat and brush it lightly with oil or clarified butter. Place one bread (more if you have a large griddle) on the griddle and cook about 1 minute until light brown blisters appear. Brush the bread lightly with butter, flip it over, and bake the other side for 30 seconds. If you feel it needs cooking a little longer, turn and cook both sides 10 or 20 seconds longer. Keep the bread warm in a covered dish while you cook the remaining bread. Serve hot. As you cook the breads, regulate the heat so that they do not brown too quickly before they cook. On the other hand, if the griddle is not hot enough, the bread will dry. They should be slightly crispy outside but still soft.

Variation: As you coat the dough with tahini mixture, sprinkle with a little sugar. After they are baked, sprinkle again with some sugar for a lightly sweetened version.

Olive Oil Bread with Black Olives

✿✿✿

2 LOAVES

[ZEYTİNLİ EKMEK]

1¼ cups black olives (see Glossary)
2½ teaspoons active dry yeast
Pinch of sugar
1 cup plus 3 tablespoons warm milk
3¾ cups unbleached all-purpose flour
½ cup minced onion
⅓ cup minced fresh mint leaves
⅓ cup fine olive oil
1 teaspoon salt
Cornmeal

This extremely delicious and fragrant bread is a specialty of the Turks of Cyprus. It is permeated by the robust taste of fruity olive oil which is intensified and enriched by the nuggets of creamy, full-flavored black olives. The crust is tender, the interior moist. Serve it fresh from the oven, when the aroma is at its height; it also keeps well for several days.

✿   ✿   ✿

Pit the olives, split into halves, and set aside.

Dissolve yeast and sugar in the milk and let stand on a warm surface for 10 minutes, until frothy. Put flour in a large bowl, make a well in the center, and put in the onion, mint, olive oil, yeast mixture, salt, and olives. Knead on a lightly floured surface for 10 or 15 minutes until smooth and springy. Place in an oiled bowl, cover with plastic wrap, and let rise in a warm place for 2 hours, or until doubled.

Put dough on work surface and knead lightly. Divide it in half; kneading and folding, shape each half into a taut oval loaf, plump in the center and tapered toward the ends. With a razor, make a lengthwise slash in the middle. Sprinkle a wooden paddle with cornmeal and place the loaves on it. Sprinkle lightly with flour, cover with a slightly damp towel, and let rise in a warm place for 2 hours.

Preheat oven to 450 degrees; heat tiles, for 30 minutes. Just before baking the bread, reduce heat to 400 degrees, sprinkle tiles with cornmeal, slide loaves onto tiles, and bake 30 minutes. Cool on racks.

Feta-and-Dill-Filled Small *Pide*

✼✼✼

8 *PIDE*

[PEYNİRLİ PİDE]

1 recipe pide *dough
(page 187)*

FETA CHEESE FILLING

*2½ cups crumbled feta
cheese*

3 eggs, lightly beaten

*6 tablespoons unsalted
butter, at room
temperature*

⅔ cup chopped fresh dill

GLAZE

1 egg yolk, beaten

TOPPING (OPTIONAL)

*Nigella seeds (see
Glossary)*

*Melted butter to brush
on baked* pide

Filled *pide* are the Turkish counterpart of Italian calzones. The union of the freshly baked bread with fragrant and savory fillings produces a heady mixture of scents and flavors.

✼   ✼   ✼

Make *pide* dough, place in a buttered bowl, cover with plastic wrap, and let rise 1 hour.

For the filling, mix all the ingredients in a bowl and blend thoroughly.

Put the *pide* dough on a lightly floured work surface and roll into a log. Cut into 8 equal pieces and roll each into a tight ball. Cover them with a towel and allow to rest 30 minutes.

Preheat the oven to 550 degrees and heat tiles 30 minutes before baking.

Roll each ball with a rolling pin on a lightly oiled surface into a 6-by-12-inch oval. Spread one-eighth of the filling over the *pide*, leaving a ½-inch border all along the edges. Fold the two long sides of the *pide* over the filling, their edges meeting along the center. Press down on the folded sides gently to help them stay down during baking. Pinch together a 1-inch portion of both sides at both ends to seal; you will have something resembling the shape of a canoe. Brush the top with the egg yolk, sprinkle, if you wish, with a few nigella seeds and, using a paddle, slide it onto the hot tiles. Bake about 6 minutes. As one *pide* bakes, shape another and continue this way until all of them are baked. As they come out of the oven, brush them with butter and keep them stacked in a large covered pan or in the folds of a towel. If you like them crustier, bake a little longer. Also remember to let oven temperature return to set heat after baking one or two *pide*.

Small *Pide* with Eggplant Filling

[PATLICANLI PİDE]

1 recipe pide *dough (page 187)*

EGGPLANT FILLING

4 to 6 Japanese eggplants (about 2 pounds)

Salt

Olive oil

6 small tomatoes, peeled and chopped

2 cups combination of chopped fresh peppers and chilies such as sweet red and green bell peppers, poblanos, or Hungarian peppers

2 red or green jalapeños, topped, seeded, and chopped

2½ tablespoons minced garlic

Crushed red pepper flakes

1 cup chopped flat-leaf parsley

1 cup combination of chopped cilantro and basil

GLAZE

1 egg yolk, beaten

Olive oil to brush on pide

Make *pide* dough, place in a buttered bowl, cover with plastic wrap, and let rise 1 hour.

For the filling, cut off the tops of the eggplants, halve them lengthwise, and slice into ¼-inch-thick pieces. Sprinkle generously with salt and let stand 1 hour. Rinse the eggplant thoroughly with water and squeeze dry by hand. Fry the slices in olive oil on both sides and drain on paper towels. Chop coarsely and set aside.

Cook the tomatoes, peppers, and chilies in oil over medium heat for 5 or 6 minutes until they become soft and form a sauce. Stir in the garlic and eggplant and cook 1 or 2 minutes longer. The mixture should be very soft. Season with salt and red pepper flakes, stir in the herbs, and remove from heat.

Follow the directions on page 192 for shaping, filling, glazing, and baking the *pide*. As they come out of the oven, brush with olive oil and serve hot.

Open *Pide* with Spicy Lamb Filling

✿✿✿✿✿✿✿✿✿✿✿✿✿✿✿✿✿✿✿✿✿✿✿✿✿✿✿✿✿✿✿✿✿✿✿✿

8 *PIDE*

[LAHMACUN]

1 recipe pide dough
(page 187)

FILLING

1 cup medium-fat ground
lamb (ground veal or
chuck can be
substituted)
¾ cup very finely
chopped onions
1 cup finely chopped
peeled tomatoes
¾ cup finely chopped
combination of semihot
peppers and chilies
such as tender long
green peppers,
Hungarian peppers,
poblanos, or Anaheim
chilies
1 jalapeño, seeded and
chopped
¼ to ½ teaspoon crushed
red pepper flakes
Salt
¼ cup chopped mint
leaves
½ cup chopped flat-leaf
parsley
2 tablespoons water

Olive oil to brush on
pide

Make *pide* dough, place in a buttered bowl, cover with plastic wrap, and let rise 1 hour. Put it on a lightly floured surface and roll into a log. Cut into 8 equal pieces and roll each one into a tight ball. Place the balls on a floured surface and let rest 30 minutes under a towel.

Put all the filling ingredients in a bowl and mix thoroughly with fingertips. Set aside.

Preheat the oven to 550 degrees and, if desired, heat tiles 30 minutes before baking.

Roll 1 ball on a floured surface with a rolling pin into a circle ¼ to ⅛ inch thick and 8 inches in diameter. Brush the top with olive oil and spread one-eighth of the filling over it, leaving a ½-inch border around the edge. Bake 5 or 6 minutes and repeat with the remaining ones. As they come out of the oven, stack them in a large pan and keep covered until all are baked. Remember to let the oven temperature return to set heat after baking 2 or 3 *pide*. Serve hot. They can also be reheated wrapped in foil.

ENRICHED BREADS AND ROLLS

Sesame Rounds

✻✻✻

12 ROUNDS

[SOSYETE SİMİDİ]

DOUGH

3½ teaspoons active dry
yeast
Sugar
¼ cup warm water
3¾ cups unbleached
all-purpose flour
1 teaspoon salt
1 egg
4 tablespoons unsalted
butter at room
temperature, divided
into small pieces
1¼ cups lukewarm
water

TOPPING

2 eggs, lightly beaten
2 to 3 cups sesame seeds

Dissolve the yeast and a pinch of sugar in the warm water and let stand 10 minutes in a warm place until frothy. Sift the flour and salt onto the work surface, make a well in the center and put in 2 tablespoons sugar, egg, butter, yeast mixture, and half of the luke-warm water. Gradually work in the flour and the remaining water, to make a very soft and sticky dough. If you have a heavy-duty mixer, knead the dough 6 minutes with the dough hook. Or knead on a floured surface 10 or 15 minutes, frequently beating it against the surface, until smooth and springy. Sprinkle the surface with flour as needed. Put the dough in a lightly buttered bowl, cover with plastic wrap and let stand 30 minutes.

Knead the dough lightly on the floured work surface, roll into a log, and divide into 12 equal pieces. Cover them with a slightly damp towel and let rest 20 minutes.

Coat the work surface and your hands lightly with oil and roll each ball into a rope ½ inch thick. Twist the rope around itself and shape into a ring 4½ inches in diameter, pressing and rolling the overlapping ends on the work surface.

Dip each ring in eggs, then in sesame seeds, making sure they are evenly coated with seeds. Place them on a greased baking sheet and allow to stand 30 minutes until they are puffed.

Preheat the oven to 400 degrees and bake 20 minutes until they are golden brown.

Sesame Rings

✻✻

8 *SIMIT*

[SİMİT]

DOUGH

*3½ teaspoons active dry
yeast*
Pinch of sugar
¼ cup warm water
*4 cups unbleached
all-purpose flour*
1¼ teaspoons salt
*About 1 cup lukewarm
water*

*2 cups molasses or
pekmez (see
Glossary)*
2 cups water

TOPPING

2 to 3 cups sesame seeds

The visitor to Turkey, whether native or foreign, is always delighted to hear the cry of the *simit* seller; it is a sound of welcome. *Simit*, sesame rings, crispy and crusty on the outside and soft and chewy on the inside, are perhaps the most democratic element in all Turkish cuisine. They are beloved of rich and poor alike and within the reach of everyone.

One of the first and certainly most welcome sounds of the morning is the cry of the *simit* seller making his first rounds. He will pass again in midafternoon, with a freshly baked batch of *simit* for people to enjoy with their traditional afternoon tea.

The *simit* vendor is also a welcome figure at train or bus stations during stops on long journeys across Anatolia.

There are specialty bakeries that make only *simit* and distribute it throughout the city. For many years I tried without success to create its unique chewy texture, which is similar to bagels. I finally learned the secret by working in a small *simit* bakery in a back street behind the Spice Bazaar in Istanbul.

✻   ✻   ✻

Dissolve the yeast and sugar in ¼ cup warm water and let stand 10 minutes in a warm place until frothy.

Place the flour on the work surface, make a well in the center, and put in the yeast mixture, salt, and 1 cup lukewarm water. Gradually work in the flour to make a very stiff dough. If you have a heavy-duty mixer, it is best to knead 10 minutes with the dough hook. By hand, knead it at least 15 minutes, until the dough is very smooth and springy. Put the dough in a buttered bowl, cover with plastic wrap, and let rise 2 hours.

Knead the dough a few times on a lightly floured work surface, roll into a log, and divide into 8 equal pieces. Roll each piece into a tight ball and let rest under a slightly damp towel about 30 minutes.

Roll each ball into a 14-inch long rope. Hold down one end of the rope with one hand while twisting it with the other. Then form this twisted rope into a ring, pressing and rolling the overlapping ends together on the work surface with one hand to seal. Place on a greased baking sheet and let rest 1 hour.

Dissolve the molasses in 2 cups water in a bowl. Put the sesame seeds in another bowl and set it next to the molasses water. Dip each *simit* in molasses water first, then in the sesame seeds, making sure the *simit* is completely and thickly coated with the seeds on all sides. Put it back on the baking sheet and let rest 30 minutes.

Preheat the oven to 550 degrees and heat tiles 30 minutes before baking. Put a few cups of water in an ovenproof pan and place it in the oven. Sprinkle the paddle with some cornmeal.

Meanwhile take each ring and rotate it gently through your hands, enlarging it into a 7-inch circle. Place the rings back on the baking sheet and let rest 15 minutes or until well puffed. Put each *simit* on the paddle and slide it onto hot tiles, sprinkled with cornmeal. Bake about 15 to 20 minutes until rich brown in color. They are at their best eaten fresh out of the oven. They will be good all day. You can also reheat them wrapped in foil to freshen them.

Delicate and Buttery Yeast Rolls

12 ROLLS

[AÇMA]

DOUGH

3½ teaspoons active dry yeast
¼ cup warm water
3¾ cups unbleached all-purpose flour
⅔ teaspoon salt
3 tablespoons sugar
4 tablespoons unsalted butter
1 egg
1¼ cups lukewarm water

6 tablespoons unsalted butter, at room temperature but firm enough to hold its shape

GLAZE

1 egg, lightly beaten

These delicate tender rolls have a flaky interior. Sold in large glass-covered boxes by street vendors, they are shaped to look like flower petals.

I went to a bakery in Ankara in the early hours of the morning to watch these rolls being made together with seemingly endless varieties of such savory and sweet yeast dough creations as *poğaça,* various sesame rings, *kandil simit,* and Easter bread, and all the lovely things that accompany the glasses of tea Turks drink throughout the day.

To make these particular rolls, pieces of butter-enriched yeast dough are rolled out to a thin sheet and then shaped into a cylinder. The cylinder is then twisted and shaped into a doughnut-shaped roll. When the rolls are baked, they look delicate and impressive. What was most interesting was the way the baker rolled out the small pieces of pastry. Instead of rolling them with a rolling pin, he held a piece of flattened dough with both hands and, with a brisk motion, made a half circle in the air with the pastry and slapped it against a marble surface. After he had repeated this operation two or three times, there lay on the marble a paper-thin piece of pastry. This recipe does not demand such acrobatics. The same result can be had by stretching the pastry by hand.

❋ ❋ ❋

Dissolve the yeast in ¼ cup warm water, let stand in a warm place 10 minutes until frothy.

Sift the flour with salt onto the work surface, make a large well in the center, and put in the sugar, yeast mixture, butter divided in small pieces, egg, and half the lukewarm water. Work these ingredients with your fingertips to make a creamy mixture. Gradually work in the flour and add the remaining water to make a very soft and sticky dough. If you have a heavy-duty mixer, knead the dough 6 minutes using the dough hook. Then knead it on the floured surface another few minutes. Alternatively, you can knead it by hand on a floured surface, frequently and rhythmically lifting the dough, folding it over itself while slapping against the surface, and sprinkling the surface with a little flour. Knead about 10 or 15 minutes until it is silky smooth and elastic. Put the dough in a buttered bowl, cover with plastic wrap, and let stand 30 minutes.

Knead the dough on a lightly floured surface for half a minute, roll into a log, and divide into 12 equal pieces. Roll each into a tight ball. Divide the butter into 12 equal pieces and place one on top of each ball. Place a piece of parchment paper loosely over the balls and let rest 15 minutes.

Press one ball into a 6-inch circle, spreading the butter over it. Now gently stretch the pastry into a very thin 12-inch rectangle. Fold in half, fold in half again, and then roll into a 5½-inch cylinder. Repeat this with the remaining balls and let rest for 20 minutes.

Gently stretch each cylinder to measure about 14 inches long. At the same time, twist it around itself and shape into a ring. Press and roll the overlapping ends to seal. Now you will have a donutlike roll about 4 inches in diameter. Place on a lightly greased baking sheet and allow to stand 30 minutes.

Preheat the oven to 375 degrees. Brush the rolls with the egg and let stand 5 minutes. Brush once more and let stand 5 minutes. Bake for 20 to 25 minutes. Cool on racks.

Paskalya Bread

❋❋❋

1 LOAF

[PASKALYA ÇÖREĞİ]

SPONGE

2½ teaspoons active dry
   yeast
Pinch of sugar
¼ cup warm milk
¼ cup unbleached
   all-purpose flour

DOUGH

1 teaspoon mastic (see
   Glossary)
About ½ cup milk
2½ cups unbleached
   all-purpose flour
1½ teaspoons mahleb,
   pulverized (see
   Glossary)
2 eggs, lightly beaten, at
   room temperature
1 egg yolk
½ cup sugar
8 tablespoons (1 stick)
   unsalted butter,
   softened

GLAZE

1 egg yolk
½ tablespoon cream

TOPPING

Chopped almonds and/or
   hazelnuts

This slightly sweetened bread, with its highly glazed, almost glistening caramel-brown exterior and comfortingly soft yellow interior, adorns the window displays of every bakery shop. If you pass by the bakery at the right time early in the morning, you will catch a whiff of the *mahleb* with which the bread is perfumed standing out in the midst of the scents of all the other breads and pastries. The name *Paskalya* bread (Easter bread) proclaims of course its Greek and Christian origin, but the Turks made this sweet bread their own by adding fragrant *mahleb,* a spice much favored in the Near East.

❋   ❋   ❋

To make the sponge, dissolve the yeast and sugar in the warm milk and let stand in a warm place 10 minutes until frothy. Stir in the flour, cover with plastic wrap, and let rise 30 minutes.

Tie the mastic in a folded piece of cheesecloth and pound gently to crush it. Place bag in a small saucepan with milk and simmer 20 minutes. If the milk evaporates too quickly add a little more. Remove from heat, take out the bag containing mastic, hold it above the saucepan and squeeze dry to extract all the liquid; discard the bag. Measure the infused milk and add more milk if necessary to make ¼ cup. If it exceeds that, boil it briefly to reduce to desired amount and cool to lukewarm.

Sift the flour into a bowl, make a well in the center, put in the *mahleb,* mastic-infused milk, eggs, egg yolk, sugar, butter, and the sponge. Mix the ingredients in the center with fingertips and gradually work in the flour to make a soft dough. The dough is very soft and sticky, and it is best to knead it in a mixer. Using the dough hook, knead for 5 minutes. It will be a sticky and gummy mixture. Turn it onto a floured work surface and knead at least 5 more minutes by hand, until the dough is very smooth and springy. If a mixer is not available, knead the dough on a floured surface at least 15 minutes until it is smooth and springy. Put the dough in a buttered bowl, cover with plastic wrap, and let rise in a warm place about 3 hours or until doubled in bulk.

Knead the dough lightly on a lightly floured surface, roll into a log, and divide into 3 equal pieces. Roll the pieces into tight balls, cover them with a barely damp towel, and let rest 20 minutes.

Roll each ball into a 20-inch rope, slightly plump in the middle and tapered at the ends. Let them rest, covered, 20 minutes, then shape the ropes into a braid. Pinch the ends and tuck under. Place the braid in a greased baking pan and let rise until almost double in bulk. This will take 1 to 3 hours, depending on the warmth of the room.

Preheat the oven to 350 degrees. Mix the egg yolk with the cream and brush over the bread. Wait 5 minutes and brush with the glaze once more. Sprinkle the top with nuts. Bake the bread 25 or 30 minutes or until a tester inserted in the thickest part comes out clean. It should be gloriously golden brown and very fragrant. Cool on a rack. It is delicious freshly baked but will keep very well for days wrapped in plastic or foil.

Flaky and Buttery Turnovers

✻✻✻✻✻✻✻✻✻✻✻✻✻✻✻✻✻✻✻✻✻✻✻✻✻✻✻✻✻✻✻✻✻✻✻✻✻✻✻

14 SMALL TURNOVERS [POĞAÇA]

SPONGE

1 teaspoon active dry
  yeast
Pinch of sugar
¼ cup warm water
¼ cup unbleached
  all-purpose flour

DOUGH

1½ cups plus 1
  tablespoon unbleached
  all-purpose flour
¼ teaspoon salt
11 tablespoons (1⅓
  sticks) unsalted butter,
  at room temperature,
  pliable but still firm
1 egg

CHEESE AND HERB FILLING

1 cup crumbled feta or
  goat cheese
1 egg, lightly beaten
⅓ cup chopped flat-leaf
  parsley or fresh dill

GLAZE

1 egg yolk
1 tablespoon cream or
  milk

TOPPING (OPTIONAL)

Nigella seeds (see
  Glossary)

Poğaça is a meltingly tender and flaky turnover. It is a favorite snack to be enjoyed with tea, and a staple item in the offerings of bakeries and street vendors. Quite often housewives make poğaça at home for their families and guests, especially for afternoon tea. However, the recipe they use is different from the one I give here, learned from professional bakers. I highly recommend it to you as one of great value capable of being used with any filling you choose.

✻   ✻   ✻

For the sponge, dissolve the yeast and sugar in the warm water and let stand in a warm place 10 minutes until frothy. Stir in the flour, cover with plastic wrap, and let rise 30 minutes.

Sift the flour and salt on the work surface, make a well in the center and put in it the sponge, butter, and egg. Mix the ingredients in the center with fingertips, then gradually work in the flour with a smearing motion of the ball of one hand until the dough comes together. Knead the dough gently on a lightly floured work surface just until smooth. This will be a very soft dough but it will not stick to hands. Put it in a bowl, cover with plastic wrap, and let stand 20 minutes.

Mix all ingredients for the filling until well blended.

On a lightly floured work surface, divide the dough into 14 equal pieces. Shape each piece into a tight ball and let rest 15 minutes under a towel.

Press each ball into a 3½-inch circle. Put a small amount of filling on one half of the circle and fold the other half over to cover. Place the pastries on a greased baking pan.

Preheat the oven to 375 degrees. Mix the egg yolk with cream or milk and brush on the pastries. Sprinkle with nigella seeds and let stand 15 minutes. Bake 25 or 30 minutes. They are good freshly out of the oven or cold.

Kandil Rings

❋❋❋❋❋❋❋❋❋❋❋❋❋❋❋❋❋❋❋❋❋❋❋❋❋❋❋❋❋❋❋❋❋❋❋❋❋❋❋

10 RINGS　　　　[KANDİL SİMİDİ]

SPONGE

1 teaspoon active dry
　yeast
Pinch of sugar
¼ cup warm water
¼ cup unbleached
　all-purpose flour

DOUGH

1½ cups plus 1
　tablespoon unbleached
　all-purpose flour
½ teaspoon salt
1 rounded teaspoon
　mahleb, finely ground
　(see Glossary)
11 tablespoons (1⅓
　sticks) unsalted butter,
　at room temperature,
　pliable but still firm
1 egg

GLAZE

1 egg yolk
1 tablespoon cream or
　milk

TOPPING

Nigella seeds (see
　Glossary) and/or
　sesame seeds

On those five special nights of the year, known as Kandil Geceleri, when the mosques are illuminated (see page 20), the occasion is marked by the sudden and welcome appearance of these picturesque little rings. Crisp and flavored with *mahleb,* glazed with egg yolks, they are topped with sesame or nigella seeds. Rushing home on such evenings, people stop at bakeries to pick up a bagful of *kandil simidi.* At dusk, the cry of street vendors hawking them can also be heard.

❋　　❋　　❋

To make the sponge, dissolve the yeast and sugar in the warm water and let stand in a warm place until frothy. Stir in the flour, cover with plastic wrap, and let rise 30 minutes.

Sift the flour and salt onto the work surface, make a well in the center and put in *mahleb,* butter, sponge, and egg. First mix the ingredients in the center with fingertips then gradually work in the flour with a smearing motion of the ball of one hand until the dough comes together. Knead the dough until it is smooth, put in a buttered bowl, cover with plastic wrap, and let rest 20 minutes.

Working on a lightly floured surface, divide the dough into 10 equal pieces and roll each piece into a tight ball. Cover with a towel and let rest 15 minutes.

Roll each ball into a 12-inch rope and then form it into a ring. Place the rings on a greased baking sheet.

Mix the egg yolk with the cream or milk and brush generously on the rings. Sprinkle half of them with sesame seeds and the other half with nigella seeds, or use only one kind of seeds if you wish. Let them rest 15 minutes.

Preheat the oven to 375 degrees and bake 25 minutes.

Crispy Sesame Tea Rings with *Mahleb*

✸✸✸

20 SESAME RINGS   [KÜÇÜK YAĞLI SİMİT]

DOUGH

1 teaspoon active dry
   yeast
Pinch of sugar
¼ cup warm water
3¾ cups unbleached
   all-purpose flour
1 teaspoon salt
1 egg
3 tablespoons sugar
½ pound (2 sticks)
   unsalted butter, at
   room temperature,
   divided into small
   pieces
2 teaspoons pulverized
   mahleb *(see Glossary)*
About ¼ cup plus 2
   tablespoons water

TOPPING

2 eggs, lightly beaten
Sesame seeds

Dissolve the yeast and sugar in the warm water and let stand in warm place 10 minutes until frothy. Sift the flour and salt onto the work surface. Make a well in the center and put in the egg, sugar, butter, yeast mixture, and *mahleb;* mix with your fingertips. Gradually work in the flour and add water to make a fairly stiff dough. Knead on the work surface just until smooth (do not overwork the dough), put in a buttered bowl, cover with plastic wrap, and let rest 30 minutes.

Preheat the oven to 375 degrees. Divide the dough into 20 walnut-sized pieces, roll each piece into a rope ¼ inch thick, and shape it into a ring, pressing the overlapping ends together. Then dip each first in egg, then in sesame seeds, making sure they are well coated with the seeds on all sides. Bake on a greased cookie sheet 15 minutes, until they are golden brown.

BÖREK

****

Rolling the thin pastry sheets required for *börek* (and also *mantı*) is a skill that takes practice to master, but once learned it becomes almost automatic. If you treat the following instructions as guidelines, you will ultimately acquire the necessary feel for making pastry dough.

You will need a large and smooth work surface or a tabletop. Wood, marble, or formica surfaces work well. To roll the dough you will need a regular rolling pin and a special Turkish rolling pin, which is about 25 inches long and about ¾ inch in diameter. A wooden curtain rod of similar dimensions will also work very well. I once tried a metal curtain rod, the only item I could find around the house at the time, and I happily found that it too worked.

Roll the dough first into a tight ball. On a lightly floured surface, flatten it with your hands. Using a regular rolling pin, roll it out to an 8- or 9-inch circle with a back-and-forward motion, slowly rotating the dough counterclockwise.

Sprinkle a little flour on the work surface both under and over the dough. With the special long rolling pin, starting at the lower edge of the circle, wrap about 3 inches of the pastry around the rolling pin. Place the stretched-out fingers of both hands on the center of the pin and begin rolling it slowly forward toward the edge of the circle with a quick back-and-forward motion, until the whole pastry is wrapped fairly tightly around the pin.

As you roll the pastry around the pin, keep your stretched-out hands constantly and rhythmically moving horizontally outward along the pin toward the ends, and quickly bringing them back to the center to begin the same motion again until the whole pastry is wrapped around the pin. As you do this, the downward pressure of the fingers and balls of the hands stretches the pastry horizontally.

Once the whole pastry is wrapped around the pin, lift the pin at both ends and flip open the pastry, slapping it against the work surface; unroll. Now rotate the pastry slightly (maybe 30 degrees) counterclockwise, sprinkle it with flour, then take an edge of pastry next to the one with which you started, and repeat the whole process. Every now and then turn the pastry over and sprinkle some flour under it. Continue stretching the pastry by rolling until it reaches the desired thickness.

A thickness of less than $\frac{1}{16}$ inch would be difficult to measure. *Börek* is quite often made with pastry sheets $\frac{1}{25}$ inch thick, or even less. For this reason, in addition to specifying an ideal thickness, I usually give the dimensions of the rolled pastry sheet in my recipes.

Rolling thin pastry sheets for *börek* may also be done with a pasta machine: First, set the rollers of the machine at the highest number and roll the dough into a log, dividing it into 1-cup portions. On a lightly floured work surface flatten a piece of dough under the palm of your hand and feed it through the rollers of the machine. Fold it in half and feed it again, and again, dusting it with unbleached all-purpose flour or rice flour each time. Now turn the dial down one notch and feed the dough through the rollers but this time do not fold the pastry. Continue lowering the notches on the dial, feeding the pastry and dusting it with flour as needed until the rollers are set at the lowest number. Unfortunately, with some machines you will be able to roll the dough only until the second-lowest notch is reached. Set at the lowest one, the machine begins to tear the dough.

Pastry stretched by a pasta machine will be approximately $\frac{1}{16}$ inch thick at best. This is fine for Italian pasta recipes, Turkish *mantı,* or even for some *börek*. But for most Turkish *börek* we need a pastry sheet that is much thinner—about $\frac{1}{25}$ inch or sometimes even less. In such cases, carefully and gently stretch the pastry further by hand.

Anatolian *Börek*

✽✽✽

6 SERVINGS

DOUGH

2½ cups unbleached
    all-purpose flour
1 teaspoon salt
3 eggs
¼ cup water

FILLING

½ pound feta cheese,
    crumbled (2 cups)
2 eggs, lightly beaten
¾ cup chopped flat-leaf
    parsley
Wheat starch or
    cornstarch to use for
    rolling pastry
12 tablespoons (1½
    sticks) unsalted butter,
    melted

[SU BÖREĞİ]

Here I am honestly obliged to use superlatives. This superb creation, jewel in the crown of the *börek* family, is the final and perfected outcome of the process that began when Turks first rolled dough in their Central Asian homeland almost a millennium ago.

At least 11 very thin sheets of an egg-based dough are first boiled and layered with butter and filling. Then the *börek* is baked until it shows a glorious golden crust. The basic method of making this *börek* resembles that of lasagna. However, neither its texture nor its flavor resembles lasagna. I must also emphasize that the pastry sheets of this or any other *börek* are far thinner than any rolled pasta sheets; they create a different and more delicate taste and texture. You will need a large work surface of wood, marble, or formica. You will also need a special rolling pin at least 27 inches long and ½ to ¾ inch in diameter. You can roll the *börek* on a pasta machine (page 206), but the result, although good, will not be the same as that achieved by hand rolling. A 12-inch cast-iron frying pan with 2-inch sides works best. You can also use a round baking pan of the same size.

✽   ✽   ✽

Put the flour on a work surface, make a well in the center and put in the salt, eggs, and water. Gradually work in the flour to make a fairly stiff dough. Knead it on a lightly floured surface 10 minutes or until silky smooth and elastic. Put in a buttered bowl, cover with plastic wrap, and let stand at least 1 hour.

Mix well all the ingredients for the filling in a bowl and set aside.

Roll the dough into a log on a lightly floured surface and divide it into 6 equal pieces. Now divide 5 of them in half to have 11 pieces of dough. One of them, of course, will be larger than the rest. Roll each one into a tight ball and place on a floured surface. Cover with a slightly damp towel and let rest 40 minutes.

Fill a large kettle with cold water, stir in some salt, and keep it over low heat. Place a large bowl of cold water next to the kettle. You will also need a few absorbent towels. After you roll the sheets of pastry, you will cook them briefly, rinse in cold water, and dry before layering them in the baking pan. *(continued)*

Following the instructions for rolling pastry by hand or with a pasta machine on pages 205–6, roll each of the 10 equal-sized balls into a thin circle of pastry 12 or 13 inches in diameter. They should be at least ¹⁄₂₅ inch thick. Roll the remaining large ball of dough almost twice as large as the others. For this particular *börek,* use wheat starch or cornstarch in place of flour to coat the pastry and the work surface. Spread the rolled circles of pastry on clean surfaces around the room. Obvious places would be countertops and table-tops. You can also put sheets of newspaper or other clean paper over sofas or chairs and place the pastry on them. At home women who roll pastry frequently use clean sheets for this purpose.

Bring the salted water to a rolling boil and preheat the oven to 350 degrees. Spread the largest sheet in a buttered 12-inch round baking pan with 2-inch sides or a 12-inch cast-iron frying pan, letting the edges of the pastry hang over the sides. Sprinkle the pastry with 2 tablespoons butter. Gently drop a pastry sheet into the boiling water and, using a perforated spoon, try to spread the pastry out so that it will not bunch together. Press down gently with the spoon to keep the pastry submerged. Leave it in water for only 10 seconds; gently take it out and drop it into cold water. Take it out and dry it in the folds of towels. Place the pastry in the pan over the first sheet. The pastry will be larger than the pan, so arrange it with fingertips in a crumpled fashion. It is not supposed to lie flat. Again coat or sprinkle with butter. Continue cooking and layering 3 more sheets, then spread the filling evenly over the pastry. Continue cooking and layering the remaining sheets.

Fold the extending parts of the first sheet to seal everything. Pour the remaining butter on top and bake the *börek* 40 or 50 minutes, until the top turns gloriously golden brown. Take it out of the oven and turn it upside down on a platter. I put a larger plate or a cookie sheet over the baking pan containing the *börek* and turn the pan upside down. Then I slide the *börek* onto a platter to serve. Cut the *börek* into wedges and serve hot. If you are not serving it right away, reheat it just before you serve. It keeps for days and needs only to be reheated to taste freshly baked.

Note on layering machine-made pastry for *börek:* If you use a pasta machine to roll the pastry sheets, you will have long strips of pastry rather than circles that fit in the baking pan as a whole piece. You will therefore need to cut the strips into manageable pieces to cook in boiling water and to place in the baking pan. It is perfectly all right to make *börek* with small strips of pastry rather than larger circles. Remember to place them in the baking pan in a gathered fashion rather than entirely flat. Also remember that the machine will probably not roll them as thin as they should be (*börek* pastry is much thinner than a pasta sheet). To remedy this, simply stretch them further by hand, without making them so thin they break or disintegrate in boiling water.

Circassian *Börek*

✻✻

26 *BÖREK*

[ÇERKEZ PUF BÖREĞİ]

DOUGH

2¾ cups unbleached
   all-purpose flour
¾ teaspoon salt
2 tablespoons unsalted
   butter, very soft or
   barely melted
1 egg yolk
¾ cup plus 3 tablespoons
   milk

GOAT CHEESE FILLING

1¼ cups crumbled goat
   cheese
½ cup chopped flat-leaf
   parsley
1 egg

Oil for deep-frying

These golden pastry puffs have crisp outsides and hollow interiors containing slightly sharp Circassian cheese made with goat's milk mixed with fresh herbs. Here I substitute goat cheese for the Circassian cheese. I use flat-leaf parsley, but you can use any herb or combination of herbs you like.

✻   ✻   ✻

Sift the flour and salt onto the work surface. Make a well in the center and put in the butter, egg yolk, and milk. Mix these ingredients with the fingers and gradually work in the flour to make a dough. Knead 10 minutes or until smooth and elastic, put in a buttered bowl, cover with plastic wrap, and let rest 1 hour.

Place the dough on a lightly floured surface, knead lightly, and divide into half. Roll each half into a tight ball, cover with a slightly damp towel, and let rest 30 minutes.

Place one ball of dough on the lightly floured surface, flatten it to a disk and with a regular rolling pin roll it into a 9-inch circle. Now, following the instructions on pages 205–6, roll the pastry into a thin circle about 20 or 21 inches in diameter. (If you use a pasta machine, you will need to divide the pastry into smaller portions in order to roll it.)

Mix all filling ingredients with a fork to blend. With a 4-inch pastry cutter, cut circles out of the rolled pastry. Put about ¾ teaspoon filling on half of each circle and fold the other half over the filling to cover. Dampen the edges and seal, pressing them together gently or using a pastry crimper. Cover the filled pastries with a towel and roll out and shape the other half of the dough.

Heat the oil for deep-frying and slip in 2 or 3 *börek*. In a second or two they will puff up and rise to the surface. Turn and remove after a few seconds when they turn golden brown. Drain on paper towels and serve hot. They are also good cold.

Griddle *Börek* with Spicy Veal Filling

6 LARGE BÖREK [ÇİĞ BÖREK]

DOUGH

2¼ cups unbleached
    all-purpose flour
½ teaspoon salt
1 tablespoon melted
    butter
¾ cup plus 2 tablespoons
    water

SPICY VEAL FILLING

1¼ cups ground veal
⅓ cup finely chopped
    onion
2 tender long green
    peppers or 2
    Hungarian chilies or
    your choice of fresh
    peppers, topped,
    seeded, and finely
    chopped
1 jalapeño, seeded and
    chopped (optional)
½ cup peeled and
    chopped tomatoes
½ cup chopped parsley
½ cup chopped fresh dill
Salt and freshly ground
    pepper
2 tablespoons water

Oil

This delicious *börek* is easy to make and a good choice for beginners as it is cooked on a griddle. In Turkey tender, semihot, long green peppers are used in this filling, but in North America I use somewhat similar, semihot chilies called Hungarian peppers that are sold at my local greengrocer. When they are not available I use poblanos, always adding a few slivers of jalapeños, which I like very much. If you have to use sweet peppers, add a few crushed red pepper flakes to the filling.

❋   ❋   ❋

Sift the flour and salt onto the work surface. Make a well in the center and put in the butter and water. Gradually work in the flour to make a dough. Put the dough on a lightly floured work surface and knead 10 minutes until very smooth and elastic. Put in a buttered bowl, cover with plastic wrap, and let rest 30 minutes.

Mix all the ingredients for the filling in a bowl and blend thoroughly.

Put the dough on the work surface and roll into a log. Divide the log into 6 equal pieces, knead each one into a tight ball and let stand 20 minutes under a towel.

Roll each ball into a 10-inch circle. Spread about ¼ cup filling over half of the circle, cover the filling with the other half, and crimp the edges to seal. Heat a griddle to medium hot, lightly brush with oil, and cook the *börek* on both sides until golden blisters appear on their surfaces. Serve immediately.

Talash *Börek* (Lamb and Pistachio Filling in Puff Pastry)

✸✸✸✸✸✸✸✸✸✸✸✸✸✸✸✸✸✸✸✸✸✸✸✸✸✸✸✸✸✸✸✸✸✸✸✸

3 SERVINGS

[TALAŞ BÖREĞİ]

FILLING

1¾ pounds boneless
   lamb shoulder,
   trimmed of fat and cut
   into strips ¼ inch
   wide, 1 inch long, and
   ⅛ inch thick

2 onions, sliced
   paper-thin

4 tablespoons unsalted
   butter

2 teaspoons chopped
   garlic

3 sprigs thyme

3 sprigs flat-leaf parsley

1 large tomato, peeled
   and chopped

½ teaspoon ground
   allspice

½ teaspoon ground
   cinnamon

Salt and freshly ground
   pepper

½ cup unsalted
   pistachios

¼ cup currants

1 cup chopped flat-leaf
   parsley

1 package frozen puff
   pastry (approximately
   1 pound)

Unlike most other *börek*, Talash *börek* is meant to be served as an entrée. However, it is not an everyday dish. Visually attractive as well as delicious, it is usually prepared for special occasions. Once the buttery, delicate layers of pastry are punctured, a perfumed steam rises from the moist lamb and pistachios contained in it.

Puff pastry is also used quite often for making various *börek*. However, because of its wide familiarity I did not give a recipe for it in this section. I suggest a frozen puff pastry for this particular *börek*, but your own pastry will do more justice to this traditional dish.

✸ ✸ ✸

To make the filling, heat a heavy pan over medium heat. Stir in the lamb, onions, and butter and cook, stirring frequently. The lamb will release its juices, which will evaporate; then it will begin to brown. Stir constantly to brown all the pieces evenly, then stir in the garlic and continue cooking 1 or 2 minutes. Add the herb sprigs, tomato, and spices and turn them a minute or so. Season the lamb with salt and pepper and test for tenderness. If it is tender, stir in the pistachios, currants, and chopped parsley, mix well and drain into a bowl, reserving the liquid. If the lamb is not tender enough, cover and simmer 10 minutes or until tender, then proceed as above.

Set aside the filling and reduce the reserved cooking liquid. Stir this into the filling, which should be very moist but not watery.

Defrost the puff pastry according to package instructions. There are usually 2 sheets of pastry, each measuring approximately 10 by 10 inches. Cut each sheet lengthwise into 3 equal strips. Then cut each strip in half. You will have 12 rectangles. On a lightly floured surface, roll 6 rectangles and stretch them into 4½-by-6-inch rectangles. Roll the remaining ones to measure 5 by 6 inches.

Put one-sixth of the filling over the 6 smaller rectangles, leaving a ½-inch border on all edges. Dampen the edges with water and place the larger pieces of pastry directly on top of the smaller ones,

1 egg yolk

½ tablespoon cream or milk

covering the filling. Seal the edges with a pastry crimper or press gently with a fork to seal.

Preheat the oven to 375 degrees.

Mix the egg yolk with the cream or milk and brush the tops of the *börek* with the egg wash. Place on a baking sheet and bake 20 to 25 minutes until they are golden brown. Serve hot.

Börek with Spinach Filling

❋❋

8 TO 10 SERVINGS   [ISPANAKLI TEPSİ BÖREĞİ]

SPINACH FILLING

2 pounds fresh spinach leaves, washed, drained, and chopped

2 tablespoons peanut oil

2 tablespoons unsalted butter

2 cups chopped onions

3 eggs, lightly beaten

Salt and freshly ground pepper

½ cup kasseri cheese, grated

14 tablespoons (1¾ sticks) unsalted butter, melted

3 eggs, lightly beaten

3 tablespoons milk

1 pound filo pastry

To make the filling, cook the spinach in a large pot with ½ cup water until wilted. Drain and squeeze dry. Heat the oil and butter in a large skillet and cook the onions until they begin to brown around the edges. Stir in the spinach and sauté for 5 minutes. Off the heat, stir in the eggs, season with salt and pepper, mix in the cheese. Place back on the heat and cook a few seconds until the eggs are set and the mixture looks very moist but not watery. Set aside.

Preheat the oven to 350 degrees.

Mix the butter with eggs and milk in a bowl. Have a buttered 9-by-12-inch baking pan ready. Unfold the filo and keep covered under a slightly damp towel. Work with one sheet at a time. Place one half of a pastry sheet on the bottom of the pan, leaving the other half extending over the side.

Brush the pastry in the pan with butter-and-egg mixture, fold over the part draped over the side and brush it with the butter-and-egg mixture. Repeat this until one-third of the pastry is used. Spread the spinach filling evenly over the pastry.

Continue layering and brushing with the butter-and-egg mixture until all the pastry is used. Pour the remaining butter-and-egg mixture over the top, tuck the edges under, and cut the assembled *börek* through to the bottom, forming squares.

Bake for 30 to 40 minutes, or until the *börek* is puffed and golden brown.

Filo Triangles with Spicy Filling of Meat and Pine Nuts

✹✹✹

8 SERVINGS

[BAKLAVA YUFKASIYLA KIYMALI MUSKA BÖREĞİ]

SPICY MEAT AND
PINE NUT FILLING

3 tablespoons peanut oil
1 teaspoon cumin seeds
1½ cups finely chopped
  onions
¼ cup pine nuts
2 garlic cloves, chopped
¾ teaspoon ground
  allspice
1 cup chopped
  combination of fresh
  peppers and chilies
  chosen from sweet red
  peppers, green bell
  peppers, and poblanos
1 or 2 (to taste) red or
  green jalapeños,
  seeded and chopped
1 pound ground lamb,
  veal, or chuck
1 cup peeled and
  chopped tomatoes
¼ cup currants
½ cup chopped flat-leaf
  parsley
¼ cup chopped fresh dill
Salt and freshly ground
  pepper

1 pound filo pastry
Melted unsalted butter to
  brush on the pastry

Heat oil until hot and add cumin seeds. Cook and stir until they turn several shades darker. Take care not to burn them. Stir in the onions and pine nuts; cook, stirring frequently, until the onions begin to brown around the edges and the pine nuts turn light brown. Stir in the garlic and allspice and cook a few seconds, stirring. Add the peppers, chilies, and meat; cook, stirring frequently, until the meat browns. Stir in the tomatoes, currants, and 2 tablespoons water; simmer, uncovered, 5 minutes. Mix in the herbs and season with salt and pepper. The filling should be moist but not at all runny or watery. If it gets too dry while cooking, add water in very small quantities.

Unfold the filo and cut the whole stack lengthwise into 3 equal stacks of strips. Keep the pastry covered under a slightly damp towel. Place a single strip of pastry on the work surface, with short end near you. Brush it lightly with butter and place another strip directly on top of the first one. Put 1 heaping tablespoon filling on the bottom end of the strip about 1 inch in from the edge. Fold the end of the strip diagonally over the filling, creating a triangle. Fold it once and then fold it diagonally to the right. Continue folding to the end. Place the triangle seam down on a greased baking pan. Continue with the remaining pastry and filling. Brush the tops with butter.

Preheat the oven to 350 degrees.

Bake the triangles about 20 to 25 minutes, until golden brown.

Börek with Eggplant Filling

✱✱

6 *BÖREK*

[PATLICANLI BÖREK]

1 recipe eggplant filling
   (page 193)
1 pound filo pastry
12 tablespoons (1½
   sticks) unsalted butter,
   melted

GLAZE

1 egg yolk
1 tablespoon cream or
   milk

Prepare the eggplant filling and set aside.

Unfold the filo and keep the sheets in a stack under a slightly damp towel. Place 2 sheets directly on top of each other on the work surface. Brush very sparingly with butter and place another double layer on top of the first pair. Brush again very lightly with butter and fold the layered sheets together in half, creating a rectangle.

Place one-sixth of the filling in the center and spread it to cover a 4-inch square. Fold one side over the filling and brush very lightly with butter. Fold over the opposite side and brush. Do the same with the remaining sides, creating a package.

Put the *börek* on a greased baking pan seam down. Continue forming the *börek* with the remaining pastry and filling. (Some packages contain 22 sheets and others 24. If you have only 22 sheets, the last *börek* you assemble will have only 2 sheets instead of 4, but do not be concerned.) Brush the tops lightly with butter.

Preheat the oven to 375 degrees.

Mix the egg yolk with cream or milk and brush on the *börek*. Bake for 20 minutes, or until golden brown. Serve hot.

Börek with Chicken Filling

✹✹

6 *BÖREK*

[TAVUKLU BÖREK]

CHICKEN FILLING

1 chicken, cut into thighs,
  legs, and breast halves
3 tablespoons olive oil
3 cups chopped onions
2 garlic cloves, chopped
3 sprigs thyme
3 tomatoes, peeled and
  chopped
Salt and freshly ground
  pepper
1 cup water
1 cup chopped flat-leaf
  parsley
Handful of basil leaves,
  cut into ribbons

1 pound filo pastry
8 tablespoons (1 stick)
  unsalted butter, melted
Glaze (page 215)

Brown the chicken pieces lightly on all sides in the olive oil. Stir in the onions and garlic, push the chicken pieces to the side and cook the onions for 8 minutes. Add the thyme, tomatoes, salt and pepper, and water; cover and simmer for 45 mintues or until chicken is done. Remove chicken pieces, bone and skin them, and cut into small pieces. The sauce should be thick; if it looks watery, boil it briefly to reduce. Remove and discard the thyme sprigs. Return chicken to pan and discard the skin and bones. Stir in the parsley and basil, mix the filling thoroughly, adjust with salt and pepper, and set aside. The filling should be moist but not watery.

Unfold the filo and keep the sheets in a stack under a slightly damp towel. Follow the instructions on page 215 for assembling, glazing, and baking the *börek*.

DESSERTS

* *

Turkish cuisine is particularly rich in the variety of its desserts. Well-known is baklava and other desserts made with thin pastry sheets and sweetened with syrups. Another category consists of desserts made with yeast dough or egg-enriched dough, deep-fried and also sweetened with syrups. Cake-type desserts are similarly sweetened with syrups. Lighter and more refreshing perhaps are those many dairy desserts for which Turkey is famous, as well as a wide range of fruit desserts made with fresh or dried fruits. Helva, or halvah, is also a rich category of desserts.

* * *

Baklava is common to all the cuisines of the Eastern Mediterranean and the etymology of the word, being a mystery, provides no clue to the origin of this highly popular pastry. The technique involved in making the ultrathin pastry, popularly known in the West by its Greek name *filo,* may have evolved from the ancient Turkish *yufka* (see page 184). That energetic investigator of culinary etymology, Charles Perry, has effectively disproved the claim of UCLA historian Spero Vryonis that something akin to baklava existed among the Byzantines. Indeed Perry points out on another occasion that there is no record of baklava having existed before the Ottomans, which makes an Ottoman origin for it more likely.

Be that as it may, baklava has always played an important part in Turkish history. Beginning in the sixteenth century with Süleyman the Magnificent, it was customary for baklava to be sent from the palace to the Janissaries on the fifteenth day of Ramadan. The Janissaries would go to a certain gate of the palace, receive their baklava, and take it in a procession back to their barracks. The procession was often disorderly and an occasion for boisterous behavior.

* * *

Helva (an Arabic word) is, of course, a universal favorite throughout the Middle East and embraces many different varieties. In its simplest form, it is an intimate and familiar companion of Turkish households under many circumstances. According to a well-known anecdote, it even invaded the dreams of the legendary Turkish humorist, Nasrettin Hoca. Awakening in the middle of the night and overcome with a sudden desire for helva, he rouses the grocer and asks, one by one, if he has the ingredients needed to make it. When he learns that the grocer indeed does have them, he asks in exasperation, "Then why not make some and eat it?"

Helva is an indispensable part of the menu on festive occasions. In addition to offering it as an expression of good wishes on such occasions as the birth of a child, buying a new home, establishing a new business, returning from abroad, or recovering from sickness, a gift of helva also expresses sympathy with the bereaved.

✴ ✴ ✴

One of the most endearing sights of Istanbul is the window display of the *muhallebici*. This specialist in dairy desserts and associated delights represents a tradition unique to Turkey and the lands that have come under its culinary influence. It is difficult to pass by a *muhallebi* shop without becoming convinced one is hungry enough to eat something, however small, from the array of foods offered. The mention of dairy desserts or milk puddings is likely to arouse in the British and American reader memories of tasteless, lumpy concoctions imposed in childhood; Turkish milk puddings belong to a quite different species. Each subtly different from the other, they are all characterized by a creaminess and lightness that is never more appreciated than on a hot summer day when the palate refuses anything heavier. The appeal of *muhallebi* becomes totally irresistible when a scoop of ice cream is placed on top of it.

The dairy desserts offered by the *muhallebici* come in different flavors and textures: they may be enriched and flavored with almonds, pistachios, and unfamiliar items such as mastic, scented with rose water or vanilla beans; some are simmered, some are baked, and some are burnt in the fashion of crème brûlée. It follows that in this wide range of delicacies everyone will choose a personal favorite and even a shop where in his opinion that particular dessert is prepared most excellently. If the search for the perfect dessert of one's choice takes one to the other side of the city, so be it!

Hazelnut Baklava

✱✱

ABOUT 30 PIECES,
SERVING 12 TO 15

[FINDIKLI BAKLAVA]

In the West, commercially prepared baklava is for the most part of very poor quality, made with throat-burning syrup. Moreover, it comes in only one variety, as if none other existed, whereas true baklava comes in a whole series of contrasting varieties. These are created by the use of different fillings, syrups, and ways of layering and shaping.

Turkish cuisine insists on specialization as a condition for excellence. The craft of making baklava is therefore separate from that of the baker or the maker of other pastries. Baklava is sold in specialty shops that have been selling it for generations. Some cities, notably Gaziantep in southeast Turkey, are particularly celebrated for their excellent baklava, and the owner of every baklava shop in Istanbul advertises himself as hailing from Gaziantep. Baklava from the Black Sea region, which is made from hazelnuts, also deserves special mention.

PASTRY

1 pound hazelnuts
¼ cup sugar
1 pound filo pastry
*½ pound (2 sticks)
    unsalted butter, melted*

SYRUP

1¾ cups sugar
1½ cups water
1 teaspoon lemon juice

Grind the hazelnuts with the sugar in a blender or food processor, but do not make a powder. Coat a 9-by-13-inch baking pan with butter. Preheat the oven to 350 degrees.

When ready to assemble the baklava, open the package of filo, unfold the pastry, and keep it well covered under a heavy towel, for it dries out very quickly. Place half of one sheet of pastry in the baking pan and let the other half hang over the side. Brush the pastry in the pan lightly with the melted butter, fold the extending half over, and brush again with butter. Continue layering and brushing the pastry until one-third of the filo is used. Spread the nuts over the pastry and proceed layering the remaining pastry sheets, brushing each with the melted butter. Coat the top with the remaining butter and press down on the surface of the layered pastry with your hands to compress the whole thing. With a sharp knife cut the pastry all the way through, forming diamond-shaped pieces.

(continued)

Bake the baklava for 20 minutes. Reduce oven to 300 degrees, place a piece of parchment paper loosely over the baklava to preserve its pale color, and bake 30 minutes longer.

To make the syrup, dissolve the sugar in the water, bring it to a boil, and simmer gently for 5 minutes. Stir in the lemon juice and simmer 4 minutes longer. Let cool.

As soon as the baklava comes out of the oven, drain off any excess butter and pour the syrup over the pastry. Recut the pieces and allow it to stand several hours before serving.

Pistachio Bird Nests

✳✳

8 BIRD NESTS, OR 4 SERVINGS

[BÜLBÜL YUVASI]

FILLING
1 cup shelled unsalted pistachios
¼ cup sugar
Rose water

These small, innocent-looking coils of paper-thin pastry, sprinkled generously in the center with pistachios, do indeed resemble miniature bird nests. To shape them I use a long Turkish rolling pin which is ½ to ¾ inch in diameter (see page 185). However, a curtain rod of similar thickness will work nicely.

✳   ✳   ✳

SYRUP
¾ cup sugar
1 cup water
1 teaspoon lemon juice
2-inch piece of vanilla bean, split and scraped

For the filling, grind pistachios to a powder in a blender or food processor with the sugar. Put the mixture in a bowl, moisten lightly with some rose water and set aside.

To make the syrup, dissolve the sugar in the water, bring to a boil, and simmer gently for 5 minutes. Stir in lemon juice, bring it to a boil again, and remove from fire. Stir vanilla bean into the hot syrup and let it steep until the syrup is cool. Remove vanilla bean and reserve the syrup.

Preheat the oven to 350 degrees.

8 sheets filo pastry
6 tablespoons unsalted butter, melted
Ground pistachios for topping

Place one sheet of pastry on work surface and keep remaining sheets well covered with a damp towel. Brush the pastry lightly with the butter and fold in half, bringing the short sides together to create a rectangle. Place the shorter side near you. Brush surface lightly with butter and place the rolling pin horizontally over the pastry one-third of the way from the edge next to you. Now fold the part of the pastry that is between you and the rolling pin over the pin to cover it.

Place about 3 tablespoons of filling on the pastry along the covered rolling pin. Begin rolling the pastry strip loosely together with the rolling pin. When the whole strip is rolled around the rolling pin, brush the pastry roll lightly with butter and gently push both ends in toward the center of the roll to create a pleated or gathered look. Now, with one hand firmly holding one end of the pastry roll, with the other hand pull the rolling pin out. Twist the gathered pastry roll into a coil. Place it in a greased muffin pan and brush with butter.

Continue making the bird nests with the remaining pastry. Bake about 25 minutes, until golden brown. Fill the centers with ground pistachios and sprinkle them with syrup. Let them rest several hours and serve plain or with clotted or whipped cream.

Semolina, Saffron, and Pistachio Helva

❊❊❊

6 SERVINGS

[İRMİK HELVASI]

½ teaspoon saffron
    threads
2 tablespoons hot milk
⅓ cup shelled unsalted
    pistachios
9 tablespoons unsalted
    butter
1 cup plus 2 to 4
    tablespoons sugar
2 cups milk
1 cup semolina

Soak the saffron in the hot milk for at least 30 minutes. Heat a heavy frying pan and toast the pistachios with 1 tablespoon of the butter for 2 minutes, until they are lightly toasted but still green. Remove as much skin as you can from them and set aside.

Dissolve the sugar in the milk over low heat and keep the mixture hot. Melt the remaining butter in a heavy saucepan, add the semolina, and cook, stirring, over low heat for about 8 to 10 minutes.

Stir the saffron milk into the hot sugared milk and add to the semolina, stirring vigorously. Remove the helva from the fire, cover, and allow to stand in a warm spot for 15 minutes. Fold in the pistachios and serve warm or at room temperature in bowls.

Poached Dried Apricots Filled with Yogurt Cream and Sprinkled with Pistachios

❋❋

[KAYMAKLI KAYISI TATLISI]

6 ounces dried apricots
¼ cup sugar
3½ cups water
¾ teaspoon lemon juice
About ½ cup Sweet Yogurt Cream (page 228), whipped cream, or sweetened crème fraîche
Ground unsalted pistachios

The amber of the apricots framing white cream in a pool of golden apricot syrup forms a picture pleasing to the eye. In Turkey, *kaymak*, a thick cream, is used to fill the apricots. Here I suggest Sweet Yogurt Cream, slightly sweetened whipped cream, or sweetened crème fraîche.

❋   ❋   ❋

There are several varieties of dried apricot on the market. Some look very dry and shriveled, while others look quite smooth and plump. If the apricots look very dry it is best to soak them in water several hours before cooking them. Otherwise you can cook them without soaking.

Dissolve the sugar in the water, bring it to a boil, stir in the apricots, cover, and simmer gently for about 25 to 30 minutes, until tender. Remove the apricots with a slotted spoon and cool them. Meanwhile boil up the already thick syrup for 1 minute, stir in the lemon juice, cool, and chill.

The cooked apricots separate easily along their ridges. When you open them, take care not to separate the halves. Fill them to overflowing with the sweet yogurt cream, whipped cream, or sweetened crème fraîche—the cream should be very visible. Cover and chill the stuffed apricots and serve drizzled with the chilled apricot syrup. Sprinkle a little ground pistachios on each apricot and serve.

Kaymak

✳✳✳

Kaymak is a thick clotted cream made from buffalo milk. It is used on bread with honey or jam for breakfast, as a topping on certain desserts, or as a filling for others such as baklava. It was once so popular and widespread that special shops were devoted to it. The most famous of these were located at Eyüb, where they appear to have functioned, at least in the sixteenth century, as trysting places, with the result that a decree issued in 1573 prohibited women from frequenting them.

Poached Dried Figs Stuffed with Walnuts

✳✳✳

4 SERVINGS

[KURU İNCİR TATLISI]

6 ounces dried figs
3½ cups water
About ½ cup ground walnuts
¼ cup sugar
¾ teaspoon lemon juice
Sweet Yogurt Cream (page 228) or sweetened crème fraîche for topping (optional)

In Turkey we associate dried fruit with nuts. In fact, they are sold together in the same specialty shops. In winter, children are offered dried fruits and nuts for snacks: toasted hazelnuts with raisins, apricots with toasted almonds, dried figs with walnuts, and so on. Candy, considered a special treat, is given to children much more rarely.

✳   ✳   ✳

Remove the stems and gently cook the figs in the water for 25 to 30 minutes, until soft. Remove with a slotted spoon and reserve the cooking liquid.

Open the figs with a knife, taking care not to separate them, and stuff with the ground walnuts. Dissolve the sugar in the cooking liquid and boil the syrup for 2 minutes or so, until it is slightly thickened; stir in lemon juice and pour over the stuffed figs. They can be served warm or chilled. Sweet yogurt cream or sweetened crème fraîche thinned to pouring consistency goes well with them.

Sweet Saffron Rice with Pistachios and Almonds

* *

8 SERVINGS

[ZERDE]

1 teaspoon saffron
    threads
⅓ cup plus 1 tablespoon
    uncooked long-grain
    rice
6 cups water
¾ to 1 cup sugar
¼ cup rose water
2 heaping tablespoons
    sliced blanched
    almonds
2 heaping tablespoons
    skinned pistachios
Pomegranate seeds
    and/or pistachios

This dessert was traditionally served at weddings and other festive occasions. In this there is a certain paradox, because the name of the dish is taken from Persian *zard,* meaning yellow, and in the conventional language of classical poetry yellowness of face was an expression denoting sorrow. The yellowness of *zerde* derives, however, from saffron, a substance supposed to bestow tranquillity and even joy.

❋   ❋   ❋

Crumble the saffron threads with your fingertips and soak in 3 tablespoons hot water for 1 hour.

Wash the rice several times, soak in water to cover for 30 minutes, and drain.

Bring the 6 cups water to a boil in a saucepan, stir in the rice, and cook over low heat, partially covered, for 25 minutes. Stir in the sugar, saffron water, rose water, and almonds; simmer for 10 minutes. Fold in the pistachios. The pudding should have a thick soup consistency that will thicken further as it stands. If it looks thicker than described, thin with a little water, boil up once, and pour into serving bowls. Serve warm or chilled, decorated with pomegranate seeds and/or pistachios.

Quince Stewed in Pomegranate Syrup and Served with Yogurt Cream

4 SERVINGS

[AYVA TATLISI]

1½ cups fresh
   pomegranate juice
   (see Glossary)
2½ cups water
½ cup sugar
2 large quinces
A few cloves
Sweet Yogurt Cream
   (page 228), clotted
   cream, or whipped
   cream

In Turkey, quinces are used abundantly in winter to make compotes, desserts, preserves, and marmalades. One variety turns a lovely shade of claret when cooked. To compensate for the diminished flavor and color I find in all too many domestic quinces, I usually cook them with a pomegranate-juice-flavored syrup. This gives them a beautiful color and intensifies the taste.

❋　❋　❋

Make the pomegranate juice several hours before you make the compote so that the residue will settle to the bottom. Take the clear part of the juice and discard the residue. This will give you about 1 cup of clear, brilliant juice. Combine with the water and sugar in a small pan.

Peel the quinces, cut them into halves, remove their cores and hard centers, and drop them into the pomegranate juice mixture in the saucepan. Add the quince seeds and cloves, cover, and cook the quinces slowly for 1½ hours, until they are very tender. Strain the syrup, discarding the quince seeds and cloves. Cool in the liquid and remove to a bowl. Boil the liquid about 20 minutes and reduce to 1 cup. Pour the syrup over the quinces and chill. When ready to serve, brush 4 serving plates with a little of the syrup, place a quince half on each plate, pour over the syrup, and serve with a dollop of sweet yogurt cream, clotted cream, or whipped cream.

Sweet Yogurt Dessert with Pomegranate Sauce

❋❋❋❋❋❋❋❋❋❋❋❋❋❋❋❋❋❋❋❋❋❋❋❋❋❋❋❋❋❋❋❋❋❋❋❋❋❋❋

4 SERVINGS

[NAR ŞURUBUYLA YOĞURT]

Sweet Yogurt Cream (see below)

POMEGRANATE SAUCE

1½ cups pomegranate juice, freshly extracted (see Glossary)
1 tablespoon sugar
1½ teaspoons arrowroot
2 tablespoons water

Pomegranate seeds for garnish

Beat the sweet yogurt cream with a wooden spoon until creamy. If you have heart-shaped or other decorative molds, use them to chill the cream overnight.

To make the sauce, bring the juice to a simmer with the sugar. Stir to dissolve sugar. Dissolve the arrowroot in the water and add to the juice; cook, stirring, 15 seconds. Remove from heat and chill.

Pool some sauce onto 4 dessert plates and unmold the cream over the sauce. Decorate with a few pomegranate seeds.

Sweet Yogurt Cream

✳✳✳✳✳✳✳✳✳✳✳✳✳✳✳✳✳✳✳✳✳✳✳✳✳✳✳✳✳✳✳✳✳✳✳✳✳✳✳

ABOUT 2½ CUPS

[TATLI YOĞURT]

2 cups Mellow Yogurt Cream (page 276)
½ cup heavy cream, whipped
Powdered sugar to taste
2 vanilla beans

With a wooden spoon beat together the yogurt cream, whipped cream, and sugar in a bowl. Scrape the seeds out of the vanilla beans and mix into the cream mixture; chill.

Apricot Fruit Rolls

✳✳✳

MAKES 2 POUNDS

[KAYISI PESTİLİ]

5 pounds ripe, sweet
    apricots
¼ cup water
Sugar or honey to taste
    (optional)
Lemon juice (about 1
    tablespoon for 2 to 3
    cups fruit puree)

Pestil means dried sheets of fruit. Any kind of fruit can be used. The fresh fruit is reduced to a paste and spread in sheets to dry in the summer, in order to be enjoyed in winter. The sheets can be folded and stored or rolled into small cylinders. Sometimes people roll them around dried nuts and enjoy them as a sort of fruit-and-nut sandwich.

✳ ✳ ✳

Place washed apricots in a heavy pan with the water and simmer gently, stirring frequently, until very soft. Pass them through a strainer placed over a bowl, pressing hard so that all the juice and pulp pass through and only the skin and pits remain in the strainer. (Alternatively, remove peels and pits and puree the fruit in a food processor.)

Sweeten (optional) and simmer the mixture gently just until all moisture evaporates and you have a thick and creamy paste. Flavor with lemon juice and pour 1/16-inch layers onto lightly greased or parchment-lined baking sheets; set them out to dry in direct sunlight for several days. When dry, detach the edges with a knife and peel them off the baking sheets. Fold or roll them in the desired sizes, wrap carefully, and store in airtight containers.

Variation: Using slightly tart purple plums, make exactly like the apricot fruit rolls.

Aşure

❋❋❋

8 SERVINGS

1 cup hulled wheat (see
  Glossary)
¼ cup chick-peas
1 cup walnuts
½ cup hazelnuts
5 dried figs
6 dried apricots
½ cup raisins
1 cup sugar
¼ cup rose water
Pomegranate seeds, 3
  sliced figs, currants,
  and pine nuts for
  decoration

[AŞURE]

Made with whole grains, legumes, dried fruits, and nuts, aşure is interesting and perhaps unique among Turkish desserts in its legendary associations. The word aşure, originally Arabic ashura, means the tenth day of the month of Muharram, the first month of the Islamic calendar. According to tradition, a number of significant events took place on this particular day: Adam met Eve; Abraham was delivered from the fire; and Jacob was reunited with Joseph. It was also on this day that the waters of the great flood subsided and Noah and his family were able to leave the Ark. Before doing so, they gathered all the foodstuffs remaining on board—wheat, beans, chick-peas, raisins, dried fruits, and nuts—and made them into a sweet soup.

In memory of that last meal taken on the Ark, a similar dessert called aşure is prepared and distributed among neighbors in Turkey on the tenth of Muharram. The overwhelming significance of this day for Muslims is that it witnessed the tragic martyrdom of Imam Husayn, grandson of the Prophet. As a result, the custom of preparing aşure and sharing with others has become in effect a commemoration of that event.

❋   ❋   ❋

In separate bowls soak the wheat, chick-peas, walnuts, and hazelnuts in cold water to cover overnight. In the morning drain the chick-peas, squeeze off the skins and discard, reserving the chick-peas.

Bring 8 cups water to a boil in a large pan. Drain the wheat, stir into the water, and simmer, covered, until the grains are tender. Set it aside in its cooking liquid.

Meanwhile, cook the chick-peas separately in water to cover until they are tender. Drain and reserve both the chick-peas and the cooking liquid.

Soak the figs in water for 10 minutes to soften them a little, then put them through a coarse sieve and reserve. Chop the apricots and reserve. Drain the walnuts and hazelnuts and rub them with fingertips to remove as much skin as possible. Chop half the walnuts and all the hazelnuts coarsely and reserve. Reserve the remaining walnuts for decoration.

Drain the cooked wheat into a bowl, measure the cooking liquid, and add enough water to make 5 cups liquid. Return the liquid to the large pan. Process half the wheat in a blender or food processor with a little of the liquid in the pan, and return the whole thing to the pan. Add the remaining wheat, cooked chick-peas, figs, apricots, raisins, walnuts, hazelnuts, and sugar and simmer for 20 minutes, stirring occasionally. The mixture should have the consistency of soup and will thicken as it stands. If it looks too thick, thin it with some of the reserved chick-pea cooking liquid. Stir in the rose water and remove from heat. Pour into dessert bowls and serve warm or chilled, decorated with walnut halves and some or all of the ingredients listed for decoration.

Pistachio *Muhallebi*

❀❀❀

4 TO 6 SERVINGS   [FISTIKLI MUHALLEBİ]

⅓ cup uncooked rice
   soaked in ⅔ cup
   water overnight
1 rounded cup unsalted
   pistachios
⅔ cup plus 2 tablespoons
   sugar
3 cups hot milk
2 cups half-and-half

Process rice and water mixture to a paste in blender. Put through a cheesecloth-lined sieve and reserve.

Grind the pistachios with 2 tablespoons of sugar almost to a powder. Add 1 cup of the milk and blend. Line a sieve with a cheesecloth folded in two layers and pour the pistachio milk into it. Bring the ends of the cloth together to form a sack and squeeze hard to extract all the pistachio milk. Pour 1 cup of hot milk over the pistachio residue and squeeze again. Repeat this once more with the remaining milk and discard the residue. Put the pistachio milk in a heavy pan with the half-and-half and the remaining sugar and bring it to a boil. Mix some of the hot mixture with the rice water in a bowl and gradually pour it all in a thin steady stream back into the pan, stirring all the time. Simmer gently for about 15 or 20 minutes, stirring almost constantly. Strain into serving bowls and chill.

Rice Pudding Perfumed with Rose Water

****

4 TO 6 SERVINGS

[GÜL SUYU KATILMIŞ SÜTLAÇ]

1¾ cups water
7 tablespoons uncooked
   short-grain rice
1 quart milk
¾ to 1 cup sugar
¼ cup rice flour
2 tablespoons rose water
Cinnamon

Bring the water to a boil in a small saucepan, stir in the rice, cover, and simmer until almost all the liquid is absorbed. Meanwhile, put the milk in a heavy pan with the sugar and let the sugar dissolve over low heat. Add the cooked rice to the milk, raise the heat to medium, and bring the mixture to a boil. Dissolve the rice flour in ¼ cup water, stir in some of the hot milk, and pour this into the simmering milk in a steady stream, stirring all the time. Gently cook the pudding over low heat for about 20 minutes, stirring constantly. Remove from heat and stir in the rose water. Serve chilled in individual bowls sprinkled with cinnamon, if desired.

Pudding Made with Breast of Chicken

****

12 SERVINGS

[KAZANDİBİ TAVUK GÖĞSÜ]

This may sound like a strange name for a dessert, but having tried it you will be obliged to confess that it is extremely delicious. Also bear in mind that something similar was known to medieval Europe under the name of Blank Mang, the distant and barely recognizable ancestor of *blancmange*. Whether this is mere coincidence or both dishes, the Turkish and the medieval European, go back to a common source, I am unable to say. Ideally you should use a freshly slaughtered chicken. Otherwise you will find it more difficult to separate the fibrous strands of the chicken breast; this is imperative for the success of the dish. Traditionally it is made with buffalo milk, but cow's milk will work just as well.

Whole breast of a
*   3-pound chicken*
8½ cups milk
1½ cups sugar
1⅓ cups rice flour

Poach the chicken breast in water until tender and drain. Cool slightly and divide into small pieces (2 inches square). Fill a bowl with cold water, rub each chicken piece between the thumb and forefinger of both hands, immerse in water, and shake vigorously. You will see that the pieces will separate into very thin threadlike fibers. Separate all of them and leave them in the bowl of water.

Put 7 cups of the milk in a heavy pan with the sugar and allow the sugar to dissolve over low heat. Put the remaining milk in a small bowl and dissolve the rice flour in it. Bring the milk in the pan to a boil and pour in the rice flour and milk mixture in a thin stream, stirring constantly.

Drain the chicken fibers, rinse them with cold water, and drain thoroughly. Squeeze dry and put them in a bowl, add a cupful of the hot pudding and beat the mixture vigorously with a wooden spoon. Then stir the whole thing into the pudding. Simmer gently for 20 minutes, stirring almost all the time. To test whether it is done, put some on a saucer and cool in the refrigerator. When you turn the saucer upside down, the pudding should adhere to it. The pudding can now be poured into serving bowls and enjoyed as it is when cooled. However, for this particular version we shall proceed as follows.

Pour the mixture into a large baking pan to a thickness of ¼ inch. Set the pan, or rather part of the pan, over a burner and carefully allow the undercrust to turn caramel in color, taking care not to burn it. While you do this stir the upper layers with a spatula without going too deep. Keep shifting the pan over the burner to allow the whole bottom to be exposed to heat and to become brown. Remove the pan from the stove and let the pudding cool. Cut the pudding into rectangles; with a spatula scrape each portion off the bottom of the pan, rolling up the piece as you go. The pudding is served in rolled-up slabs with the seam down on the plate. Serve chilled, plain or with a dollop of vanilla ice cream.

Turkish Beignets Sweetened with Vanilla Syrup

ABOUT 2 DOZEN PASTRIES

VANILLA SYRUP

3 cups sugar
1½ cups water
1 teaspoon lemon juice
2-inch piece of vanilla bean, split and scraped

⅓ cup milk
½ cup water
6 tablespoons unsalted butter, cut into small pieces
1 cup all-purpose flour mixed with 1 tablespoon each semolina and arrowroot
3 eggs
Oil for deep-frying

[TULUMBA TATLISI]

Dissolve the sugar in the water and simmer 5 minutes. Stir in the lemon juice, bring to a boil, and remove from heat. Stir in the vanilla bean and set aside to cool until ready to use.

Boil milk, water, and butter together, remove from heat as soon as it comes to a boil, and add the flour mixture all at once, stirring vigorously, until a stiff paste forms. Return to heat and cook, stirring over gentle heat, for 2 minutes.

Transfer the paste to a mixer bowl and let it cool for 8 to 10 minutes. Beat in the eggs one at a time, beating well after each addition. Do not be hasty in adding and incorporating the eggs. The paste will be very soft and sticky and will look smooth and glossy. Put the paste into a pastry bag with star-shaped nozzle and pipe 2-inch ribbons into lukewarm oil. It is very important that the oil not be hotter than lukewarm at this time for the pastry to puff properly. Do not crowd the pastries in the oil, for they will expand dramatically.

As they puff up and slowly rise to the surface (this will take about 5 minutes), increase the heat to medium and cook them until they turn rich brown on all sides. Before you add another batch of pastries, make sure to cool down the oil. It is important to cook them slowly. After rising to the surface they should take about 12 to 15 minutes to brown.

Drain them on paper towels and drop into cold syrup. Leave them in the vanilla syrup for a few minutes for a lightly sweetened dessert. The longer you leave them in syrup, the sweeter they will be. Traditionally they are left in syrup for several hours to soak up some of it. Serve them warm or cold.

Golden Fritters

✻✻✻

6 TO 8 SERVINGS [LOKMA]

SYRUP

1½ cups sugar

2 cups water

1 teaspoon lemon juice

1 teaspoon active dry
yeast

1½ cups warm water

Pinch of sugar

2 cups unbleached
all-purpose flour

1 tablespoon melted
unsalted butter

Pinch of salt

Peanut oil for deep-frying

Lokma, meaning morsel, describes perfectly these glistening, small sweet balls, hollow on the inside and crispy on the outside. They are often prepared on Kandil Geceleri (Lamp Nights) and other special occasions (see page 20) and are favored at seaside resorts, where they are fried in a vat of bubbling oil.

✻　　✻　　✻

Make the syrup by simmering the sugar and water for 5 minutes. Stir in the lemon juice, bring to a boil, and set aside.

To make the *lokma* dough, dissolve the yeast in the warm water with a pinch of sugar and leave in a warm place for 10 minutes until frothy.

Put the flour in a large bowl, make a well in the center, and put in the butter, salt, and yeast mixture. Mix into a batter and beat for 5 minutes, using a dough hook or paddle. Alternatively, work it with a slapping, beating motion of one hand. Cover and let rise for 1 to 2 hours.

Heat the oil for deep-frying (a small square of bread should brown in 30 seconds). Keep the heat at medium. Take a handful of batter, make your hand into a fist, squeezing out a teaspoonful of batter through the opening between your thumb and index finger. Sever the dough with a knife and drop the dough into the hot oil. Drop 5 or 6 *lokma* into the oil, depending on the size of the pan, but do not crowd them. As soon as you drop them, they will rise to the surface and puff up. Stir them to ensure an even browning. They should become caramel brown in 3 or 4 minutes. If they take longer or brown too quickly, adjust the heat. Drain on paper towels. Dip them briefly in the syrup. Serve warm or cold. If you like them sweeter, leave them in the syrup longer.

Yogurt and Pistachio Cake

✱✱✱

ONE 10-INCH CAKE,
8 TO 10 SERVINGS

1 cup pistachios
1 cup all-purpose flour
¾ teaspoon baking soda
¼ teaspoon baking
   powder
¼ teaspoon salt
6 eggs, separated, at
   room temperature
1 cup sugar
¾ cup yogurt
½ cup extra-virgin olive
   oil
½ teaspoon cream of
   tartar

[YOĞURTLU YEŞİL FISTIKLI KEK]

This is a pale green, delicate, and very moist cake. You must use a fine-quality extra-virgin olive oil, without any trace of rancid aftertaste.

✱　✱　✱

Preheat the oven to 300 degrees.

Toast the pistachios in the oven until crisp, about 15 minutes. Do not let them brown. Rub them between your hands to remove as much skin as possible. Grind the nuts finely.

Butter and flour a 10-inch springform pan. Raise the oven to 350 degrees. Sift flour with baking soda, baking powder, and salt.

Beat egg yolks with half of the sugar until pale and very thick. Mix in the yogurt and then the olive oil. Fold in flour and nuts.

Beat egg whites with cream of tartar to soft peaks. Add remaining sugar and beat to firm peaks. Whites should look shiny and not dry and granular. Gently fold egg whites into the batter. Pour into the pan and bake 55 minutes, or until done. Cool on a rack.

This cake is good plain, with coffee or tea. It is also very good with slices of fresh fruit.

Semolina-Pistachio Cake with Apricot Cream

❋❋❋❋❋❋❋❋❋❋❋❋❋❋❋❋❋❋❋❋❋❋❋❋❋❋❋❋❋❋❋❋❋❋❋❋❋❋❋

10 SERVINGS

[FISTIKLI REVANİ]

VANILLA SYRUP

2 cups sugar
3½ cups water
1 teaspoon lemon juice
2-inch piece of vanilla
  bean, split and
  scraped

CAKE

½ cup pistachios
¾ cup semolina
½ cup cake flour
6 eggs, at room
  temperature
1 tablespoon finely
  grated mixed orange
  and lemon peel
½ cup sugar

Pistachios
Whipped cream
  (optional)

This dessert is traditionally served with *kaymak* (see page 225). In the absence of *kaymak,* whipped cream or sweet yogurt cream flavored with apricot puree or apricot jam, sprinkled with pistachios, is also very good.

❋   ❋   ❋

Dissolve sugar in water and simmer 5 minutes. Add lemon juice; simmer 1 minute more. Stir in the vanilla bean and set aside. Keep warm.

Butter and flour a 10-inch springform pan. Preheat oven to 350 degrees.

Grind pistachios finely, combine with the semolina and flour in a bowl; mix with fingers to blend.

Beat the eggs with citrus peel and sugar until they hold a 5-second ribbon. Gently fold in dry ingredients. Pour into prepared baking pan and bake 30 or 40 minutes, until a toothpick inserted in the center comes out clean.

Cut cake into diamond-shaped pieces and put it, still in the springform, in a large baking pan and pour the warm vanilla syrup over it. Put it all into the turned-off oven and leave 15 minutes. Some syrup will leak out of the springform into the baking pan; pour this back over the cake, release the springform and remove the cake, leaving it in the baking pan to soak up all the syrup while it chills in the refrigerator for several hours.

Serve the cake plain, sprinkled with pistachios, or with whipped cream or apricot cream and a sprinkling of pistachios.

Apricot Cream

❋❋❋❋❋❋❋❋❋❋❋❋

2 cups Sweet Yogurt
  Cream (page 228), or
  whipped cream
Apricot jam or puree

To make the apricot cream, mix sweet yogurt cream or whipped cream with apricot jam or slightly sweetened puree.

Butter Cookies

[KURABİYE]

8 tablespoons (1 stick)
    unsalted butter, at
    room temperature
½ cup confectioners'
    sugar
¾ teaspoon vanilla
    extract
1 cup unbleached
    all-purpose flour
Confectioners' sugar for
    dusting cookies

These snow-white, delicate cookies are rich and tender. However, they need a lightness of hand, for if the dough is worked too much they will lose that melt-in-the-mouth quality.

❋   ❋   ❋

Preheat the oven to 300 degrees.

Cream the butter, sugar, and vanilla until light and fluffy. Add the flour by degrees, working lightly, to form a dough. Pat the dough into a 6-by-7-inch rectangle and cut into about 20 squares. Place the cookies slightly apart on a cookie sheet and bake 20 minutes.

Coat generously with confectioners' sugar while still warm and store in airtight container.

Almond Macaroons

[ACIBADEM KURABİYESİ]

These chewy macaroons with a hint of bitter almonds are part of the stock-in-trade of almost every bakery. They were always childhood favorites of mine. Even now, they belong to that select group of foods the mere thought of which instantly transports me back to my homeland. In Turkey they are not made at home, and in my yearning for them I had to obtain the recipe from a professional baker.

4 cups blanched almonds
3 cups sugar
1 tablespoon blanched
　apricot kernels, ground
　to a powder (or 2
　teaspoons almond
　extract)
2 tablespoons lemon juice
8 egg whites
About 1 dozen blanched
　almonds, halved, for
　decoration

Put 1 cup of the almonds with 2 tablespoons of the sugar in the blender and grind almost to a powder. Continue with the rest of the almonds, adding 2 tablespoons sugar for each cup of nuts. It is important that the almonds be ground very finely. Put the ground almonds in a large bowl and stir in the remaining sugar, blanched apricot kernels or almond extract, lemon juice, and egg whites and blend with a spoon. Process to a paste in a food processor.

Cook the paste in a heavy pan over very low heat, stirring all the time, for 15 to 20 minutes. Be careful not to let the almonds burn or brown. If you cannot regulate the heat to very low, put a heat diffuser under the pan or raise it on a wok ring. Pour the almond paste on a cool work surface (marble would be ideal). Cool the paste, working it with a lifting and folding motion, using a large spoon or a dough scraper. This is the time to determine whether the paste has the right consistency. If it looks and feels too thin or runny you will need to mix in a little more ground almonds. Should it be too heavy on the other hand, difficult to lift and fold, thin it with a little more egg white. To recognize these conditions usually takes a bit of experience but the proportions of the ingredients given in the recipe should yield a paste of the right consistency. The best clue to the correct consistency of the almond paste is that when cool it keeps its shape and does not spread over the surface.

Preheat the oven to 300 degrees.

Place some almond paste in a pastry bag and pipe walnut-size pieces onto a parchment-lined baking sheet, leaving ½ inch between the macaroons. Flatten slightly and place half an almond on the center of each. Bake for 20 minutes, then raise the oven temperature to 375 degrees and continue baking for an additional 15 to 20 minutes. Do not let the macaroons get brown. Place a piece of foil over them if necessary. They should be pale brown or beige, and the tops should look parched.

FLOWER AND FRUIT, COLOR AND SCENT

✦✦

An oft-reproduced picture of Sultan Mehmed Fatih, the conqueror of Istanbul and true founder of Ottoman glories,
shows him meditatively smelling a rose. This delicate pose of the
great warrior is a striking illustration of the fondness of the Turks for
scents and perfumes, a fondness that like so much else has its roots
in the great Islamic civilization to which the Ottoman Turks were
heirs. The Prophet Muhammad himself mentioned perfumes as one
of the three things of this world in which he took delight. The love
of scents goes together naturally enough with the love of color, and
these twin loves are reflected in many aspects of traditional Turkish
life.

In poetry, the beloved was praised, among other things, for her
reng -ü bû, her color and fragrance, a fixed compound expression
indicating all the desirable qualities of beauty and youth. Incense
was constantly burned in the palace, in mosques during religious
festivals, and the rich washed in musk-perfumed water. Before going
to the mosque on Fridays men lightly perfumed their beards. A
frequent scene on Turkish streets, at least until a few years ago, was
the *esansçı,* an itinerant seller of perfumes who squeezed onto the
back of his customer's hand a few potent drops of concentrated
perfume. The *esansçı* is becoming a figure of the past, but even now
part of the ritual of every bus journey is to have some eau de cologne
shaken into one's cupped hands soon after departure. An offer of eau
de cologne is also the unvarying first stage in the program of hospitality that envelops the visitor to even the humblest Turkish home.

So far as food and drink are concerned, the combination of vivid
color and scent is most apparent, perhaps, in sherbets, iced drinks
that are equally pleasing to the palate, the eye, and the sense of
smell. The English word *sherbet* is identical to the Turkish *şerbet,*
which in turn is derived from the Arabic *sharbat* (from the root

shariba, to drink), and it is to the Arabs that we must look for the origins of this summer refreshment. Sherbets were made fresh from fruit juices and flower blossoms, and—among the affluent—were perfumed with musk and ambergris. Alternatively, and especially in winter, they would be made by diluting syrups (*şurup,* again derived from the same Arabic root as sherbet) that had been prepared during the summer out of flowers and fruit juices.

This abundance of iced drinks in premodern times may appear surprising, but in fact it was precisely the Arabs who first manufactured ice on a large scale, through the simple expedient of bringing snow and ice down from the mountains in winter and then burying them deep in the ground until it became time to disinter them in summer. The Ottomans used the same technique; Evliya Çelebi tells us, for example, that ice used to be brought down from Mount Olympus (Uludağ) to the nearby city of Bursa. By organizing the ice trade on a large scale, the Ottomans were able to popularize sherbet throughout the Eastern Mediterranean.

Sherbets were served in a variety of settings and on a variety of occasions, from the most exalted to the most humble. The palace was well supplied with these fragrant icy drinks, which were served to guests in goblets made of gold, silver, or crystal. On some occasions, their presentation involved even greater artistry. Thus Sultan Mahmud II, invited to break the fast of Ramadan one evening by his Şeyhülislam (head of the religious hierarchy), Dürrizade, admired the crystal goblet in which his host served him sherbet only to discover that it was made from carefully carved ice! Sherbet flowed especially freely when marriages and births were celebrated in the palace; as a former inmate of the harem put it, sherbet then flowed "as if it were water gushing from a fountain."

A cooling drink of sherbet was particularly welcome after enduring the warm vapors of the bathhouse. Lady Mary Wortley Montagu, that sympathetic and generally acute observer of Turkish life in the eighteenth century, has left this voluptuous yet innocent picture of sherbet being drunk in the women's *hammam* (bathhouse): Describing the "majestic grace" that the women preserved despite their nakedness, she mischievously suggests that a certain Jervis, a contemporary portrait painter, would find his art "very much improved . . . to see so many fine women naked, in different postures, some in conversation, some working, others drinking coffee or sherbet, and many lying negligently on their cushions, while their slaves (generally pretty girls of seventeen or eighteen) were employed in braiding their hairs in several pretty fancies."*

One curious use to which sherbet was put was to indicate the absence from home of the master. A guest arriving for an unannounced visit could not leave immediately on finding the master of the household absent; this would have been impolite. So he would first be served coffee, in the hope that the master would soon be back. If the coffee was followed by sherbet, this was a discreet sign that the master's return was not anticipated any time soon, and the self-invited guest might as well leave.

Sherbet was sold in the streets from tall and elaborate brass containers, surmounted with little crescent-bearing turrets as if they were miniature mosques; the seller loudly proclaimed the type of sherbet he was selling, and decanted it into little glasses he carried and perfunctorily rinsed between customers. These figures have virtually disappeared from the streets, and when they are encountered they generally have little to offer but watery lemonade and sour cherry juice.

Colorful ices or sorbets of Western type, made with fruit juices and impregnated with all the flavor and taste of the fruit, are now more generally available than sherbets. Every *pastane* offers them during the heat of the summer, the open windows displaying a whole colorful range to passersby. My own favorite is Morello cherry sorbet.

Icy-cold compotes called *hoşaf* (a loanword from the Persian *khushab*) would often adorn the traditional Ottoman table together with sherbet; indeed, they are still much favored, although now designated by a loanword from Italian, *komposto*. Such compotes were made with fresh or dried fruits and perfumed with flower essences, musk, and ambergris, and served to cleanse the palate between courses.

❋   ❋   ❋

Another fine combination of scent and color was provided by such jams and flower sugars as rose or violet. Traditional Turkish jams have a taste and a fragrance both delicate and vivid. They were a food in their own right, something to be savored in small quantities,

* *Letters and Works* (New York, 1893), Volume 1, 235.

not smeared over bread. I can remember how the whole house was sweetly redolent of stewed fruit on the days when my grandmother made jam.

My mother recalls a charming custom of jam tasting that seems now to be extinct. Different jams would be put in little silver bowls and a spoonful taken from each, rinsing the spoon in a bowlful of water before moving to the next. This is a custom that evidently existed in the Balkans as well, especially Macedonia. Jam played a particular role during the fasting month of Ramadan; the weeks leading up to the month might in fact be a principal jam-making season. At the first spread laid to relieve the hunger of the fasters, numerous jams would be laid out, side-by-side with different cheeses, olives, and dried meats.

❋   ❋   ❋

Ideal in its combination of color and fragrance, the rose was the most favored flower of the Ottomans. Made a symbol of unattainable beauty in the Persian poetical tradition that so profoundly affected the Ottomans, the rose is ubiquitously depicted in fabrics and ceramics. The southwest Anatolian city of İsparta became the Turkish answer to Shiraz as a main center of rose cultivation. The petals of the rose are used for making jams, syrups, sherbets, and confections, and the uses to which rose water have been put are endless: flavoring desserts, syrups, nut fillings, and even sprinkled over meat dishes. Probably with good reason, the rose was thought to be healthy.

Other flowers—oleaster, jasmine, lily, jonquil, gardenia, clematis, violet—were also used in similar ways. A flower that had no culinary application but nonetheless served to define the cultural ethos of a whole period was the tulip. For about twelve years in the early eighteenth century, the Ottoman elite devoted itself to the cultivation of tulips and was soon imitated by the people at large. The fashion passed, but not before the tulip had become a standard motif in all the decorative arts.

To the student of Turkish history, the name Gülhane (Chamber of Roses) calls to mind the Imperial Rescript decreeing governmental reforms that was promulgated there in November 1839. But the origin of the structure, situated on the grounds of Topkapi Palace, is more fragrant and romantic, for it was devoted to the making of sherbets and preserves, not only from roses but also from gardenias, pansies, linden flowers, and chamomile, further perfumed with musk, ambergris, and aloes. Mouradjea d'Ohsson, in his valuable *Tableau général de l'Empire Ottoman,* describes the Gülhane as it was in the eighteenth century and makes an apt comparison between the care the Turks lavished on sherbet and the devotion of the French to wine making.*

SHERBETS AND SYRUPS

Rose Petal Syrup and Sherbet

ABOUT 1 QUART

[GÜL ŞURUBU VE GÜL ŞERBETİ]

1 pound rose petals from highly scented pink or red garden (not store-bought) roses
3 cups water
5 cups sugar
Juice of 1 lemon

The recipe is adapted from the nineteenth-century cookbook of Mehmed Kamil. Do take care that the roses you choose for this and other recipes have not been treated with any poisonous insecticide, and be sure to wash them thoroughly.

❋   ❋   ❋

To make the syrup, cut off the white ends of the rose petals and put them in a bowl. Boil the water, pour over the petals, cover, and allow to stand overnight. The next day, strain the liquid from the roses into a saucepan; add the sugar. Let the sugar dissolve, bring the syrup to a boil, and remove from heat. Add the lemon juice, strain the syrup and pour into clean, warm, airtight bottles.

To make sherbet, dilute some rose petal syrup with icy cold water and serve with shaved ice.

* Quoted in Alev Lytle Croutier, *Harem: The World Behind the Veil* (New York, 1989), 93.

Syrup of Violets and Violet Sherbet

❋❋

[MENEKŞE ŞURUBU VE ŞERBETİ]

Violets held a prominent place among the flowers from which beverages were produced. We learn from the historian Fuat Bayramoğlu that they were used in making not only syrups and sherbets but also wines that were praised in poetry for their curative benefits.

The following recipe for syrup is from Türabi Efendi's cookbook, published in 1862, the first Turkish cookbook to appear in English.

"Procure a pound of fresh-gathered violets, cut the stalks off, and put the leaves in a basin; pour two pints and a gill of boiling water over, immediately cover it, and let it remain for 12 to 15 hours; then pass the liquor through a clean cloth into a stewpan, add about 3 pounds of crushed sugar, stir with a wooden spoon till the sugar is dissolved, and set it on a charcoal fire. Just as it commences to boil up, instantly remove it, and let it remain covered till nearly cold; pass it again through a cloth, bottle and cork it up till wanted."

❋ ❋ ❋

To make violet sherbet, dilute some violet syrup in icy cold water and serve with shaved ice.

Almond Sherbet

ABOUT 1 1/2 QUARTS

[BADEM ŞERBETİ]

1 pound blanched almonds
1 tablespoon blanched apricot kernels
5 cups water
6 cups sugar

This recipe is adapted from the nineteenth-century Turkish cookbook by Mehmed Kamil.

❋ ❋ ❋

Grind the almonds and apricot kernels to a powder and put in a bowl with 3 cups of water to soak for several hours.

Line a sieve with a cheesecloth folded in two layers and pour the almonds with their soaking liquid into the sieve. Bring the ends of the cloth together to form a sack, and squeeze hard to extract all the almond milk. Pour 1 cup of the water over the almond residue and squeeze again. Repeat this with the remaining 1 cup water, squeeze the almonds dry and discard the residue. Put the almond milk in a heavy pan with the sugar and let the sugar dissolve over low heat, stirring frequently. Simmer to a thick syrup that will coat the back of a spoon. Strain through cheesecloth. Pour into clean warm bottles or jars and close tightly. Dilute with very cold water and serve with crushed ice.

Apricot Ice

ABOUT 1 QUART

[KAYISILI DONDURMA]

2 pounds apricots, pitted and peeled
1 cup sugar
3 to 4 tablespoons lemon juice

Simmer apricots, covered, in a noncorroding pan with 1/4 cup water until they are soft. Process in a food processor and strain. Dissolve sugar in 1 cup water over low heat, boil 5 minutes and cool. Stir syrup into apricot puree and mix thoroughly. Add lemon juice to taste, refrigerate until very cold, and freeze in an ice cream freezer.

COMPOTES

Jasmine-Perfumed Raisin Compote

•••

4 SERVINGS

[ÜZÜM HOŞAFI]

1 cup sugar or to taste
3 cups water
¼ pound raisins, washed
  and drained
1 cup jasmine blossoms
  (optional), or a few
  drops flower essence

Icy cold fruit compotes were very much part of the traditional Turkish meal. Like sherbets, they were enjoyed in their own right and also served to cleanse the palate so that the flavor of each dish might be separately enjoyed. They were perfumed with flower essences as well as musk and ambergris. They are still prepared today, especially in winter. In the absence of fresh fruits, compotes called *hoşaf* are made with dried fruits.

Here I suggest jasmine blossoms if you happen to have them in your garden, for they impart a delicate perfume to syrups and can be used in ice creams and sorbets. However, you need to make sure that your blossoms do not belong to a poisonous variety. In any event you can also add a few drops of flower essence instead of fresh blossoms.

❋   ❋   ❋

Dissolve the sugar in the water and simmer 5 minutes. Stir in the raisins and simmer just until the raisins are swollen. Remove the raisins from the syrup and set aside. Remove the syrup from heat.

If you are using jasmine blossoms, put them in a glass bowl that will fit snugly over a simmering pan of water. Pour the hot syrup over the blossoms, put the bowl over the simmering water, and let steep for 30 minutes. Strain the syrup, pressing against the flowers. Cool slightly and return the raisins to the syrup. If on the other hand you are not using flowers, stir a few drops of flower essence into the syrup. Pour the compote into serving bowls and chill thoroughly.

Quince, Apple, and Pomegranate Compote

✳✳✳

6 SERVINGS

[KARIŞIK KOMPOSTO]

3 large pomegranates
½ cup sugar
4 cups water
2 large quinces
3 cloves
1 stick cinnamon
2 large tart apples

Break the pomegranates into halves, then divide them into small sections. Remove the seeds into a bowl, working with fingertips and separating them from the skin and membrane. Reserve half of the seeds. Put the remaining ones in a noncorroding bowl, place it in the kitchen sink, and crush the seeds with one hand. Put the mixture through a sieve and let stand at least 2 hours for the sediment to settle in the bottom of the bowl. Then strain through a cheesecloth-lined sieve and chill.

Dissolve ¼ cup sugar in 2 cups water in a saucepan. Peel the quinces and quarter them, cutting each piece into 3 or 4 slices. Remove the cores and hard centers, put them in the syrup with quince seeds, cloves, and cinnamon, cover, and cook slowly until the fruit is tender. Remove the quinces from the syrup and reduce the syrup to 1 cup. Remove from heat and strain. Put the quinces in the reduced syrup in a bowl, cover, and chill.

Peel the apples, quarter them, then cut each piece into 3 or 4 slices and remove the cores. Cook them in a syrup made with 2 cups water and ¼ cup sugar until they are tender and translucent. Remove the apples from the syrup and reduce the syrup to 1 cup. Put the apples in the syrup, cover, and chill in a bowl. When you are ready to serve remove the pieces of fruit from the syrup and arrange them in serving bowls. Mix in the pomegranate seeds. Pour over the fruit a little of the apple and quince syrup and all of the pomegranate juice. Serve sprinkled with shaved ice.

Chilled Summer Fruit in
Rose Petal–Infused Syrup

❈❈

6 SERVINGS

[YAZ MEYVELERİYLE KOMPOSTO]

SYRUP

*1 cup tightly packed
highly scented pink or
red garden rose petals,
untreated with
insecticides and
washed thoroughly*

⅓ cup sugar

1 cup hot water

1 sweet melon

3 nectarines

2 cups strawberries

1 tablespoon lemon juice

Cut off the white ends from the petals and rub them in a bowl with the sugar a few minutes until they look like a paste. Put them in a small bowl that will sit snugly over a saucepan. Put some water in the saucepan and keep it at a simmer. Pour the hot water over the rose petals and steep them, covered, over the simmering water for 1 hour. Cool the rose water and chill in the refrigerator until ready to use.

Cut the melon into halves and remove the seeds. With a melon baller or a spoon, scoop out balls of melon and place them in a bowl. Cut the nectarines into ¼-inch slices and add to the melon balls. Hull and slice the strawberries and add them to the fruit. Sprinkle lemon juice over them. Strain and pour the rose syrup over the fruit, cover, and chill several hours. Serve the fruit in its syrup in serving bowls sprinkled with shaved ice.

FLOWER SUGARS AND PRESERVES

Rose Sugar

❋❋

[GÜLBE ŞEKERİ ŞEMSİYYESİ]

Old Turkish cookbooks are full of recipes for flower sugars—preserved flower essences. They are made from all sorts of highly scented flowers, in particular roses and violets, and are used to flavor drinks, to preserve the flower to use later in making jams, and also as a medicine for stomach ailments and as laxatives. Nowadays, rose sugar especially is widely used in Turkey.

Recipes for flower sugars, particularly for rose or violet sugars, are to be found in many medieval European sources. There can be no doubt that they derive from Arabic recipes, for it is no coincidence that sugar cane was first grown in Sicily and Spain, the two areas of Arab colonization in Europe.

The following nineteenth-century recipe comes from Türabi Efendi, who suggests that violets can also be used.

❋ ❋ ❋

"Procure a pound of very fresh rose leaves, cut the white ends off with a pair of scissors and throw them away, put the other parts in a basin with two and a half pounds of white sifted sugar, and work it together with the hands until the rose leaves are reduced to a pulp or paste; then fill the preserve jars or glass bowls, cover, arrange them on a tray, and put it where the sun is powerful. When near sunset, put the cover over and take them in. The next day uncover the jars, and expose the preserve to the sun as before, and continue the same for a month, or until the top of the preserve is nicely crystallized. It is a delicate confection, and may be taken at breakfast, or used with pastry."

Rose Petal Preserve

* *

ABOUT 3 1/2 CUPS   [GÜL REÇELİ]

4 ounces rose petals from
  highly scented pink or
  red garden roses,
  untreated with
  insecticides and
  washed thoroughly
4 cups sugar
15 ounces water
2 tablespoons lemon juice

Cut off the white ends from the petals and layer them in a noncorroding bowl with 1 cup sugar, ending with a sugar layer on top.
Cover the bowl and let stand 1 or 2 days.

When you are ready to make the preserve, rub the petals with
one hand until they are reduced to a paste. This will take only a few
minutes. Dissolve the remaining 3 cups sugar in the water in a
noncorroding saucepan over low heat, making sure the syrup does
not come to a boil until sugar is dissolved completely. Stir in the rose
petal mixture and boil over medium heat about 20 minutes, until it
reaches a jam consistency—214 to 217 degrees on a candy thermometer. Another way to test for correct consistency is to drop some
of it on a plate that has been chilled in the freezer. If the drops more
or less retain their shape on the plate, the preserve is ready. When
it reaches the desired consistency and temperature, stir in the lemon
juice, bring to a boil, and remove from heat. Skim the top and pour
the preserve into perfectly clean, warm jars and seal. Keep in a cool
and preferably dark place.

Sun-Cooked Apricot Jam

* *

ABOUT 4 16-OUNCE
JARS   [GÜNEŞTE KAYISI REÇELİ]

Turkish housewives often take advantage of the sun's rays to finish
cooking their jams and marmalades. It is pleasant to see colorful
bowls of jam lined up in rows on the edge of balconies and in
backyards. My friend Türkan Ersin tells me that jams matured by
being left in the sun keep longer and never crystallize, a frequent
hazard of jam making.

❋   ❋   ❋

2 pounds firm apricots
(weight after pitting)
2 pounds sugar
15 ounces water
Juice of 1 lemon

Wash and drain apricots and remove pits, leaving fruit whole.

Dissolve sugar in the water in a noncorroding saucepan over low heat, making sure syrup does not come to a boil until sugar is dissolved completely. Raise heat to medium and boil syrup about 15 minutes to thicken slightly. This will be about 214 to 217 degrees on a candy thermometer. Add apricots and simmer about 4 minutes. Remove from heat and let stand several hours or overnight.

With a slotted spoon remove apricots to a bowl; simmer the syrup, which is thinned with the juices from the apricots, for about 10 minutes, until it thickens. Return apricots to the syrup and simmer 2 minutes. Stir in lemon juice and cook 1 or 2 minutes longer; remove from heat.

Put jam in a large shallow noncorroding container, drape with cheesecloth, and set out in direct sunlight until it has thickened to the desired consistency. Under the hot Mediterranean or Aegean sun the jam is ready in only a week or so. Store in clean airtight jars.

Sun-Cooked Purple Plum Marmalade

✹✹

[ERIK MARMELATI]

Plums
Sugar
Lemon juice

Apricots, peaches, and tart apples can all be prepared this way.

✹ ✹ ✹

Wash plums and put in noncorroding pan with just enough water to prevent the fruit from burning. Cook 5 or 10 minutes until the fruit is soft; put through a colander set over a bowl. Press against the fruit until only the pits and skins remain in the colander. Measure fruit pulp and for each cup add 1 cup of sugar. Put fruit and sugar back into pan and simmer 5 minutes. Stir in lemon juice (about 1 tablespoon for each pound of fruit), simmer 2 minutes longer and remove from heat. Pour into a large shallow noncorroding container and cover with cheesecloth. Set out in the sun for several days, stirring every day, until the marmalade thickens to the desired consistency. Store in clean and airtight jars.

Türkan's Quince Preserve

✱✱

ABOUT 7 OR 8
16-OUNCE JARS

[AYVA REÇELİ]

4 pounds quinces
4 pounds sugar
4 tablespoons lemon juice

One does not come across quince preserve in the West, but it is much liked and frequently made throughout the Balkans and Middle East, where quinces with delicate fragrance and flavor are found in abundance. This recipe was given to me by my dear college friend Türkan Ersin, who explained that through slow simmering in a covered pan the preserve attains its splendid deep rose color.

✱　　✱　　✱

Peel quinces and remove cores, grate coarsely. Tie seeds in a muslin bag. Put quinces in a noncorroding pan with water just to cover and simmer 15 to 20 minutes. Stir in sugar and let it dissolve over low heat. Put the muslin bag in the pan, cover, and simmer very gently over very low heat about 1 hour or longer, until it reaches the desired jam consistency. Stir in lemon juice and boil 1 minute longer; remove from heat. Store in clean warm jars; cover when cool.

COFFEE AND OTHER BEVERAGES

✳✳✳✳✳✳✳✳✳✳✳✳✳✳✳✳✳✳✳✳✳✳✳✳✳✳✳✳✳✳✳✳✳✳✳✳✳

****

Two ferocious-looking fellows most politely made room for me on the straw-covered divan; and the coffee which I obtained there was certainly better than the black decoction of the best cafés of Paris.
—Théophile Gautier, *Constantinople,* 1875

Gönül ne kahve ister, ne kahvehane;
Gönül sohbet ister, kahve bahane!
One's heart wants truly neither coffee, nor the coffeehouse;
One's heart desires company, coffee's the pretext!

T his line of verse, which has attained almost proverbial status, summarizes neatly the importance of coffee drinking as a mainstay of social life. The Turkish affection for coffee is in fact reflected in numerous poems and proverbs that show how fully this beverage penetrated both literary culture and everyday life. One proverb states, for example, that "a sip of coffee is to be remembered with thanks for forty years!" This apparent hyperbole shows concisely how coffee may serve as a means for the exchange of modest hospitality and lasting gratitude, and thus contribute—however humbly—to the network of social relationships we need to sustain us. How comforting and reassuring is the attitude expressed in this proverb, and how sadly lacking in our contemporary life!

Coffee has always had a special association with the Turks; when the first coffeehouses were opened in London, they proclaimed their presence with signboards depicting a Turk in his turban. The story of the origin and spread of coffee is fairly well known. Originating in the mountains of Ethiopia, the coffee bean was carried by dervishes, who found coffee drinking effective in warding off sleep, to the Yemen, soon to become a province—albeit an unruly one—of the

259

Ottoman Empire. It then spread northward, meeting with instant acclaim on its arrival in Istanbul early in the sixteenth century. Within a few decades, the city was full of coffeehouses. Both the substance and the institution to which it gave rise were new, and aroused the suspicions of both the religious and the civil authorities. It was clear that coffee altered the mental state of the drinker, and the coffeehouse might easily become a center for frivolous amusement or, worse still, for seditious intrigue. The enemies of coffee therefore issued a decree prohibiting it as religiously forbidden, on the basis of a dubious analogy with wine, and more than once the coffeehouses were closed down or even destroyed. But the triumph of coffee could not be prevented, and it became so ubiquitous that a Venetian visitor to Istanbul in 1615 remarked with amazement, "It rarely happens that Turks should meet, whatever the occasion, without their drinking coffee together."

Coffee was now freed from its dubious association, in certain minds, with intoxicants and stimulants, and even benefits were ascribed to it. Thus the great polymath Katib Çelebi recommended the drinking of "a great deal of strong coffee" to "those of moist temperature, and especially women," the inherent "dryness" of coffee serving to offset their "moisture."

Soon after its conquest of the Ottoman Empire, coffee moved on to further victories in Europe. It made its first appearance in France in the second decade of the seventeenth century, but did not become triumphantly fashionable until 1669 when an Ottoman envoy, Süleyman Mustafa Ağa, delighted his numerous guests by serving them coffee. His diplomatic mission was not particularly successful, but it put coffee firmly on the map. After his departure, coffee was successfully marketed by itinerant sellers dressed in pseudo-Turkish garb as a mark of their profession. It was also Turks who brought coffee to Vienna, under somewhat different circumstances. It is said that when the Turks unsuccessfully besieged Vienna in 1683 they left behind on the battlefield several sacks of coffee they had brought with them as part of their supplies. A Pole named Franz Kolschitsky who had once served as an interpreter in the Ottoman army recognized the strange beans for what they were and introduced the Viennese to the delights of coffee drinking.

But the serving and consumption of coffee never acquired in Europe the quasiritual aspect it has retained in Turkey down to the present, at however reduced a level. Not surprisingly, this dimension of coffee was most fully developed at the Ottoman court, despite the misgivings coffee had inspired in some sultans. The preparation and serving of coffee to the sultan in his private quarters was the prerogative of a skilled female coffee maker (*kahveci usta*), assisted by no fewer than forty underlings, all with distinctive uniforms; on festive occasions they would parade on the grounds of the harem, in perfect formation. If the sultan was of musical disposition, he would often take his coffee while listening to music—a complete sybaritic experience!

The exact manner in which coffee was served was common both to the palace and to many aristocratic households. Emine Foat Togay has left a vivid description of after-dinner coffee in such a household at the turn of the century:

> Two maids, one on either side, each held a handle of the oval coffee tray and also with it one corner of a round piece of crimson velvet, richly embroidered and fringed with golden thread, which, being folded in the middle and held so as to cling firmly under the tray, depended from its edges, the gold-fringed crimson thus showing off to perfection the noble polished silver of the tray itself. Tiny handle-less porcelain cups stood on the tray, each in front of its enamelled stand, these being shaped like egg-cups and studded with pearls and diamonds. A third maid carried, suspended from chains, a silver brazier heaped with burning charcoal, and embedded in the centre of this stood the coffeepot. A fourth maid then poured out the coffee, while two others placed the full cups on the stands, and handed them round on smaller trays.*

Elaborate ceremonies involving priceless artifacts were beyond the reach of all but the most affluent, but many well-to-do households had coffee makers whose sole function was to see to the selection, roasting, grinding, and making of the coffee. The place of coffee in the running of the household was underlined by the fact that it was not prepared in the kitchen but in a pantry immediately adjacent to the reception rooms of the house. This permitted coffee to be served swiftly and on demand.

Traditional Turkish homes were divided into separate zones, the

* *Three Centuries: Family Chronicles of Turkey and Egypt* (London, 1963), 267.

selamlık, where the master of the house received his guests, and the *harem,* where the womenfolk lived and received their guests. The consumption of coffee appears to have been particularly high in the harem as an accompaniment to the large quantities of confectionery that were eaten. The coffee was delivered to the harem from the coffee-making pantry in a "turning cupboard" (*dönme dolap*), a device set in the wall that permitted items to be transferred from one side to the other without either party catching a glimpse of the other. These devices were also a means of subtle romantic communication and intrigue; an alluring voice on the other side of the wall could always excite the imagination.

Though part of the daily routine of many households, coffee had a greater impact on Turkish life through the institution to which it gave rise, the coffeehouse. Coffeehouses came into existence with the appearance of coffee. The first coffeehouses were opened in Istanbul in 1555 by two Syrians, and they were an instant success as places where time might be pleasantly idled away in games such as chess or in leisurely conversation. Despite attempts to check their growth, coffeehouses spread rapidly and were found everywhere. Particularly favored were those spectacular vantage points from which panoramic views of the city, the Golden Horn and the Bosphorus, were to be had. In many coffeehouses entertainment was provided: singers and musicians would perform, and popular stories and legends would be narrated.

The coffeehouse even became an adjunct to prayer. Next to many a mosque stood a coffeehouse where people would sit waiting for the call to prayer or to while away the time between sunset and evening prayers in conversation with other members of the congregation. In numerous villages and towns of Anatolia, the mosque and the adjacent coffeehouse became, in fact, the two dominant social institutions.

The place of coffee as the beverage of choice has now been usurped by tea, in large part because of the steeply rising cost of coffee, which unlike tea cannot be grown domestically. In one particularly austerity-stricken period a few years ago, the import of coffee was even banned to save precious hard currency. Nonetheless, the value of coffee as a gesture of hospitality remains. A cup of coffee may still be offered, for example, to the mailman or to the porter who has delivered some heavy appliance, and in general it is regarded as more effective than tea in dispelling weariness. How pleasant it is to arrive on a visit and be immediately offered *yorgunluk kahvesi*—a coffee to revive the tired!

Turkish Coffee

✸✸✸

2 SERVINGS

[TÜRK KAHVESI]

¾ cup cold water
1½ teaspoons sugar (for medium-sweet coffee)
3 tablespoons freshly ground, medium roast, pulverized coffee

A perfect cup of Turkish coffee is prepared caringly with freshly ground coffee. It is covered with a thick layer of rich brown foam, it is hot, fragrant, and sweetened according to taste. Most important, it is offered with grace and a gesture of respect for the guest who is (in the Turkish belief) sent to us by God. To make this coffee, a special Turkish coffeepot, a *cezve*, is used. Of enameled metal, the *cezve* has a long handle and a lip for pouring.

✸   ✸   ✸

Combine all ingredients in the *cezve* and mix with a spoon. Put it on very low heat and do not stir. Watch carefully, about 3 or 4 minutes, until a thick foam rises at least 1 inch above the original level. Remove the *cezve* from the flame immediately, just before it begins to boil and overflow. Carefully divide the foam into 2 demitasse cups, taking care not to disperse it. Put the *cezve* back on the flame only for a few seconds and pour the coffee, again carefully and slowly, with a steady hand down the sides of the cups, taking care not to disturb or disperse the foam. Serve immediately.

TEA

Despite the Turkish role in assuring the universal spread of coffee, today it is tea, served in an unbroken succession of small glasses, that lubricates the activities of the day. Tea is drunk for breakfast; served in offices or other places of business; taken at home in the afternoons, accompanied by a pastry or other appropriate morsel; and served as conclusion to dinner, the fullest meal of the day. Tea is also consumed in leisurely fashion at the countless thousands of teahouses found throughout the country, those very stores that were formerly coffeehouses.

Much the same might be said about the ubiquity of tea among the Russians and Persians, and the three nationalities used to have in common the use of the samovar to make tea. Today, samovar use has somewhat declined in Turkey (as well as Iran), but a similar method of preparing tea has been improvised through the use of a kettle with a mouth wide enough to hold a teapot. The aim is to make a strong infusion in the teapot while keeping it constantly warm over boiling water and then to dilute this infusion with hot water in a cup.

Fill the kettle with fresh cold water, bring it to a full boil but do not let it boil too long. Rinse a 2-cup teapot with hot water. Put in 2 or 3 tablespoons of loose tea and pour in 2 cups of boiling water. Put the teapot on top of the kettle (if the kettle has a large opening on top) or keep the teapot very warm without letting the tea boil. Put a folded towel over the teapot and let the tea brew 5 or 6 minutes. Strain some tea infusion into each glass or cup and then fill with hot water. Most people sweeten their tea with sugar and some like it with lemon slices.

BOZA

❧

•••

*B*oza is a fermented drink made in Turkey from millet and occasionally from other grains. It originated among the Turkic-speaking peoples of southern Russia and its Tatar origins were never forgotten. In a late nineteenth-century lithograph where various stimulants and intoxicants are personified and dispute with each other their respective virtues, *boza* is depicted as a pale-faced Tatar, just as coffee is a sunburned Yemeni (these colors corresponding to those of the two drinks).

Sarı Saltuq, the saint who preached Islam in the Crimea and along the Danube, is said to have concocted this drink. Despite these saintly associations, *boza* is often described by European travelers as alcoholic; the Frenchman Tavernier, who encountered *boza* among the Circassians in the seventeenth century, claimed it was fully as intoxicating as wine. Nonetheless, properly brewed and drunk on time, *boza* need not be intoxicating, and it is regarded as religiously licit by the Hanefi school of Islamic law, which has always prevailed among the Turks. Beneficial effects are ascribed to it; according to the great Evliya Çelebi, who himself found *boza* as refreshing and delicious as rose-water sherbet, pregnant mothers ought to drink it to produce healthy offspring, and nursing mothers to have abundant milk.

Primarily a winter drink, capable of fortifying the body against cold winds, *boza* used to be sold—like so many other drinks and foodstuffs—by itinerant vendors, recognizable by their distinctive dresses and cries. It is now sold only at a few specialized shops in the major cities, the most important being the Vefa *boza* shop in the district of Istanbul bearing the same name. There it is still possible to step back in time to late nineteenth-century Istanbul and enjoy a leisurely drink of *boza,* surmounted with dried chick-peas and cinnamon, in a stately and ornate room full of gilt-framed mirrors and marble.

KIMIZ AND AYRAN

Drinks made from milk products have long been a part of Turkish cuisine, going back to the days when Turks were primarily nomads and herdsmen. One ancient drink, *kimiz* (*kumys* is perhaps a more familiar form of this word), forms an almost legendary part of the lore concerning Central Asia. This is fermented mare's milk, brewed with the birth of the first foal in the spring, and its drinking—which results in mild inebriation—is a happy rite marking the end of the severe winter that ravages the region. The Russians have not failed to note the apparent benefits of *kimiz,* for they prescribe drinking it in sanatoria and commercially produce a modified version of it from skimmed cow's milk.

Most readers of this book will not have a herd of horses at their disposal, so I refrain from providing a recipe for *kimiz.* Another drink, however, is just as delicious and is accessible to us all. This is *ayran,* made from diluted yogurt. It is also an ancient drink and of Central Asian origin, but unlike *kimiz* it is still universally popular among Turks. It is served in restaurants, especially kebab shops, to accompany meals; hawked on city streets to refresh one in the struggle through the noise and bustle of a hot summer day; and nowadays sold in bottles at grocery stores. The status of *ayran* as a simple, unpretentious, and indispensable drink is reflected in this charming proverb, which mocks the ambition of those who seek to live beyond their means: "There's no *ayran* in his house, yet he wants a bridge made of silver to walk over!"

Yogurt Cooler

✿✿✿✿✿✿✿✿✿✿✿✿✿✿✿✿✿✿✿✿✿✿✿✿✿✿✿✿✿✿✿✿✿✿✿✿✿✿✿

2 SERVINGS

[AYRAN]

2 cups yogurt
1 to 1½ cups water
   (depending on
   consistency desired)
½ cup heavy cream
   (optional—it makes
   the drink creamier
   and frothier)
Salt
Crushed ice

This miraculously refreshing yogurt drink that is the best cure for thirst on the stifling hot days of summer.

✿   ✿   ✿

Blend all ingredients except the ice in a food processor or blender until frothy. Serve in tall chilled glasses with crushed ice.

SOME TURKISH INGREDIENTS

* *

YOGURT

* * *

The contemporary achievement-oriented urbanite, eager to increase his sources of world-conquering stamina, might be interested to know that the Turkish and Mongol horsemen who subdued most of Asia in the thirteenth century subsisted largely on yogurt. Even for those whose ambitions are not quite so vast, yogurt has much to recommend it. Although its popularity in Europe and America is fairly recent, yogurt is an ancient food and probably the sole major contribution of the nomadic peoples to the gastronomic resources of the world.

It is difficult to assign a time and place of origin to yogurt, for it may well have arisen in different areas and locations. But two factors must have been involved: a hot climate, to cause the first, unintended curdling of the milk; and a nomadic, pastoral way of life in which men depended entirely on their livestock for sustenance and had little or no access to vegetables or grains. The ancient Near East certainly knew yogurt; the Bible alludes to it (Job 10:10), and both the Egyptians and the Hebrews made use of it. It is probable, however, that yogurt originated with the Scythians, a nomadic people of Central Asia, and was conveyed by them to ancient Iran, whence it spread to the rest of the Near East (as well as to India). Yogurt was appreciated by the Greeks, and Galen praised its curative as well as nutritional benefits. Of all the peoples bordering on Central Asia, only the Chinese, with their tendency toward culinary chauvinism, resisted the appeal of yogurt, indeed of milk products in general.

The Huns, the first of the Asian nomadic peoples to enter Europe, consumed a kind of yogurt called *lo,* but they bequeathed virtually nothing of their rather modest culture to Europe. In the seventh century the Bulgars—originally a Turkic people until their environment slavicized them—knew yogurt. But of all the Central Asian peoples, it was certainly the Turks who did the most to popularize yogurt and incorporate it in sophisticated cuisine. The very word *yogurt* is often said to be of Turkish origin, coming from an ancient Turkish root meaning "to thicken." When Turks arrived first in Anatolia and then in the Balkans, yogurt was a staple part of their diet. The Ottoman Turks always had yogurt and yogurt-based dishes on the menu at the palace and Istanbul had no fewer than five hundred yogurt shops in the middle of the seventeenth century, all subject to a careful quality control by the market authorities. It was from Istanbul that the first recorded transmission of yogurt to post-medieval Europe took place: François I of France was cured of intestinal disease by a diet of yogurt prescribed by a courtier who had spent some time in Turkey.

The modern popularity of yogurt in the West is quite recent and connected with the medicinal properties attributed to it. In 1913, Ilya Metchnikoff, head of the Pasteur Institute in Paris, noted the curious fact that Bulgars, one of the least developed peoples in Europe, had in the early years of the twentieth century a remarkably long life expectancy. This he attributed in part to their regular consumption of yogurt. Numerous medical traditions, both formal and folk, had long discerned all kinds of properties in yogurt: it was thought to ward off sleeplessness, nervousness, impotence, allergies, ulcers, and arthritis; to act as an intestinal detoxicant; and to be a remedy for sunburn when applied to the skin. Current research suggests that yogurt may indeed have certain therapeutic benefits. In particular, yogurt is helpful to infants, the aged, the convalescent, people with sensitive stomachs who for various reasons cannot tolerate the lactose in milk. The bacteria in yogurt break down and reduce the lactose, thus making yogurt more digestible than milk. For this reason, yogurt is the first food given after mother's milk in certain countries, including Turkey. There, yogurt forms part of the daily diet of almost all hospital patients. Professor John Bruhn of the Department of Food Technology at the University of California at Davis tells me that a number of research centers across the country are now investigating why and how yogurt should benefit some people in this way, in the hope that the beneficial effects of yogurt may be extended to everyone.

There is, in any event, a consensus that yogurt is a nutritive, gentle, and relatively low-calorie food, as well as being a source of energy. If we truly aspire to longevity, we should perhaps begin looking to the centenarian yogurt eaters of Turkey, the Balkans, and the Caucasus!

To tell the truth, however, I regard yogurt mostly as a delicious food eaten by itself and as a versatile cooking ingredient to be used in a wide variety of dishes, not as an aid to dieting or the pursuit of longevity we may or may not deserve.

❋ HOW TO MAKE YOGURT

Yogurt is milk fermented and coagulated by benign bacteria. To make your own all you need is milk and yogurt culture or starter. The milk can be almost any kind available: sheep's milk, cow's milk, or goat's milk. If you use raw milk, however, it must be pasteurized by heating to 145 degrees and holding it at this temperature for at least 30 minutes. Milk and then the yogurt can vary in richness from nonfat to half-and-half. Whatever milk you use, make sure it is fresh.

You need yogurt to make yogurt. Use 2 tablespoons yogurt for 1 quart of milk. The yogurt can be homemade or storebought. Read the expiration date on the carton of storebought to be sure you are using very fresh yogurt. The longer yogurt stands, the sourer it gets. Sweet yogurt produces sweet yogurt, and sour yogurt produces sour yogurt.

Yogurt bacteria need heat to germinate and thicken the milk; 105 to 115 degrees is the temperature range for that process. The milk must first be heated to 180 to 195 degrees and then cooled to 105 to 115 degrees. (By the way, if you hold the milk at 180 to 195 degrees—in a double boiler, to prevent it from scorching—for a period of 5 to 20 minutes, the yogurt will be firmer and more intense in flavor. The longer you hold it at this temperature the firmer the yogurt becomes. This procedure, however, is optional.)

Once the milk has cooled to 105 to 115 degrees, mix the starter—which should be at room temperature—with 2 to 3 tablespoons of the warm milk and then stir it back into the rest of the milk quickly. As soon as the starter has been introduced into the milk, it should be maintained at this temperature constantly throughout the incubation period; the yogurt bacteria are very sensitive to changing heat.

The temperature of the environment in which the bacteria incubate affects the taste and texture of the yogurt as well as the time needed for it to set. All these things are interrelated.

If the temperature of the milk is maintained at 110 degrees

during the incubation period, it will set within 4 to 5 hours and the yogurt will be pleasantly sweet. However, yogurt incubating in the folds of blankets in a cold room (in which case the temperature of the milk will fall) will take 8 to 14 hours to set.

Once we understand the importance of maintaining the milk at a temperature of 105 to 110 degrees during the incubation period, the next question is how to do so. One sure way is to cover the bowl and place it immediately in a pan of water at 110 degrees before the temperature drops. Keep the water temperature constant by placing the pan on a warm spot over a gas stove or in an oven with the pilot light burning. Then monitor the temperature of the water with a thermometer. If you do not have a gas stove be inventive!

Traditionally the milk is kept warm within the folds of warm woolen blankets, put somewhere warm—perhaps next to a radiator—and draft free. Every yogurt maker eventually finds his or her ideal place for yogurt making. But to begin with I strongly recommend maintaining a constant warmth in a pan of warm water as described above.

It is also important not to overincubate yogurt. Kept warm long after it has set it will get more sour with every passing hour. If you like sweet, mellow yogurt, you must check it after 4 to 5 hours. If you wish to have sour yogurt, leave it for as long as 24 hours. If you are making it in the folds of blankets, for example in a cold room, check after 8 hours. If it has not yet set, cover it again and check after 1 hour.

Whichever way you choose to make yogurt, once the starter has been introduced into the milk, do not disturb it, shake it, or move it from one place to another. Do not use it right after it has set. Let it stand in the refrigerator for a few hours to thicken further.

When you make yogurt at home, using your homemade yogurt as starter each time, the bacteria may lose some of the organisms after a while; your yogurt may taste different and the texture may change. If this happens, you must use fresh starter: buy some yogurt and start over.

Finally, I recommend that you experiment, making certain changes each time you make yogurt. You may heat the milk to varying temperatures within the range of 180 to 195 degrees. You may hold it there for just a few minutes or as long as 20 minutes. You may cool it down to 105 to 110 degrees. Sometimes you may keep it warm for 4 to 5 hours, at other times much longer. Try these variations and you will ultimately discover the kind of yogurt you like best.

Yogurt Cream

❊❊❊

MAKES 2 CUPS

[TORBA YOĞURDU]

2 quarts yogurt

Yogurt drained of its moisture becomes very thick and creamy. Every true yogurt devotee will find it a worthwhile discovery.

A white, pillowcaselike sack, gathered together at the top with string and hung over the sink to drain the yogurt, is a familiar sight in Turkish homes. Yogurt cream made this way is called literally "sack yogurt." Allowed to drain for a day or two at room temperature, the yogurt becomes creamy in texture and pleasantly sharp and tangy in flavor and can be used in many imaginative ways. Made from goat's milk yogurt, it produces a particularly delicious and tangy, soft cheeselike substance. At home, yogurt cream is mostly used to make yogurt soups and, flavored with garlic, to make sharp sauces. It's also eaten as a spread on bread. *Ayran,* a yogurt drink (see page 267), is particularly good made with yogurt cream instead of regular yogurt.

❊   ❊   ❊

Line a colander with 3 layers of cheesecloth. Pour the yogurt into the lined colander. Bring the ends of the cloth together to form a sack, twist the ends, and tie with a string. Hang this sack over the sink and let the yogurt drain 1 or 2 days. Remember, the longer it drains, the sharper or tangier it will become. Remove the yogurt from the sack and store in a covered container in the refrigerator. It keeps for days.

Mellow Yogurt Cream

❋❋❋❋❋❋❋❋❋❋❋❋

Throughout my years of experimenting with yogurt, I came to realize that if you drain a sweet-tasting yogurt in the refrigerator for 8 hours or longer the resulting yogurt cream is a mellow, rich-tasting and creamy substance. When sweetened it makes a perfect and healthy replacement for thick cream or sweetened cream cheese. And once drained, yogurt stays fresh much longer.

To make mellow yogurt cream, pour the yogurt into a cloth-lined colander. Place all over a bowl to catch the liquid and refrigerate for 8 hours or overnight. Remove the yogurt from the colander and store in a covered container in the refrigerator.

BUTTER

* *

There is a distinct separation in Turkish cuisine between dishes cooked with meat and butter and served hot, and meatless ones cooked with olive oil and served cold or at room temperature. When cooking with butter, except for pilafs, the distinct flavor of clarified butter is preferred. Turks consider it a sacrilege to use anything but fresh butter of the best quality for pilafs. Clarified butter, yellow and subtly nutty in flavor, is commercially available in bulk. Certain provinces, such as Urfa, are renowned for high-quality clarified butter. I remember hearing solemn announcements in my grandmother's house that the pantry supply of butter from Urfa was running low and should be reordered promptly to avoid the awful fate of running out. The pantry replenishing usually took place in the spring and with the expectation that its stock would last at least until the next spring. But some years one would miscalculate or have more houseguests than anticipated. And there was one time each year when it would be disastrous to run out of things: Ramadan.

Of course that was a different era. The bad news about cholesterol and saturated fats has reached Turkey, and desperate attempts are being made to replace butter with oils or at least use half of each—except for pilafs.

My recipes call for unsalted butter, which is fresher than salted, and I like its flavor. You can try using oil in most of the recipes. Even some pilafs, such as those made with bulgur, will be quite good with oil.

EGGPLANT, PEPPERS, AND TOMATOES

E very traveler to Turkey is struck by the almost arrogant profusion of fruits and vegetables that greets him wherever he turns. You may well have heard of the legendary figs and sultana grapes of Smyrna (Izmir), the apricots of Anatolia, the peaches of Bursa, the cherries and hazelnuts of Cerasus (Giresun), the pistachios of Gaziantep, etc. But if you have actually visited Turkey and tasted its fruits and vegetables you will know that what we have in North America pales in comparison.

I sometimes wonder what it is that makes the difference: the seed, the soil, or the climate. No doubt all these factors play a role, but many people are of the opinion that methods of cultivation aimed at mass production and high profit are at fault. This is not the place for lamenting or attempting to solve the problem. Let me tell you instead of the ways I have discovered over the years to substitute for some of the flavors missing here, sometimes by replacing unavailable ingredients with those that are available and sometimes by using certain flavor-enhancing techniques.

Eggplant

If I were a poet, I would compose a panegyric in honor of the eggplant! A hallmark of Turkish cuisine is its wide and consistent use of eggplant, an extraordinarily versatile ingredient that can be cooked in many different ways and combined with many different flavors. When roasted and incorporated into a cream sauce, as in the case of Smoked Eggplant Cream for example (page 96), eggplant has a mild, creamy, almost subdued taste that introduces itself gradually to the palate, while in another dish, Fried Eggplant with Fresh Tomato-Garlic Vinegar Sauce (page 53), the eggplant fuses with the flavors of olive oil, garlic, tomatoes, and vinegar to invade the palate with a sudden rush of vigorous taste.

The cooking method also changes the character of the eggplant. Roasted over a fire, it acquires a unique smoky taste that no other vegetable cooked the same way could acquire. Fried in olive oil, it gains an earthy flavor and a creamy texture. It can be chopped, sliced, pounded, braised, cooked whole, stuffed, pickled, or even turned into a jam.

At the risk of disappointing the reader, however, I am obliged to declare that it is difficult to match the exact taste of the eggplant found in Turkey, where its flesh has greater density and it is creamy and full of flavor. It has a slightly elongated shape, similar to the Italian eggplant, and is generally 2 to 2½ inches wide and 8 to 9 inches long, dark velvety purple in color. With a little care in selection and preparation, you can still create wonderfully authentic dishes with the type of eggplant available to you.

Keep in mind that eggplant must be cooked thoroughly until it is meltingly soft and tender, whether it is fried, roasted, or braised. Occasionally I encounter in restaurants a piece of eggplant that is half cooked and therefore rubbery, hard, and tasteless. With eggplant, chefs must put aside the principle of cooking *al dente*.

Roasting and frying are the most suitable methods for cooking eggplant. Even when braised or stewed with other ingredients, frying lightly beforehand improves its taste considerably. Sprinkling with salt or soaking in salted water for a while and then rinsing and drying to rid it of all the moisture before frying greatly reduces the amount of oil the eggplant will absorb.

Turks peel eggplant in a striped fashion. I am not aware of any reason for this except to make it look attractive. Peel the eggplant lengthwise, removing a ½-inch strip and leaving on the next ½-inch strip. A vegetable peeler is ideal, as it removes a strip exactly the right width.

To fry eggplant slices, regardless of their ultimate use, simply sprinkle with salt and let stand for at least 30 minutes (they will become discolored), or let them stand in salted water (at least 3 tablespoons salt to 6 cups of water) for the same amount of time, covering with a heavy object to keep them submerged. Rinse thoroughly and squeeze dry to remove as much moisture as possible before frying. This procedure is particularly important for large eggplants, which absorb more oil than small ones. In Turkey we do not always salt whole eggplants before frying because whole ones do not absorb as much oil as sliced ones.

To roast a whole eggplant on an open fire or a gas fire, simply put it directly on the grill or burner. As one side gets all charred and black, turn on the other side until the whole eggplant becomes black and charred and the flesh is thoroughly soft when pierced with a skewer close to the stem, where it is hardest. Let it cool enough to be handled and peel the black skin with wet hands, removing all the particles.

Open the eggplant and carefully scrape off as many of the seeds as you can. If there are tough or hardened parts of eggplant covered with black seeds, remove these sections, for otherwise they will ruin the taste and texture of the dish for which you are using the eggplant.

Turks pay attention to keeping the roasted eggplant pale and take care to prevent discoloration, especially for dishes such as smoked eggplant cream and some eggplant salads. We put the peeled, roasted eggplant immediately in water to which some lemon juice has been added, and leave it for 20 minutes or until we are ready to use it. Then it is squeezed dry and used as desired. This prevents discoloration and further bleaches the eggplant, making it very pale.

Peppers and Chilies

A wide variety of capsicums are cultivated in Turkey. Particularly in the southeastern provinces, a large number of different peppers and chilies, varying in shape and color, play an important role in the spicy and hot cuisine. In addition, throughout Turkey quaint shops sell all sorts of spices, seeds, and barks, both familiar and unfamiliar. In burlap sacks they display dried powdered red peppers ranging in color from orange-red to caramel red and in hotness from sweet to fiery hot.

Classic Turkish cuisine that evolved from the royal kitchens in Istanbul, and may sometimes be called Istanbul cuisine in the provinces, is never thought of as hot or spicy, even though it has made use of various spices such as cinnamon, allspice, cloves, cumin, black pepper, and sweet and semisweet red peppers. Occasionally a small dose of hot peppers has been used in dishes such as Circassian Chicken (page 50). As for the fresh peppers and chilies, sweet peppers have been used both as vegetables and flavor enhancers and semihot ones sparingly as flavor enhancers.

TENDER LONG GREEN PEPPERS.

These are slightly curvy pale green peppers, about 6 to 7 inches long, varying in flavor from sweet to hot. All are used abundantly for the lovely flavor they impart, raw with meals, as salads and pickles, and as garnish on most summer meat and vegetable dishes. Unfortunately they are unavailable in North America. Substitute green and red bell peppers, Hungarian peppers, Mexican poblanos, and sometimes jalapeños as directed by individual recipes.

POBLANOS.

These are sometimes mistakenly called *chile ancho* or *pasilla*. *Chile ancho* is in fact a ripened and dried poblano, and *pasilla* is another type of dried chili. The poblano varies in shape and size. Shiny black-green in color, it is usually triangular in shape, about 5 inches long and 2 to 3 inches wide. Its flavor varies from mild to hot. Roasted poblanos give an earthy and pleasant flavor to dishes, and they can also be served on grilled meats or made into salads. They must always be roasted until the skin is black and charred, and then peeled.

JALAPEÑOS.

These small dark green or bright red fresh chilies vary in hotness; use carefully to suit personal taste. Remove the seeds, which are the hottest part. Serranos—smaller, more slender, and very hot—can be substituted for jalapeños.

BULBOUS SWEET GREEN PEPPERS.

Dolmalık biber, "peppers for dolmas," are known as bell peppers in North America. They are pale green, very tender, fragrant, and flavorful, much smaller than their North American counterparts, and they cook faster. Cooked in dolma dishes they exude an incredibly delicious and distinct aroma. Select the smallest bell peppers you can find. For dolmas, use also red bell peppers, which are somewhat sweeter and more tender than the green ones.

HUNGARIAN PEPPERS.

These are tender, long, semi-hot chilies pale green in color. They are the best substitute for tender long green peppers.

HOW TO ROAST AND PEEL PEPPERS AND CHILIES

If you have a gas stove, the easiest way to roast peppers is to place them directly on the burner flame, turning frequently until the skins are black and charred. A Mexican *comal* or a metal grid can also be used and would be ideal for small chilies that cannot be roasted directly on the burner. If you must use an electric stove, again use a *comal* or any kind of metal grid or a cake rack. Or heat a cast-iron skillet until hot and roast the peppers over medium heat, turning on all sides until the skins are charred and black. Immediately seal them in a plastic or brown paper bag: the steam will separate the skin from the flesh. Leave them in the bag for 15 minutes and peel off all the skin. Remove the tops and seeds and use as directed—whole, sliced, or chopped.

Tomatoes

Turkish tomatoes are the vegetable I most miss. They are large, a little irregular in shape, nubby here and there and ribbed, and they always seem warm to the touch. Juicy, fragrant, full of flavor, and sweet and tangy at the same time, they tempted us to eat them like apples when we were children. I still do when I am home, sprinkling them with a little salt. A plateful of sliced tomatoes sprinkled with salt and accompanied by fresh crusty bread and maybe some white cheese and black olives always makes a perfect lunch. Dribble a little Aegean olive oil over them, scatter some thyme or mint leaves if you like, and the only other thing you will need is a big chunk of bread to soak up the juices.

Use fresh tomatoes only when they are in season. Substitute good canned tomatoes and ban tasteless, hard, meaty ones. Roasting improves the flavor of tomatoes. You can roast them on a charcoal grill if you happen to be roasting meats, or on a *comal* or any other metal grid over a gas burner as Mexican cooks do, turning them on all sides until dark brown blisters appear all over their surfaces. Then peel them. Lacking a gas burner, roast them in a cast-iron skillet until blistered.

GLOSSARY

✳✳

ALMONDS. *Badem.* Street vendors sell skinned freshly harvested almonds, in ice cold water. They taste sweet and creamy. Do not buy almonds already blanched, for they lose their moisture and flavor. To blanch them, drop in boiling water, remove from heat, and let stand in hot water for 2 minutes. Drain, refresh with cold water, and squeeze the kernels to remove the skins. To toast almonds, place them on a baking sheet in a preheated 325 degree oven for about 15 minutes, until they turn golden. Or fry them in butter or oil until golden brown, particularly if they are to be used for garnishing pilafs.

BULGUR. *Bulgur.* Wheat partially cooked, dried, and crushed to various degrees of coarseness. Bulgur has been a staple ingredient throughout Anatolia since ancient times. You can replace the rice in any pilaf recipe with bulgur.

CHICK-PEAS. *Nohut.* In addition to soups, stews, *mantı,* pilafs, and salads, perhaps the most interesting use of chick-peas in Turkey is *leblebi,* a delicious snack sold in the same places as roasted nuts. *Leblebi* comes in two varieties: white and yellow. White *leblebi* is nutty, tender, and crunchy. It is made by partially cooking the chick-peas and then drying them. Yellow *leblebi* is crunchy and tender with a roasted flavor. It is made by partially cooking the chick-peas and then roasting them. The distinctive aroma of roasting chick-peas is quite powerful and seductive.

CUMIN SEEDS. *Kimyon.* These are yellowish brown in color, and resemble caraway seeds in shape. They are available in powdered form, but if freshly ground just before cooking, they retain their fragrance and freshness. To grind cumin seeds, put them in the jar of a coffee grinder, a spice mill, or an electric blender, and grind to the consistency of a powder.

GARLIC. *Sarımsak.* Garlic is used abundantly in Turkish cooking. Turks always pound peeled garlic using a mortar and pestle with a little salt until it is reduced to a paste. One can also use a garlic press or a food processor.

HAZELNUTS (FILBERTS). *Fındık.* Hazelnuts grow in the Black Sea region of Turkey and appear on the market in summer in their husks and, like fresh almonds and walnuts, taste moist and sweet. Blanch hazelnuts in the same way as almonds. If you are going to use them toasted, there is no need to blanch them first, for the skins will come off once the nuts are toasted. Place them in a preheated 325 to 350 degree oven for 15 minutes. Rub the skins off in the folds of a towel.

HULLED WHEAT. *Aşurelik buğday.* Cream-colored, plump, and softer than regular wheat, hulled wheat resembles barley. It is used in soups and is the main grain in *aşure* (page 230). In fact, because of its use in this well-known dessert, hulled wheat is often called *aşurelik buğday,* "wheat for making *aşure.*" It is available in Middle Eastern markets and health-food stores. Barley can be substituted.

JASMINE FLOWERS. *Yasemin, jasminum.* In spring, you can use jasmine blossoms to flavor fruit salads, ice creams, or sherbets. Certain varieties are poisonous, so you must be sure to find one that is not. Also be sure to use flowers that have not been sprayed with poisonous insecticides.

KAYMAK. Very thick cream that is cut with a knife to be served. Substitute clotted cream or whipped cream.

LINDEN BLOSSOMS. *Ihlamur,* linden tree (*Tilia europaea*). Dried linden blossoms are steeped to make hot tea sweetened with sugar and sometimes flavored with cinnamon. It is believed to help cure colds and coughs.

MAHLEB. *Prunus mahaleb.* The origin of the word is Arabic, and it designates the highly fragrant, golden-brown, lentil-sized seeds from the kernels of the black cherry. It is used ground and its sweet fragrance and flavor are very much appreciated in sweet breads and sweet or savory rolls (pages 200, 203, 204). Available in Middle Eastern markets, it is sold whole and can be ground in a coffee grinder or crushed in a mortar just before use.

MASTIC. *Sakız, Pistacia lentiscus.* Mastic is resin from a small evergreen acacia tree. In my childhood, it was the only chewing gum available in Turkey. It is still sold in tiny, colorful paper packages. Used to flavor and aromatize sweet breads, milk puddings, and ice cream, it is available whole and has to be pounded or ground before use. It can also be tied in a cheesecloth sack and simmered in milk to infuse it. Mastic can be obtained at Middle Eastern markets.

NIGELLA SEEDS. *Çörek otu, kalonji, Nigella sativa (Ranunculaceae).* These fragrant tiny black seeds of a plant now grown mainly in India and the Middle East are sprinkled on certain breads and rolls before baking. They are available at Middle Eastern and Indian food markets.

NUTS. *Fındık fıstık.* Turks enjoy snacking on roasted, salted nuts of all kinds. Street vendors sell them almost everywhere, and from shops specializing in nuts and dried fruits the unmistakable aroma of freshly roasting nuts draws in the passersby. Raw unsalted nuts are used in cooking and making sweets. Nuts are at their best freshly harvested, when they taste delicate and sweet. They should be stored in airtight containers in cool dry places and not be kept longer than 5 or 6 months. Freezing will also keep them relatively fresh.

OLIVES. *Zeytin.* It is curious how certain items of food play different roles in different cultures. While in North America the olive is an incidental fruit used here and there as garnish, in Turkey it is a staple food enjoyed in its own right. Almost every morning rich and poor alike consume olives together with cheeses, butter, jam, fresh bread, and tea for breakfast. Green or black olives in a pool of full-flavored olive oil, with just a hint of lemon juice, maybe sprinkled with thyme or toasted sesame seeds together with fresh crusty bread, make a perfect snack. Dipping a piece of bread into the olive oil is an additional pleasure.

Green olives are picked when fully grown yet unripe and cured in brine, which includes some olive oil, lemon slices, and local herbs. Their colors range from green to all shades of beige, including a lovely pinkish shade.

Black olives are ripe, fleshy, full-flavored, and mellow. They look slightly wrinkled outside and their pulp has a creamy texture. You can find them in Middle Eastern markets imported from Turkey, Greece, or Morocco. Especially for Olive Oil Bread with Black Olives, do not substitute canned olives; they do not have enough flavor.

PEKMEZ. Made by boiling grape juice to a thick syrup, it is sometimes available in Middle Eastern markets canned and imported from Turkey.

PINE NUTS. *Fıstık, dolma fıstığı.* Plump pine nuts are frequently used in Turkish cooking, particularly in fillings for olive oil dolmas. Consequently they are sometimes referred to as *dolma fıstığı,* pine nuts for dolma. They are also used in fillings for fish or *börek,* as well as in pilafs. Depending on the dish, they are sautéed in butter or oil along with the onions until they turn golden.

PISTACHIOS. *Şam fıstığı.* They grow in Gaziantep, a southeastern province of Anatolia. Salted and roasted pistachios are highly appreciated as snacks and used raw in cooking and sweatmeats. Pistachio-filled baklavas of Gaziantep hold an esteemed place throughout Turkey.

POMEGRANATES AND POMEGRANATE JUICE. *Nar, nar suyu.* Pomegranates, the ancient fruit of the Middle East, are a source of legend as well as inspiration for poets and artists. Along with olives and figs, the pomegranate is mentioned in the Qur'an as an indication of divine abundance and provision for man and as one of the fruits of paradise. In summer, the pomegranate trees of Anatolia are adorned with lovely blossoms the same glorious color as transparent pomegranate seeds. In winter, sweet pomegranates are enjoyed as fruit and the seeds are used to make sherbets and syrups that are made into icy cold drinks in summer. Pomegranate seeds also decorate many milk puddings and *aşure* (see page 230).

The slightly tricky operation of removing the seeds is easiest done in the kitchen sink, to prevent the juices from splashing all over. Halve the fruit, divide it into smaller chambers removing the white membrane, and drop the seeds into a bowl. To obtain their juice, crush the seeds by hand or in a blender and strain. You can squeeze them like an orange or lemon, but then the juice is slightly bitter, flavored by the bitter-tasting membrane. Bottled pomegranate juice is available in certain health-food stores.

POMEGRANATE SYRUP. *Nar ekşisi.* Pomegranate syrup is concentrated (boiled) juices of sour pomegranates. Like tamarind, it has a sweet-and-sour flavor. Sometimes called grenadine molasses, it is available in Middle Eastern stores, in bottles imported from Arab countries.

RED LENTILS. *Kırmızı mercimek.* If you have never tasted them, I highly recommend red lentils. Tiny, lens-shaped, and bright orange-red, when cooked they turn a beautiful yellow. They have a sweetly earthy flavor and when pureed in soups yield a velvety and creamy texture. You can find them in Middle Eastern or Indian markets and in health-food stores. Those from India are larger in size and paler in color than those from the Middle East, but they are interchangeable.

RED PEPPERS. *Kırmızı biber.* See pages 281–82.

ROSE PETALS. *Gül.* Petals of highly scented pink or red garden roses are used to infuse syrups and sherbets and mostly to make Rose Petal Preserve (page 254). In Turkey rose petals for this particular purpose are sold fresh or dried and called *reçellik gül,* rose petals for preserving. In North America I use very fragrant garden roses to make preserve as well as to infuse syrups or cream to make ices and ice cream. Be sure to use roses that have not been sprayed with poisonous insecticides.

ROSE WATER. *Gül suyu.* Distilled from fragrant rose petals, rose water has been prepared in Persia from early times. It has been used in Middle Eastern cookery to flavor both savory and sweet dishes. In Turkish cooking it is used mainly to flavor syrups, cold drinks, milk puddings, and some other sweets and confectionery.

SAFFRON. *Safran, Crocus sativus (Iridaceae).* A legendary, precious spice that flavors and colors pilafs and sweets.

SESAME SEEDS. *Susam, Sesamum indicum (Pedaliaceae).* Cream-colored sesame seeds are probably the oldest plant for seed use. They have been used in the Middle East for centuries. In Turkey they are used as topping on breads and rolls and in confections and commercially made helvas.

SUMAC. *Sumak, Rhus corioria.* Sour and slightly peppery berries of a shrub. The berries are steeped in water and the aromatic liquid used in cooking. It is also used in powdered form, sprinkled on grilled meats. In kebab shops ground dark red sumac is always available in small containers, along with red pepper and crushed red pepper flakes. Sumac is available in Middle Eastern markets.

TAHINI. *Tahin.* A thick paste made from sesame seeds. In Turkey a simple and healthy snack is made by combining tahini and *pekmez* into a paste and serving it with bread on the side or spread on bread. Its flavor, color, and texture remind me of peanut butter and honey. Tahini is also used for making a commercial helva called *tahin helvası.* It also forms the basis for spreads, salads, and some sauces.

WALNUTS. *Ceviz.* Walnut trees grow throughout Anatolia and are appreciated for both their fruit and their wood. When freshly harvested, walnuts are delicate and sweet. If you soak them in cold water overnight, the skins come off easily and the exposed white flesh is tender, moist, and sweet tasting, almost like freshly harvested walnuts. In winter people enjoy walnuts with raisins, dried figs, and apricots as snacks. They are also used in cooking, particularly in sweetmeats for desserts, such as baklava and others.

BIBLIOGRAPHY

✽✽

TURKISH COOKBOOKS

Fahriye, Ayşe. *Yeni Yemek Kitabı*. Istanbul, 1882.

Fahriye, Hadiye. *Yeni Ev Kadının Yemek Kitabı*. Istanbul, 1924.

Kamil, Mehmed. *Melce'üt-Tabbahin*. Istanbul, 1844.

Makhmudov, K. *Uzbekskie Blyuda*. Tashkent, 1963.

——— and S. H. Salikhov. *Uzbek Culinary*. Tashkent, 1983.

Necip Usta. *Türk Mutfak Sanatı*. Istanbul, 1971.

Nedim, Fahriye. *Yemek Kitabı*. Istanbul, 1956.

Türabi Efendi. *Turkish Cookery Book*. London, 1864 (reprinted Rotting-dean, 1987).

Yeğen, Ekrem Muhittin. *Tatli-Pasta Öğretimi*. Istanbul, 1979.

———. *Yemek Öğretimi*. Istanbul, 1979.

OTHER SOURCES

Volumes on food history as well as dictionaries, memoirs, travel narratives, books of general history, and a few works of fiction that illuminate the topic of Turkish cuisine in one way or another.

Algar, Ayla. "Bektaşilik'te Yemeğin Yeri." In *İkinci Milletlerarasi Yemek Kongresi Tebliğleri*, 20–24. Konya, 1989.

———. "Bushaq of Shiraz: Poet, Parasite, and Gastronome." *Petits Propos Culinaires* 31 (March 1989): 9–20.

———. "Food in the Life of the Tekke." In *The Dervish Lodge in Ottoman Turkey*, edited by Raymond Lifchez. Berkeley and Los Angeles, in press.

Ali Riza Bey, Balıkhane Naziri. *Bir Zamanlar Istanbul*. Istanbul, n.d.

Ali Seydi Bey. *Teşrifat ve Teşkilatımız*. Istanbul, n.d.

Alsan, Nebil Fazıl. *Şair, Edip ve Tarihçi Kalemiyle İstanbul*. Istanbul, 1973.

Araz, Nezihe. "Türk Yemek Töresi." In *İkinci Milletlerarasi Yemek Kongresi Tebliğleri*, 31–34. Konya, 1989,

Ayverdi, Semiha. *İbrahim Efendi Konaği*, 3rd ed. Istanbul, 1982.

Bayramoğlu, Fuat. "Türk Mutfağı ve Yazılı Kaynaklar." In *Birinci Milletlerarasi Yemek Kongresi Tebliğleri*, 38–49. Ankara, 1988.

Birge, E. K. *The Bektashi Order of Dervishes*. London, 1937.

Boratav, Pertev Naili. *Türk Folkloru*. Istanbul, 1973.

Canard, Marius. "Le riz dans le proche orient aux premiers siècles de l'Islam." *Arabica* 6 (1959): 113–31.

Celal, Musahipzade. *Eski Istanbul Yaşayışı*. Istanbul, 1946.

Cenkman, Emin. *Osmanlı Sarayı ve Kıyafetleri*. Istanbul, 1948.

Çelebi, Evliya. *Seyahatname*. Edited by Zuhuri Danışman. Istanbul, 1969.

Çelik, Zeynep. *The Remaking of Istanbul: Portrait of an Ottoman City in the Nineteenth Century*. Seattle and London, 1986.

Cox, Samuel S. *Diversions of a Diplomat in Turkey*. New York, 1887.

Davidson, Alan. *Mediterranean Seafood*. London, 1981.

de Amicis, Edmondo. *Constantinople*. 2 vols. Philadelphia, 1896.

de Busbecq, Ogier Ghislain. *Vier Briefe aus der Türkei*. Erlangen, 1926.

de Tott, Baron. *Memoirs Containing the State of the Turkish Empire and the Crimea*. 2 vols. London, 1786.

Flaubert, Gustave. *Voyages: Tôme Second, Voyage en Orient*. Paris, 1948.

Fragner, Bert G. "Zur Erforschung der kulinarischen Kultur Irans." *Die Welt des Islams* 23–24 (1984): 320–60.

Gallwitz, Esther, ed. *Istanbul*. Frankfurt, 1981.

Gautier, Théophile. *Constantinople*. New York, 1875.

Geleneksel Türk Tatlıları Sempozyumu Bildirileri. Ankara, 1984.

Gibb, H. A. R., and Harold Bowen. *Islamic Society and the West*. London, 1950.

Goodwin, Gillian. "Blancmange: A Brief Sketch and Some Queries." In *Symposium Fare Two*, 30–33. Totnes, 1986.

Gray, Patience. *Honey from a Weed*. New York, 1987.

Grigson, Jane. *Vegetable Book*. London, 1988.

Grosser-Rilke, Anna. *Nieverwehte Klänge*. Leipzig and Berlin, 1937.

Gülersoy, Çelik. *Alphonse de Lamartine ve Istanbul Yazıları*. Istanbul, 1971.

Hattox, Ralph S. *Coffee and Coffeehouses*. Seattle and London, 1985.

Heine, Peter. *Kulinarische Studien: Untersuchungen zur Kochkunst im arabisch-islamischen Mittelalter*. Wiesbaden, 1988.

Hisar, Abdülhakk Şinasi. *Çamlıcadaki Eniştemiz*. Istanbul, 1978.

İşin, Ekrem. "19.yy'da Modernleşme ve Gündelik Hayat." In *Tanzimat'tan Cumhuriyet'e Türkiye Ansiklopedisi*. Vol. 2. Istanbul, 1985.

Johnson, Maria. "Notes on Turkish Contributions to Balkan Flour Confectionery." In *Birinci Milletlerarası Yemek Kongresi Tebliğleri*, 153–62. Ankara, 1988.

Kashghari, Mahmud, al-. *Diwan Lughat al-Turk, Compendium of the Turkish Dialects*. Edited and translated by Robert Dankoff. 3 vols. Harvard 1982.

Katırcıoğlu, F. M. "Ottoman Culinary Habits." In *Birinci Milletlerarası Yemek Kongresi Tebliğleri*, 163–65. Ankara, 1988.

Kemal, Yahya. *Aziz İstanbul*. Istanbul, 1974.

Koçu, Resat Ekrem. *Topkapu Sarayı*. Istanbul, n.d.

Kömürciyan, Eremya Çelebi. *İstanbul Tarihi: XVII. Asırda Istanbul*. Translated by Hrand Andreasyan. Istanbul, 1988.

Kongaz, Gülcan. "Topkapı Sarayı Mutfakları." *Tarih ve Toplum* 15 (March 1985): 22–24.

Koşay, Hamit Z., and Akile Ülkücan. *Anadolu Yemekleri ve Türk Mutfağı*. Ankara, 1961.

Kut, Günay. *Et-Terkibat fi Tabhi'l-Hulviyyat (Tatlı Pişirme Tarifleri)*. Ankara, 1986.

———. "Şehzade Cihangir ve Bayezid'in Sünnet Düğünlerindeki Yemekler Üzerine." In *III. Milletlerarası Türk Folklor Kongresi Bildirileri*, 227–38. Ankara, 1987.

———. "Şirvani'nin Yemek Kitabı Çevirisine Eklediği Yemekler Üzerine." In *Birinci Milletlerarası Yemek Kongresi Tebliğleri*, 170–75. Ankara, 1988.

———. "Türk Mutfaginda Çorba Çeşitleri." In *İkinci Milletlerarası Yemek Kongresi Tebliğleri*, 213–20. Konya, 1989.

Kut, Turgut. *Yemek Kitapları Bibliyografyasi*. Ankara, 1985.

———. "18. Yüzyılın İkinci Yarısında Hazırlanmış Bir Yemek Lugatı." In *Birinci Milletlerarası Yemek Kongresi Tebliğleri*, 181–85. Ankara, 1988.

Lamartine, Alphonse de. *A Pilgrimage to the Holy Land*. 2 vols. New York, 1848.

Leclant, V. S. "Le café et les cafés à Paris, 1644–1693." *Annales: Economies, Sociétés, Civilisations* 6, no. 1 (January–March 1951): 2–4.

Lewis, B. *Istanbul and the Civilization of the Ottoman Empire*. Norman, 1963.

Mantran, Roger. *Istanbul dans la deuxième moitié du xviieme siècle*. Paris, 1962.

Miller, Barnette. *Beyond the Sublime Porte: The Grand Seraglio of Stambul*. New Haven, 1931.

Mirzoev, Abdulghani. *Abu Ishaq va Fa'aliyat-i Adabi-yi U*. Dushanbe, 1971.

Montagu, Lady Mary. *Letters During the Embassy to Constantinople*. Vols. 1–2: *Letters and Works*. New York, 1893.

Mustafa Ali, Gelibolulu. *Ziyafet Sofraları*. Istanbul, n.d.

Mustafa, Emir. *Ramazanname*. Edited by Amil Çelebioğlu. Istanbul, n.d.

Ögel, Bahaeddin. *Türk Kültür Tarihini Giriş, IV: Türklerde Yemek Külturü*. Ankara, 1985.

Oral, M. Zeki. "Selçuk Devri Yemekleri ve Ekmekleri: i." *Türk Etnografya Dergisi* 1, no. 2 (1956).

Orga, Irfan. *Portrait of a Turkish Family*. London, 1950.

Örik, Nahid Sırrı. *Abdülhamid'in Haremi*. Istanbul, 1989.

Ozansoy, Halit Fahri. *Eski Istanbul Ramazanları*. Istanbul, 1968.

Pallis, Alexander. *In the Days of the Janissaries*. London, 1951.

Penzer, N. M. *The Harem*. London, 1965.

Perry, Charles. "Baklava Not Proven Greek." *Petits Propos Culinaires* 27 (October 1987): 47–48.

———. "The Central Asian Origins of Baklava." In *İkinci Milletlerarası Yemek Kongresi Tebliğleri*, 356–59. Konya, 1989.

———. "Grain Foods of the Early Turks." In *Oxford Symposium 1983: Food in Motion,* 19–22. Leeds, 1983.

———. "Notes on Persian Pasta." *Petits Propos Culinaires* 10 (March 1982): 48–49.

———. "The Oldest Mediterranean Noodle: A Cautionary Tale." *Petits Propos Culinaires* 9 (October 1981): 42–45.

———. "Shorba: A Linguistic Chemico-culinary Inquiry." *Petits Propos Culinaires* 7 (March 1981): 23.

———. "Three Notes, Oriental and Levantine." *Petits Propos Culinaires* 15 (November 1983): 29.

Radloff, W. *Die alttürkischen Inschriften der Mongolei.* St. Petersburg, 1895.

———. *Versuch eines Wörterbuches der Türk-Dialecte.* St. Petersburg, 1911.

Refik, Ahmed. *İstanbul Hayatı.* Istanbul, 1988.

Reyhanlı, Tulay. *İngiliz Gezginlerine Göre XVI. Yüzyılda İstanbul'da Hayat.* Ankara, 1983.

Rodinson, Maxime. "Recherches sur les documents arabes relatifs à la cuisine." *Revue des Etudes Islamiques* (1949): 95–165.

Sabban, Françoise. "Court Cuisine in Fourteenth-Century Imperial China: Some Culinary Aspects of Hu Sihui's *Yinshan Zhengyao.*" *Food and Foodways* 1 (1986): 161–96.

Saz, Leyla. *Haremin İçyüzü.* Istanbul, 1974.

Schimmel, Annemarie. *The Triumphal Sun: A Study of the Works of Jalaladdin Rumi.* London and The Hague, 1978.

Seferçioğlu, M. Nejat. *Türk Yemekleri (XVIII. Yüzyıla Ait Bir Yemek Risalesi).* Ankara, 1985.

Simeti, Mary Taylor. *Pomp and Sustenance.* New York, 1989.

Smith, R. E. F. "Kazan Tatar Diet and Russia." In *Birinci Milletlerarası Yemek Kongresi Tebliğleri,* 276–83. Ankara, 1988.

Sözen, Gürol. *Bin Çeşit Istanbul ve Boğaziçi Yalıları.* Istanbul, 1989.

Sumner-Boyd, Hilary, and John Freely. *Strolling Through Istanbul: A Guide to the City.* London, 1987.

Tannahill, Reay. *Food in History.* New York, 1973.

Tarama Sözlüğü. 6 vols. Ankara, 1963–72.

Tavernier, Jean-Baptiste. *Collection of Travels Through Turkey into Persia and the East Indies.* London, 1688.

Togay, Emine Foat. *Three Centuries: Family Chronicles of Turkey and Egypt.* London, 1963.

Türk Mutfağı Sempozyumu Bildirileri. Ankara, 1982.

Uluçay, M. Çağatay. *Padişahların kadınları ve kızları.* Ankara, 1985.

Ünüvar, Safiye. *Saray Hatıralarım.* Istanbul, 1964.

Ünver, A. Suheyl. *Fatih Devri Yemekleri.* Istanbul, 1962.

———. *Tarihte 50 Türk Yemeği.* Istanbul, 1948.

Uzunçarşılı, Ismail Hakki. *Osmanlı Devletinin Saray Teşkilatı.* Ankara, 1945.

Vambery, Hermann. *Reise in Mittelasien.* Leipzig, 1865.

van Millingen, A. *Constantinople.* London, 1906.

von Gabain, Annemarie. *Das Leben im uigurischen Königreich.* Wiesbaden, 1973.

Vryonis, Spero. *The Decline of Mediaeval Hellenism in Asia Minor.* Berkeley and Los Angeles, 1971.

Zübeyr, Hamit. "Mevlevilikte Mutfak Terbiyesi." *Türk Yurdu* 5, no. 28 (March 1927): 280–86.

METRIC CONVERSION CHARTS

✾✾

CONVERSIONS OF OUNCES TO GRAMS

Ounces (oz)	Grams (g)*	Ounces (oz)	Grams (g)
1	30	11	300
2	60	12	340
3	85	13	370
4	115	14	400
5	140	15	425
6	180	16	450
7	200	20	565
8	225	24	675
9	250	28	800
10	285	32	900

* Approximate. To convert ounces to grams, multiply number of ounces by 28.35.

CONVERSIONS OF POUNDS TO GRAMS AND KILOGRAMS

Pounds (lb)	Grams (g)* kilograms (kg)	Pounds (lb)	Grams (g) kilograms (kg)
1	450	5	2¼
1¼	565	5½	2½
1½	675	6	2¾
1¾	800	6½	3
2	900	7	3¼
2½	1,125; 1¼	7½	3½
3	1,350	8	3¾
3½	1,500; 1½	9	4
4	1,800	10	4½
4½	2		

* Approximate. To convert pounds into grams, multiply number of pounds by 453.6.

CONVERSIONS OF FAHRENHEIT TO CELSIUS

Fahrenheit	Celsius*	Fahrenheit	Celsius
170°	77°	350°	180°
180°	82°	375°	190°
190°	88°	400°	205°
200°	95°	425°	220°
225°	110°	450°	230°
250°	120°	475°	245°
275°	135°	500°	260°
300°	150°	525°	275°
325°	165°	550°	290°

* Approximate. To convert Fahrenheit into Celsius, subtract 32, multiply by 5, then divide by 9.

CONVERSIONS OF QUARTS TO LITERS

Quarts (qt)	Liters (L)*	Quarts (qt)	Liters (L)
1	1	5	4¾
1½	1½	6	5½
2	2	7	6½
2½	2½	8	7½
3	2¾	9	8½
4	3¾	10	9½

* Approximate. To convert quarts to liters, multiply number of quarts by .95.

INDEX